BULLIED!

CONFRONTING
AND
OVERCOMING
SIX MAJOR OBSTACLES
TO
CHURCH
EFFECTIVENESS

J. TODD KINGREA

eLectio Publishing
Little Elm, TX
www.eLectioPublishing.com

Bullied! Confronting and Overcoming Six Major Obstacles to Church Effectiveness
By J. Todd Kingrea

ISBN-13: 978-1-63213-135-5
Published by eLectio Publishing, LLC
Little Elm, Texas
http://www.eLectioPublishing.com

Printed in the United States of America

5 4 3 2 1 eLP 21 20 19 18 17 16

The eLectio Publishing editing team is comprised of: Christine LePorte, Lori Draft, Sheldon James, Court Dudek, Kaitlyn Campbell, and Jim Eccles.

Publisher's Note
The publisher does not have any control over and does not assume any responsibility for author or third-party websites or their content.

J. Todd King

This book is dedicated to my wonderful bride,
Felicia,
a constant source
of
encouragement, hope, laughter and love

CONTENTS

ACKNOWLEDGMENTS

NO BOOK IS the work of a single person. Even the novelist creating her own world relies on information and research to make the story as realistic as possible. Just as no single person can claim their achievements as purely their own, but as the result of those who have gone before, I am indebted to the shoulders of those I have been fortunate to stand on in writing this book.

I would like to express my grateful appreciation to the many friends and colleagues who have been instrumental in shaping this book. Some have shared their stories while others have given advice. Some have been proofreaders and some have been sounding boards. No matter the contribution, they have been valuable assets in seeing this come to light.

My gracious respect and thanks to Janis Balda, Wesley Balda, Dawn Bergstrom, William Beckham, Michelle Bowers, Graham Cooke, Sandy Garrabrant, Lynn Hill, Hugh Halter, Don Hanson, Alan Hirsch, Bill Hull, Chris Kelly, Braxton Kendrick, Felicia Kingrea, Eddie & Cheryl Kingrea, Joaquita Martin, Robin Meyers, Tina Morgan, Richard Rambo, Terry Roller, Rev. Gene Sheffield, Karen Smith, Rev. Lee Stevenson, Mary Grindstaff Thompson, Linda Tipton, and Ben Woolsey.

In addition, the following people have gone above and beyond the call of duty to make this book a reality: Delisa Allen-Hartman, Bill & Judy Beckman, Connie Beeken, Rev. Brian & DeAnne Burch, Cindy Cunnyngham, Cory & Courtney Fox, Sharon Gregory, John Guy, Cindy Hines, Vicki Hardesty, Jerry & Ann Haynes, Noel & Patsy Irwin, Teresa M. Jordan, Kathryn Mullins, Leala Munson, Brenda Newman, Rev. Joe Phillips, Keith Simmons, the late Anne Smith, Becky Stulce, and Janet Winn. Thank you so much for all you've done!

I would like to especially recognize Arnie Stulce for his time, skill and counsel.

I am also grateful to Jesse Greever, Christopher Dixon, my editor Christine LePorte, and everyone at eLectio Publishing for the opportunity to share this vision and to work in partnership with their creativity and passion.

Finally, my appreciation is extended to the members of Soddy United Methodist Church for their prayers, encouragement and support.

BULLIED!

INTRODUCTION

IN LATE OCTOBER and early November 2013, the National Football League made headlines. It had nothing to do with division rivalries, superstar rookies, or Peyton Manning's march to a record fifth Most Valuable Player award. In the midst of the NFL's ninety-fourth season, the Miami Dolphins franchise became embroiled in a scandal, one that had never before been exposed in any professional sport: bullying.

An offensive lineman was found guilty of bullying a fellow teammate. Derogatory, racist text messages and voice mails were produced as evidence. Two other linemen were also found culpable. A league-appointed investigator compiled a 144-page report that found a culture of bullying on the Dolphins practice field and in the locker room. The victim quit the team and debated continuing his NFL career before finally signing with a different team. The perpetrator was released from the Dolphins and was out of football for a period of time before signing with another team.

What made the Miami Dolphins situation so newsworthy was the fact it was the first public allegation of bullying in a major league locker room. In a sport where 300-pound athletes are paid exorbitant sums of money to pummel each other for sixty minutes, it seemed almost surreal to hear accusations of grown professionals being bullied. As the Miami Dolphins situation unfolded, we discovered that some of the schoolyard bullies of our childhood never really changed.

Sadly, organized sports at every level come with some degree of bullying. Most of it is the name-calling and put-downs many of us experienced during our time on the court or field, epitaphs designed to humiliate or motivate us. Sometimes the bullying happened as a result of anger or aggression.

With the prevalence of social media, bullying has taken a prominent place in our national consciousness. Everyone from supermodels to students, politicians to teachers, has weighed in on this important issue that we dare not look away from. Yet there is one place where we *do* look away. There remains one place where bullying continues, blatantly and unchecked.

The church.

Pastors, leaders and church members experience bullying with alarming regularity. It doesn't come in the form of physical threats or inflammatory text messages. People are not challenged to "meet outside after the bell rings." These would be too obvious, too transparent. No, bullying in the church often arises whenever change is pursued, or when some person or group does not get their way. This ecclesiastical bullying does as much damage as bullying in the locker room or on social media. It is rarely confronted, and often covertly rewarded when people turn a blind eye to it and the bullies continue to get their way.

Most bullying arises over issues of control. A Sunday school class, committee, board of deacons or founding family may have called the shots in the church for a long time. Anyone who crosses that group—or advocates for change or actually confronts the troublemakers to hold them accountable—becomes a target for bullying.

Parsonage families have endured poisonous comments and been subjected to hateful attitudes, often leading to children abandoning the faith or marriages dissolving. Talented staff members have fled the gossip and workplace harassment, often in tears. Church members who supported a leader or a new direction for their congregations have been ostracized, slandered and demeaned. Churches have been polarized, often leading to acrimonious splits.

One saintly woman, after recognizing the bullies within her local church, asked, "Can't we just ignore the troublemakers? Can't we just move forward with the good things we want to do and try to ignore all the negativity and division?" It is a natural response, especially if we do not like conflict. However, I told her it was that perspective—trying to overlook what was happening or pretend it did not exist—which helped foster and embolden the bullies in her church. For many years a handful of people had been allowed to dominate the committees, harass those with whom they disagreed, and turn the church into a dysfunctional social club. No one held them accountable for those actions.

But it is not always church members. In some instances it is the pastor who acts as the bully. He or she also seeks more power and control. Pastors can intimidate committees and browbeat staff, creating unstable and abusive work environments. However, most churches have procedures available—congregationally or denominationally—to correct or remove such a pastor. What most churches *lack* are the procedures to correct or remove congregational bullies.

* * * * * *

The church is a peculiar thing. We are called to be the physical manifestation and expression of Christ's love and grace, carrying on his mission until he returns. Yet we struggle with ourselves and with one another, often so much that the purpose of the church is eclipsed by our antics. We know that no church is perfect and never will be this side of eternity. The body of Christ is made up of weak, fallible, prideful people who have been saved by grace through faith. Sometimes—thanks be to God—we get it right. Sometimes we do the right thing at the right time and truly make "on earth as it is in heaven" happen. At other times, however, we get it wrong. Dreadfully, painfully wrong. We fail to represent the best of Jesus to those around us. We are blinded by our own desires, selfishness and need for control.

That is why I have always enjoyed Paul's first letter to the Corinthians. It exposes some of the most common problems in the church—problems that are just as real today as they were when Paul first put quill to papyrus in the mid-first century AD.

The church at Corinth was pretty bad. But it was not *all* bad.

We read about it in the New Testament and tend to think, "Wow, what a seriously messed up bunch!" It does not seem they got much of anything right. Oh, Paul used his impressive rhetorical skills to pat them on the back a few times, but we generally view the Corinthian congregations as only one step above paganism.

Not surprising, since that is exactly what they were.

Paul formed the Corinthian church sometime around 50-51 AD while on his second missionary journey (Acts 18:10-11). On his third journey Paul settled in at Ephesus for three years (Acts 19:10; 20:31) and carried out his letter-writing campaign with the Corinthian church. After only a few brief years in existence, Paul had to address a host of thorny problems that had arisen among the Christians in Corinth.

We need to bear in mind *that this was less than twenty years after the death and resurrection of Jesus.* The Corinthian believers were first-generation Christians, and let us be honest, they did not have much of a clue what they were doing. This was a collection of diverse individuals—Jew and Greek, slave and free, rich and poor, male and female—drawn by the Holy Spirit out of their former lifestyles and supernaturally joined together in this new thing called *ekklesia* (church). It should not surprise us that there were a lot of misunderstandings and confusion swirling through the congregations. In many ways they were making it up as they went along.

We have a habit of overgeneralizing the Pharisees in the gospels the same way. It is quicker and easier—but incorrect—to depict them as a single mass of legalistic fuddy-duddies or power-hungry zealots. The truth is not all of the Pharisees were against Jesus (consider Nicodemus and Joseph of Arimathea). Not all wanted him killed. Not all of them had it in for the disciples in the book of Acts. Just as the radical fringe elements of Islam do not represent the totality of that religion, neither were all the Christians at Corinth a bunch of sex-crazed, lazy, gluttonous idol worshipers.

The church at Corinth was not all bad. *And neither is your church.*

Just as the Corinthians needed a firm hand to discipline them and keep them on the right path, many of our churches are likewise

6

in desperate need of the same thing. We need to lovingly but firmly step up and address an ongoing problem: the bride of Christ is being bullied. Personal agendas, money, land and buildings, man-made traditions, and a lack of biblical discipleship are the primary oppressors. In some instances one or more of these bullies may be just beginning to be noticed. In other cases they have been deeply ingrained in the DNA of the church for decades.

But our churches do not have to keep cowering in fear or avoiding the bullies! With a new awareness of the bullies our churches face, there are ways to navigate these troubled waters, just as Paul did in Corinth. It is my hope and prayer this book will lead to new, honest conversations in every church about the ways we allow the bride of Christ to be browbeaten and intimidated, and what we can do to help restore her glory, dignity and purpose.

Why write this book?

IT IS NO secret that the church in the United States today is in trouble. The church is often considered anemic in its effectiveness and contradictory in its witness.

We are routinely viewed as out of touch and out of date, and are known more by what we oppose than by what we support. For many churches, institutional preservation has become the primary focus rather than changing the world. Declining membership, aging parishioners, insufficient funds, intolerant attitudes—the list of problems goes on and on.

A plethora of resources are available that address these issues and offer alternatives and solutions. Just pop in to any Christian bookstore and browse the church leadership section, and you will discover ideas, approaches, plans, recommendations, and examples of ways to stem the downward spiral of church decline. However, one thing I have never seen on any of these shelves is a practical discussion about the bullies that cause or perpetuate many of the problems.

This book developed from my observations and experiences as a pastor, and from study and research into the biblical purpose of the church. In over fifteen years of ministry I have witnessed much that is wonderful about the church, and I have witnessed much that causes it to fall short of its intended purpose.

My intention with this book is to offer a solid biblical understanding of the nature and purpose of the church; to expose the biggest bullies that prevent our churches from growing and functioning in healthy ways; and to provide some helpful solutions for dealing with those bullies.

It is not too much of a stretch to say that every church has within it a small number of people—often a Sunday school class, a committee or board, a family—that wields too much power and influence. They directly or indirectly determine what monies are (and are not) spent, in what ways, when and for whom. They veto anything they do not agree with regardless of its biblical foundation or missional purpose. They have been allowed to do this for many years—sometimes across family generations.

Their demands usually revolve around removing a pastor or staff person, getting their agenda pushed through with regard to finances or facilities, having the worship service cater to their preferences, and, of course, refusing anything that has to do with church revitalization or transformation. And if their demands are not met, they withhold their money, circulate petitions, gossip, go to denominational officials, and create a palpable state of tension and animosity that ruins the church's witness and effectiveness.

Faithful church members know who these individuals or groups are within their local congregation. In many cases they may consider them friends or at least acquaintances. Some have probably been together in Sunday school and in worship services for many years. Unfortunately, these same faithful members—like the saintly lady mentioned earlier—have tacitly allowed negative, poisonous, and divisive attitudes and behaviors to turn the church into a back alley where bullies thrive. Good ministry ideas, gifted pastors and staff, and opportunities for growth have all been torpedoed because a small, extremely vocal group demands its own way.

But some may say, "Why fight this battle? Why not just let things alone? It's always been this way." Some will say not to rock the boat. Others will assure us we will divide the church and lose members if we seek to stand up to the bullies. These are the comments of those who are either (a) perfectly satisfied with the status quo, or (b) who do not want to deal with the conflict and fallout that will inevitably occur. However, these excuses are unacceptable. As authors Janis Balda and Wesley Balda note in their *Handbook for Battered Leaders*, "We are at best deceived and at worst cowardly when we determine that it is not our responsibility to confront, not our job to speak out, not our Christian duty to respond to organizational culture or specific individuals who are destructive or dysfunctional."[1]

Let me offer four reasons why the issue of bullying needs to be addressed.

First and foremost, a bullied church is not the biblical model. The body of Christ was never intended to be a playground for the pet agendas of wealthy, influential or cantankerous members. The church was designed to function with all persons participating fully and equally, gathering for communal worship, then dispersing to carry the gospel into the world. The church in the West today must reclaim its biblical roots and purpose. Arguments over theology, end times predictions and other "territorial markings" will not produce the kind of fruit Jesus expects from his followers.

Second, we all know churches—maybe the one you are a member of right now—that remain ineffective in reaching new people for Jesus Christ. Many churches are alienating those in

---

[1] Janis Bragan Balda and Wesley D. Balda, *Handbook for Battered Leaders* (Downers Grove: InterVarsity Press, 2013), p. 141. Used by permission. All rights reserved.

desperate need of God's grace because sinful attitudes dominate the church. While none of us are perfect and all stand in need of God's redeeming and saving power, some remain locked in childish, self-centered perspectives where everything is expected to revolve around them. It only takes a few such attitudes to derail a church. The result is churches with no outreach or missional engagement, stale and uninspired worship, and a growing self-centeredness that "we" matter more than "them."

Third, until bullies are held accountable, churches will continue to struggle and decline. Many churches will eventually die once the last remnant of the older generation is gone. Those churches will perish because a handful of hard-hearted (and hard-headed) people were allowed to monopolize positions of leadership for their own personal agendas. Churches will close their doors permanently because of the reputation they have acquired over the years. Few people will visit these churches, and even fewer will choose to stay around long enough to become members.

And fourth, pastors and church leaders have the ability to turn their churches around *if they will confront the bullies*. Our churches can be led back from the brink. We need to develop supportive bonds within the church that allow us to stand in unity, to confront the bullies and hold them accountable. It will not be easy but it will be worth it. Using the ideas and suggestions in this book, we can be better equipped to guide our churches to revitalization and hope. To do any less is to abdicate our responsibility to the church.

I speak from personal experience. I have been part of congregations that were victimized by bullies—human and inanimate—and thanks to the Holy Spirit and passionate, visionary leaders those churches took positive steps toward renewal and transformation. So do not despair. There is hope!

We would not allow someone to bully our spouse or children. We should not—*we cannot*—allow it to happen in the church any longer. The National Football League demanded answers from the Miami Dolphins' coaches and players, and held guilty parties accountable. People do not believe bullying is acceptable in schools, in the military, in business or in sports. So why does it remain acceptable in the church? I invite you to join me as we expose some of the most common bullies in the church. I pray that what lies ahead will benefit your church in fulfilling its biblical mission and purpose.

* * * * * *

A note of clarification: throughout this book I use the word "Church" (capital "C") to refer to the universal church or to the whole of church in general. I use "church" with a lowercase "c" when referring to a local congregation or to the local congregations in general.

CHAPTER 1
GOD'S BLUEPRINT FOR THE CHURCH

"When the world asks, 'What is God like?' we should be able to say, 'Look at the church.' As the body of Christ, we are to be like Jesus; so that we too, reveal God to the rest of the world."

William R. L. Haley

IF PEOPLE WANT to know what God is like, all they need to do is look at the church. If someone wants to know what Jesus is like, all they need to do is look at a Christian, a "little Christ" (as C. S. Lewis phrased it).

Both of these sound good if the church and the Christian look the way they should. But what if they do not? What if a lot of churches look more like corporations, historical monuments or country clubs? What if a lot of Christians are indistinguishable from the non-Christians around them?

Regretfully, this is where Christianity finds itself as we move deeper into the twenty-first century. Somewhere along the way the church transformed from a grassroots movement empowered by the Holy Spirit into a bureaucratic machine dedicated to institutional preservation. What was once done by all Christians working together is now—and has been for nearly two millennia— the exclusive domain of specialized, credentialed (mostly) men. One part of the Body functions on behalf of the whole.

Imagine if everything your body does was handled by one single part (other than the brain). It would be rather difficult to make it into work every day if only the hands functioned. Forget about seeing if the only part that operates is the lungs. Hungry? Sorry, you cannot eat because your mouth does not work. Only your left arm does.

When a person nears death the body begins to shut down. Organs, and in some cases entire bodily systems, no longer operate. As this shutdown continues, the body weakens and the person eventually dies. One part cannot sustain the whole. In truth, if only one part of our bodies functioned we could not survive.

This is an apt description of the Church today.

The apostle Paul used this body analogy in 1st Corinthians 12. It is significant not only for its profound, yet easily understandable imagery; but by using the body in this way Paul was refuting a common philosophical principle of his day.

The Greeks who lived centuries before Paul developed the belief that the spirit or soul of a person was good and the physical body was bad. Although the Greeks placed a great deal of emphasis upon the perfection of the body (as seen in their art and sports), it was still thought to be less important than the spirit. The material was thought to be less valuable than the immaterial. Not surprisingly, this perspective bled over into much of early Christian thought and theology, despite the fact that God had proclaimed his human creation—all parts of it—good (Genesis 1:31). This dichotomy has perpetuated itself across the centuries so that even today we still find attitudes and perspectives that exalt the spirit but vilify the body.

Paul challenged this Greek philosophy. Writing in 1st Corinthians 12:1 he says...*just as a body, though one, has many parts, but all its many parts form one body, so it is with Christ.*

He declared the Church to be the physical body (or representation) of Jesus on earth. Paul gave prominence to what philosophical thought downplayed or denigrated. We should not forget that Jesus never subscribed to this false dualism for he was born of a woman and took on human flesh as the *bodily* incarnation of God.

Paul also emphasized the value of the human body by using a humorous illustration of how it is designed to work in harmony, and that each part plays a vital role:

Now if the foot should say, "Because I am not a hand, I do not belong to the body," it would not for that reason stop being part of the body. And if the ear should say, "Because I am not an eye, I do not belong to the body," it would not for that reason stop being part of the body. If the whole body were an eye, where would the sense of hearing be? If the whole body were an ear, where would the sense of smell be? But in fact God has placed the parts in the body, every one of them, just as he wanted them to be. If they were all one part, where would the body be? As it is, there are many parts, but one body.

The eye cannot say to the hand, "I don't need you!" And the head cannot say to the feet, "I don't need you!" On the contrary, those parts of the body that seem to be weaker are indispensable, and the parts that we think are less honorable we treat with special honor. And the parts that are unpresentable are treated with special modesty, while our presentable parts need no special treatment. But God has put the body together, giving greater honor to the parts that lacked it, so that there should be no division in the body, but that its parts should have equal concern for each other. If one part suffers, every part suffers with it; if one part is honored, every part rejoices with it.

Now you are the body of Christ, and each one of you is a part of it.

(1st Corinthians 12:15-27)

God has designed the Church like he designed the human body: with all parts working together in harmony to accomplish God's purpose. One part, no matter how well it functions, cannot sustain the whole.

The bride of Christ

WHAT EXACTLY *IS* the Church? What is its purpose? Why is it important? Before we can address bullies in the Church, we need to consider the Church itself. We need to understand what we are talking about. It is vital that we all work from the same set of blueprints.

Builders do not arrive at a construction site with final blueprints drawn up by four or five different architectural firms. There would be chaos and nothing of worth could be constructed. God has given us the master blueprint for his Church in the New Testament.

The Church in the New Testament is referred to by the Greek term *ekklesia*, which means "an assembly"—specifically like a civic gathering or a political rally. Paul and other New Testament writers adopted the term and applied it to this young gathering of Christ-followers. To be the *ekklesia* meant to be called and set apart by God and then to be sent out by God.

The New Testament uses a variety of different names and images for the Church. It is called

- "The body of Christ" (Romans 12:4-5; 1st Corinthians 12:12-27; Colossians 1:18);
- The "flock" (1 Peter 2:25, 5:2-4);
- The "bride of Christ" (Ephesians 5:22-32; Revelation 19:7, 21:2, 9-10);
- The "household" of God (1 Timothy 3:15);
- The "priesthood" (Hebrews 2:17; 1 Peter 2:9);
- The "temple" (1st Corinthians 3:11; Ephesians 2:19-22);
- The "kingdom" (Colossians 1:13; Philippians 3:20).

The relationship between Christ and the Church is a deeply intimate one, as attested by the names "body" and "bride." We are told that Christ loves the Church. He gave himself for her (Acts 20:28; Ephesians 5:25), and he nourishes and cherishes her (Ephesians 5:29). The Church is Christ's body in the world (Colossians 1:18, 24) and he himself is the Head (Ephesians 1:2-23;

Colossians 1:18); therefore, when we abuse or manipulate the Church, we are attempting to do so to Christ.

Today we think of Church in terms of buildings and property, or perhaps worship and rituals. Whenever someone asks, "Where do you go to church?" they are asking for a location and we respond by giving the name of our building or the site of our campus. However, the biblical perspective is that the Church is the living, breathing, growing and adapting representative of Jesus Christ.

The early Church met in what we refer to as "house churches." That is, it gathered in small groups in the homes of believers. For example, when Paul says...*to the church of the Thessalonians in God the Father and the Lord Jesus Christ*...(1 Thessalonians 1:1), he is addressing all the house churches that met throughout the city of Thessaloniki. Paul's letter would have been read and circulated from house to house. We must remember that the early Christians were persecuted for their faith and for refusing to acknowledge Caesar as Lord. They had no way to construct the houses of worship to which we are accustomed. But more importantly, they did not see the need to.

* * * * * *

In the Old Testament, the people of Israel believed that the presence of Yahweh dwelt among them. During their escape from Egypt and journey through the desert, the presence of Yahweh was known by a cloud and pillar of fire (Exodus 13:21). Before they settled in the Promised Land, a tabernacle was built to symbolize the Lord's presence.

The Lord dwelt among his people through the Ark of the Covenant (Numbers 7:89), and later in the Holy of Holies in the temple in Jerusalem (Psalm 26:8, 43:3, Ezekiel 37:27, Zechariah 8:3). All the major Jewish festivals were held in Jerusalem, necessitating that the people journey to the temple to be in Yahweh's presence. The ultimate expression of the presence of God was revealed in the incarnation of Jesus Christ (John 1:1, 14). Jesus made it clear that in him there was no longer any need for the temple and its sacrificial system (Matthew 12:6, 26:61; John 2:20-21). The early Christians *were* the new temple (Acts 17:24; 1st Corinthians 3:16-17, 6:19; 2nd Corinthians 6:16; Ephesians 2:21). Wherever they gathered together, Jesus was in their midst (Matthew 18:20) through the indwelling presence of the Holy Spirit.

What the nation of Israel was in the Old Testament, the Church was to be under the new covenant. Israel was chosen by God to be the bearer of his image, to set a new standard for living in relation to Yahweh and one another, and to be the people through whom all nations would come to Yahweh. Unfortunately, Israel did not always accept this divine mandate and responsibility. The Hebrew Scriptures—what we know as the Old Testament—is the poetry, stories, prayers, histories, prophecies and wisdom of a people on pilgrimage with Yahweh—a people who sometimes got it right and often got it wrong.

The Church in the New Testament also represents a people chosen by God to be the bearer of his image, to set a new standard of living in relation to God and to one another, and to be the people through whom all the world would be drawn to God. Like Israel, the Church is called and set apart, and sent into the world as ambassadors of God's reign. But as with Israel, the Church has sometimes gotten it right and often gotten it wrong.

At its simplest, the Church is the physical manifestation and representation of Jesus Christ in the world. The Church is to show a better, alternative way of living—not as the world around us does—but under God's rule. It is the way of the kingdom of heaven. At the same time the Church is commissioned to engage the world as the hands, feet, heart and voice of Christ. What Jesus did, the Church is to do. What Jesus said, the Church is to say. The people Jesus loved and welcomed into the kingdom, the Church is to love and welcome into the kingdom. At its best, the Church is a reflection of Christ and the living presence of Christ in a confused and broken world.

An incarnational presence

Occasionally, denominations engage in a lengthy process whereby they seek to identify the central purpose of the Church. Their intention is to bring all the churches in their tribe together around this common goal. Sometimes individual churches will hire consultants to help them identify their mission. While trained consultants are beneficial in many ways, and denominational plans can have their place, investing time and energy into identifying the mission of the Church is redundant. The New Testament already does that.

In Luke 4:16-21, Jesus returned to his hometown of Nazareth in Galilee and went to the synagogue on the Sabbath. He was handed the scroll of the prophet Isaiah and *...unrolling it, ...he found the place where it is written: "The Spirit of the Lord is on me, because he has anointed me to proclaim good news to the poor. He has sent me to proclaim freedom for the prisoners and recovery of sight for the blind, to set the oppressed free, to proclaim the year of the Lord's favor."* Following his reading, Jesus announced to the people, *"Today this scripture is fulfilled in your hearing."*

Jesus *intentionally* chose this passage of Hebrew prophecy as his mission statement. He could have selected any other passage from the scroll of Isaiah, yet this is the one he declared had been fulfilled that day. For Jesus, this represented why he came.

If this was the mission statement of Jesus, it is also the mission statement of the Church. The Church is anointed by the Holy Spirit to proclaim good news to the poor. How seriously does the Church take this mandate when many of our buildings and campuses are worth more than some people will earn in a lifetime? How many of our churches welcome in the poor and the outcast or better yet, go to them with the gospel?

The Church is directed by the Holy Spirit to proclaim freedom for prisoners and to set the oppressed free, to bring release for everyone who is bound by sin, oppression and injustice. We are to provide recovery of sight for the blind—that is, to help people see themselves and others from the perspective of God's grace and redemptive plan.

If Luke 4:16-21 serves as the mission statement of Jesus, then Mark 1:14-15 presents the true essence of the gospel: *...Jesus went into Galilee, proclaiming the good news of God. "The time has come," he said. "The kingdom of God has come near. Repent and believe the good news!"* The message of Jesus, and the message of the Church, is that the kingdom of God is near. This was true in first-century Israel when God became flesh and walked among people. The kingdom of God had come near to them. It is supposed to be true today.

Due to the influence of nineteenth- and twentieth-century revivalism in the United States, the good news of the gospel has been reduced to "accepting Jesus into your heart." While a personal and intimate relationship with Christ is *vital* to the Christian faith and life, the American or Western Church has veered away from the message of Jesus. He did not come asking people to accept him into their hearts. That would have been a bizarre and alien concept for the people of his day. The message of Jesus—that which he lived and taught—was that the kingdom of God was present in him, and that all who wanted could take part in it.

The Jewish religion of Jesus' day had become a top-heavy, elite collection of rituals and requirements that did little to help people connect with Yahweh. Jesus inaugurated the arrival of God's kingdom in ways that threw open the doors to everyone—scoundrel or scribe, prostitute or Pharisee, doubter or devout. It is one of the key reasons why the religious leaders so aggressively opposed Jesus. Through his life, teaching and example Jesus allowed people to experience the presence and purpose of Yahweh. This was something that had always been the exclusive role of the religious leaders.

I believe one of the greatest things the Church can do is to reclaim the message and manifestation that "the kingdom of God is near." We are discovering that fewer people are responding to the revivalist call to accept Jesus into their hearts. Make no mistake: it *is* crucial that we confess our sins and receive the atoning work of Jesus Christ for our redemption. But the phraseology of "praying the sinner's prayer" and accepting Jesus into our heart is becoming less influential. It does not resonate with emerging generations as it once did for their parents and grandparents.

What *does* resonate is an invitation to join in making God's rule and reign—his peace, justice, compassion, mercy and love—a reality in the lives of those around them. Most everyone wants to see the world become a better place; they want opportunities to help bring it about. To call people to this, and to live in a countercultural way that expresses the beauty, harmony and purpose of God, is to use the same language Jesus did. Our churches would do well to immerse themselves in the kingdom language and perspective of Jesus, for by doing so we will be returning to the core of Christ's purpose.

* * * * * *

The New Testament blueprint also gives us two other missions for the Church. In Matthew 28:19-20, Jesus told his followers, "Therefore go and make disciples of all nations, baptizing them in the name of the Father and of the Son and of the Holy Spirit, and teaching them to obey everything I have commanded you. And surely I am with you always, to the very end of the age."

It is the responsibility and mission of the Church to GO (not stay inside our sanctuary walls) and make disciples. We are to teach these disciples how to truly follow Jesus and be obedient to him. We are to baptize them into the faith and the Body of Christ. The Church's mission is to reproduce followers of Jesus, not make members for the institutional roll.

The third mission of the Church likewise comes directly from Jesus. It is found in Acts 1:8. Following his resurrection, Jesus appeared to his followers on several occasions. During one of those gatherings, the disciples wanted to know if Jesus was going to fulfill the Messianic expectations of Israel by overthrowing Rome and establishing Yahweh's eternal rule on earth. Instead of answering their nationalistic hopes Jesus told them, "...you will receive power when the Holy Spirit comes on you; and you will be my witnesses in Jerusalem, and in all Judea and Samaria, and to the ends of the earth." In other words, Jesus said, "Quit worrying about what you want the Messiah to do. Don't try to figure out timelines and don't sit around waiting for something to happen. Concentrate on carrying my message to the entire world. Tell people the kingdom of heaven is near and they are invited to jump on board!"

The mission of the Church is to go into Jerusalem and Judea (the neighborhoods, towns, counties and states where our churches are located), to Samaria (those places where we are reluctant to go or do not want to go), and to the ends of the earth, echoing the command given in Matthew 28.

A long journey down the wrong road

LET US BE HONEST: the churches we serve and attend rarely, if ever, resemble the biblical design we have just explored. Committee meetings and denominational requirements swamp us. A faithful handful of saints give tirelessly while the majority drift in and out, doing little to move the kingdom forward. Pastors and staff are besieged by unrealistic expectations and negativity. Worship is often flat or uninspired, and prayer only tends to focus on those who are sick or dying. The Church today bears faint resemblance to the New Testament blueprint.

Robin Meyers, in his book *The Underground Church: Reclaiming the Subversive Way Of Jesus*, states, "What began as communities of radical inclusiveness, voluntary redistribution of wealth, a rejection of violence as the tool of injustice, and a joyful egalitarianism that welcomed a 'nobody' to worship elbow-to-elbow with a 'somebody' *devolved* into what [Harvey] Cox calls a 'top heavy edifice defined by obligatory beliefs enforced by a hierarchy.'"[2]

---

[2] Robin Meyers, *The Underground Church: Reclaiming the Subversive Way of Jesus* (San Francisco: Jossey-Bass, 2012), p. 59. Used by permission. All rights reserved.

How did this happen?

We have seen what Scripture tells us about the mission and purpose of the Church. And in the first three hundred years of the Church's life, existing evidence bears out the claim that they did indeed spread the good news. The Christian faith traveled across the known world as the apostles and new believers lived out the life of Christ. They faithfully followed the blueprint given to them.

However, things took a massive turn around 325 AD.

The Roman Emperor, Constantine, having received a vision of the cross prior to an important battle, triumphed over his foes and attributed his victory to Jesus. It was not long before the emperor publicly declared the Christian faith to be the official religion of the Roman Empire. Almost overnight the fledgling Church, spurred by the power of the Holy Spirit and an unwavering commitment to Christ's mission, became respectable throughout the land. What had previously been small house gatherings of socially equal, radically transformed Christian brothers and sisters was suddenly elevated to equal status with the state.

There has been much speculation as to whether Constantine was truly a converted Christian. We have no way of knowing. But the emperor was a shrewd and visionary man. He saw the potential of this rapidly expanding new religion and took a gamble by pairing it with his own government. From Constantine's perspective, the gamble paid off handsomely. The Church quickly acquired a place of acceptance and prominence in the empire. It moved from persecuted to popular, receiving favor and compensation from the throne of Rome. Constantine had the power of the state and the burgeoning power of the Church at his disposal.

Part of the legitimization of the Church in the eyes of the Roman world was the creation of a hierarchy of Church leaders. These men ordered the life and structure of the Church, and they handled the ministry that had previously been shared among all believers. With these advancements it was only natural that places for meeting and worship were required.

Constantine spent exorbitant amounts of money constructing the first basilicas for Christians to gather in. Christian houses of worship soon outnumbered the shrines of the old Roman gods and basilica upkeep required ongoing resources. Christ-followers who, only a generation before, had met in homes (and occasionally catacombs or forests when persecuted) now had the largest and most lavish buildings in which to worship. Thus was born the Roman Catholic Church with its priestly structure, theology, liturgy, tradition, and later—in the fourth and fifth centuries—its finalized canon of Scripture. A different blueprint had been introduced, one far removed from the apostolic original.

A second branch of Christianity also developed in the fourth and fifth centuries, what we call the Orthodox Church. In structure and style, the Orthodox Church remains almost identical to the Roman Catholic Church. The key difference is that Orthodox Churches subscribe to a few different creedal affirmations than the Catholic Church. Over the centuries attempts were made by bishops, popes and councils to reunite Eastern and Western Christianity but with no success. These two branches were the shape of global Christianity for more than a millennium.

In the sixteenth century a third branch emerged. An ecclesiastical rebellion arose against church hypocrisy and abuse, led by a Catholic monk, teacher and scholar named Martin Luther. Yearning for reformation and renewal in the Church, he nailed a list of ninety-five grievances against the Catholic Church to the door of his own parish, thus launching a fateful, bloody and world-changing movement that came to be known as the Protestant Reformation.

Like all Church reformers before him (and there had been many), Luther wanted to see the Church return to its apostolic blueprint. To do this he called for the reclamation of the biblical precept of "the priesthood of all believers." This says that because of the sacrifice of Christ, our great High Priest, there is no longer any need for an intermediary (a priest) between people and God. Because of Christ, individuals can go directly before God themselves; and in addition, every member of the Body of Christ is to minister to one another.

Luther called for many other reforms within the Church, including an end to ecclesiastical greed and corruption, and making the Bible available in common languages so people could read it for themselves. While Luther truly longed to see renewal, and did not set out to launch a completely separate branch of Christianity, he failed to change the Constantinian blueprint. Even though a great many churches separated from the Roman Catholic Church, they retained the same basic structure and system. Only a few cosmetic changes were made to worship. Church rules, systems and order remained virtually the same. Instead of a pope and a long list of cardinals, bishops, priests and sundry attendants, Protestant churches developed their own forms of governance. Yet when the dust settled, the Protestant churches were still building with the same blueprint the Catholic Church had used since Constantine.

This is not a rant against the Catholic Church. I deeply respect my Catholic brothers and sisters, and they have done immeasurable good across the world throughout their existence. The point is not to bash Catholics. It is to recognize that once Christianity was declared the officially sanctioned faith of the empire, the Church shifted away from the New Testament blueprint. The uniting of Church and state produced a model that I believe is not what God intended. Yes, God has been able to use this model across the centuries. But it is a model of man-made origin. It is not the way God designed it.

The chart below highlights a few of the contrasts between the New Testament and Constantinian models.

The churches you and I support and serve have inherited an institutional blueprint. We continue to operate our churches using a system that grew out of Constantine's influence. The powerlessness, irrelevance, apathy and ineffectiveness experienced by the majority of churches in the West can be traced back to the wrong blueprint. If our churches are to survive and grow once more, we need to seriously consider how we can jettison the institutional model and return to what Scripture has established for us.

It is because our churches have been built with the wrong set of blueprints that the problem of bullying has become so prevalent. Let us now turn our attention to some of the most common ways in which the bride of Christ is bullied today.

New Testament blueprint	Constantinian blueprint
Mission and purpose was to carry on the work of Jesus	Mission and purpose was to maintain institutional power and control
Ministry done by everyone	Ministry done by professional clergy
Small house church gatherings	Large basilica gatherings
Practice of spiritual gifts	Spiritual gifts rarely, if ever, emphasized
Apostolic leadership	Hierarchical leadership
Openness to the Holy Spirit	Reliance upon human guidance
Ability to speak prophetically to the world's systems	Collusion with the world's systems
Equitable sharing of resources for the poor and needy	Hoarding of resources for institutional maintenance and preservation
Accountability to one another and apostolic leadership	Little to no accountability to one another or among ecclesiastical leadership
Fluid, portable	Rigid, cumbersome
People joined because of the changes they saw/experienced in the lives of Christians	People joined because they were members of a nation under Church authority or experienced enforced conversions
Worship involved all people participating	Worship done almost exclusively by clergy; little involvement by laity
Dynamic, adaptive, living	Apathetic, inflexible, resistant to change
Empowered by the Holy Spirit	Empowered by tradition, rules, fear

CHAPTER 2
GIVE ME WHAT I WANT
AND NO ONE GETS HURT

The bride of Christ is bullied by our
sinful nature and the influence of Satan

"Our sins are like a carousel where the same decorated dogs, pigs, and goats, ridden by the foolish, come around again and again until the machine wears out."

Austin O'Malley

PASTOR JAMES HUNTER reclined in his office chair and waited for the computer to boot up. He sipped gingerly at a steamy cup of caramel drizzle coffee and watched the trees across the road surrender their leaves to the autumnal wind. Gray clouds hung in the sky, occasionally teasing the promise of the sun.

James felt good this morning. Better than he had in some time. He and his wife returned last night from a couples retreat, and it had been a much-needed getaway. Hectic overlapping schedules, the stress of work, and ordinary day-to-day problems and responsibilities had worn him thin. He and Tracey had laughed more, held hands more, and spent more time together over the weekend than it seemed they had in ages.

The computer ready, James opened his e-mail. He knew there were no emergencies or pressing matters. There had been no messages awaiting him when he got home, and he had received no calls on his cell. The only texts he had gotten had been from the twins wanting to know if they could spend the night with friends. James smiled to himself, anticipating a relaxed, productive day back in the office.

His spam folder held several e-mails. There were two from Canadian pharmacies promising deep discounts on prescription drugs; one for discount tires; and two from supposed "friends" — one in Sierra Leone, the other in Taiwan—alerting him to several million dollars awaiting him if he would just reply with his Social Security number. James deleted them all and clicked on the New Mail tab. His heart tightened as soon as the folder opened. Clamminess broke over him.

There was a single e-mail in the box. It was from Edward Albridge.

The subject line read CHURCH SERVICE.

Not wanting to open the e-mail but knowing he had to, James steeled himself. *Maybe it won't be bad,* he thought. *Maybe he had a really good time in worship yesterday, and he just wanted me to know.* James rejected both thoughts outright. In the three years he had been pastor at Highland Fellowship Church, he had never once known Edward Albridge to be positive about anything.

A new window opened on the monitor, revealing Edward's e-mail. James took a deep breath and started to read.

Pastor,

It's Sunday evening and I've been on the phone ever since church was over. A lot of people were simply not happy with the worship service today. To begin with, you had a *woman* in the pulpit. You know how some of us feel about that. I've mentioned it to you several times, but yet you went right ahead and brought one in anyway.

The heat wasn't turned on when we went into the sanctuary. It was cold here yesterday. I know you wouldn't know that since you were out of town. But several of our older ladies were uncomfortable during the service.

I also think you should know that Vance and Connie Lenley had a new family with them yesterday. I don't know where the family was from but they had two small children who were very disruptive during the service. You need to start up the Children's Church again. It would give kids something to do and would keep the distractions down during the service for the rest of us.

You've made a lot of changes since you've been our pastor, but the fact is that a lot of people are uncomfortable with them and just plain don't like them. Who decided these things? I don't recall anyone bringing them before the board to vote on. I think we need some policies in place to make sure that everyone gets a say.

I intend to bring all this up at the next board meeting. Something has to be done. We've lost some good members since all this stuff started, and you just keep pushing forward with your ideas. Some of our shut-ins haven't been visited in months, and that's your job, pastor! Instead of coming up with all these changes that are destroying our church, you need to get out and start visiting. If you don't, a lot more people are going to leave and take their money with them. You need to let the members run the church and you just do your job. That's what you're being paid for.

Ed Albridge

James sipped his coffee but did not taste it. His stomach had soured and his heart was pumping rapidly. He stared at the monitor, his mind shifting back and forth between responses.

Should he yell and curse to vent the anger that had clawed to life inside him? Should he pretend he did not get the e-mail? After all, computers were known for losing electronic correspondence. But no, that would not work. He knew it. Should he just delete the e-mail and try his best to ignore it?

But what of Ed's veiled—and not-so-veiled—threats? James knew that Ed had a mean streak in him, coupled with a chip on his shoulder. Ed's Sunday school class had been directly responsible for the unfavorable departure of two previous pastors. His threats weren't to be taken lightly. Once again, just like before the couples weekend, James felt smothered by demands, threats and expectations that were slowly draining his energy, his calling and sometimes, he felt, even his life away from him.

* * * * * *

While this story is fictitious, the situation it describes is anything but imaginary. If you are a pastor, you know this all too well. If you are a regular church member, you may think it sounds a bit extreme. Let me assure you it is not.

Pastors do receive e-mails, phone calls and letters like this. Such communications are rarely meant to be constructive. Instead, they are intended to wear the church leader down, to cause him or her to second-guess themselves and what God has them doing. They serve notice that there are those in the church the pastor better not mess around with, or else all hell will break loose.

Pastors, you can see their faces in your mind right now, can't you?

Church member, you know who the Ed Albridges of your congregation are. You may have known them all your life. They may be your friends. They may even be your relatives. Perhaps you have had a run-in with them before over a line item in the budget, someone using the church building or the support of a missionary. Maybe you have never personally incurred their wrath but you know others who have. And some of those victims are no longer in your church, or any church, as a result.

The Church in North America suffers from a problem that has gone unchecked for decades, and which contributes to the ineffectiveness of the Body of Christ. The Church's witness is compromised at best, and written off or ignored at worst. Unless something is done to address this issue—which exists regardless of denomination, size, demographic makeup or geographic location—the Church in the twenty-first century will remain a joke at our own expense.

The bullied bride

THE CHURCH IS being bullied. Small contingents of members in nearly every local congregation prevent the church from fulfilling its mission. They do this in order to control what does and does not happen in the church. They are fearful of change so they fight against anything that might upset the status quo. They do not trust pastors, staff or volunteer leaders to "run the church," so they make sure those who share the same perspective remain in positions of decision-making. They threaten to withhold money, stop attending or contact denominational officials to keep the church right where they want it. These people have been in power for a long time and very few want to tangle with them. On those rare occasions when someone has confronted them, the results have been ugly. The Church is being pushed around and intimidated by bullies, just as happens in locker rooms and school hallways.

Such situations prevent churches from effectively sharing the gospel and making disciples. Monies are only spent on the "insiders" and rarely, if ever, on benevolence, outreach or missions. The church cannot grow because (a) it is unhealthy, (b) it is dysfunctional, and (c) it has likely earned a reputation as a place of discord, hypocrisy or elitism.

Many members long for a vibrant, Spirit-filled church where hope is found, joy is tangible and lives are transformed. However, they see their dreams dashed again and again by bullies who threaten the church if it does not capitulate to their demands. The longer these people are allowed to micromanage, dictate terms and bully others, the less effective the church becomes. Left unchecked, such churches will eventually close their doors permanently. They will not receive new members, and age and attrition will take their inevitable toll.

I once knew a man who had a reputation of always getting his way in the church. He would threaten and bully those around him into acquiescing to his demands. Hardly anyone confronted him. Some had tried it in the past and gotten embroiled in lengthy feuds

31

with this man, who loved to keep a fight going. When I stood my ground on a decision I made, he turned his fury onto me. It took a year and a half of near-constant anxiety, fear and second-guessing before a tenuous resolution arrived. But the damage had long since been done.

In the 2003 film *The Matrix Reloaded*, the main character, Neo, visits an elderly woman known as The Oracle. He needs some information about a powerful entity called The Merovingian. Neo sits beside The Oracle on a park bench and asks, "What does he [The Merovingian] want?"

The Oracle replies, "What do all men with power want? More power."

Bullies want more power. They want to control all that goes on in the church.

No church is bullied overnight. It happens over a period of time as denominational officials, church leaders and committees fail to hold members accountable for their words and actions. Members see opportunities to gain more control or influence in the church and seize them. Slowly and methodically, they rally around them those who have similar feelings (e.g., the pastor should go, the worship service has to stay the same, we need to be sure only "the right people" receive help from our church).

We must recognize, however, that for the most part these people have been loyal and supportive members of the church all their lives. They have given money and volunteered their time. They have cleaned and decorated and raised funds. They have attended Sunday school, special services and have seen their church through many ups and downs. While their attitudes may mark them as bullies or controllers, they are not *evil* people. So where does their behavior come from? Why do they obstinately oppose change, monopolize committees and act distinctly un-Christian when they do not get their way?

William Beckham raises similar questions in his book *The Second Reformation: Reshaping the Church for the 21st Century*: "Why has the church agreed to allow its most immature members to dictate the ministry focus of the church? Why does the church tolerate manipulation—practically blackmail—from those members who contribute the least to the work of the church?"[3]

The short answer? They are led more by their sinful nature than by the Holy Spirit. Unconfessed sin and unconverted hearts rule.

Sin is everybody's problem

THE ROOT OF the problem is sin. Every person, without exception, has a fallen nature. We all sin. There are no exemptions. From the broken innocence of the garden in Genesis to the arrogant rebellion of humanity in Revelation, the entire canon of Scripture makes it plain that sin lies at the heart of the human condition. Left to our own devices, we will indulge our every sinful inclination. God created us good (Genesis 1:31). But our own individual choices and decisions have stained us with sin.

To make matters worse, we are incapable of fixing ourselves. There is nothing we can do to atone for our sinful thoughts, words and actions. If we think otherwise, Scripture exposes our deception: *Who can say, "I have kept my heart pure; I am clean and without sin"?* (Proverbs 20:9). *If we claim to be without sin, we deceive ourselves and the truth is not in us* (1 John 1:8). The prophet Isaiah flatly declared that our greatest and highest achievements are nothing more than tattered, grimy rags compared to God's perfect holiness and glory (64:6).

It is not a pretty picture. It is not supposed to be. The Bible reveals the depths to which our sin takes us, compared to the majestic glory of the Perfectly Holy One who rules in eternity. We cannot plead, wiggle or buy our way out of the punishment our sins deserve (Romans 6:23).

---

3 William A. Beckham, *The Second Reformation: Reshaping the Church for the 21st Century* (Houston: TOUCH Publications, 1997), p. 45. Used by permission. All rights reserved.

But in his vast mercy and compassion for all he has made, God provided the solution. He sent us a Savior—Jesus Christ—whose atoning death on the cross paid the price for our sinful pride and rebellion. We also received the undeserved honor of being adopted into God's family and clothed in the righteousness of Jesus himself (Isaiah 61:10; Ephesians 1:5).

Through faith in Jesus Christ our sins are forgiven, we are cleansed and restored to the proper relationship with the Father that he intended for us. We also receive the Holy Spirit, who takes up residence within us. It is the Spirit who gives us the power and ability to turn from sin and to live in holiness before God.

This does not make us immune to sin, however. Scripture atests that we continue to struggle with temptation and sin. The Holy Spirit warns us when we are tempted and convicts us when we give in to sinful behaviors. Through the blood of Jesus, and the regenerating power of the Spirit, we can continue to find forgiveness and restoration.

This does not give us a "blank check" to continue sinning (Romans 6:1-7). If we are truly in Christ, our desire is to become more like him. To that end, the Spirit guides us away from sin and toward godly and holy lives. Yes, we will still mess up. Yes, we will still sin. But our goal should be to sin less and less. Figure 1 shows how we move from death to life, from sinfulness to holiness.

FIGURE 1

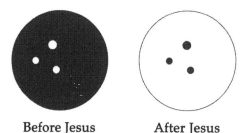

Before Jesus   **After Jesus**

The black circle on the left represents a person under the curse of sin. There remain "pockets" or spots of goodness within us, but we are dominated and led by our fallen human nature. We seek our own best interests. We do not know God or love

God, nor do we love others as we should.

The white circle on the right represents a person under the grace of Jesus Christ. We have been forgiven of our sins and made new in Christ (2nd Corinthians 5:17). We are no longer under the curse of sin and the law. However, we are not made fully perfect. There are still pockets or spots of sinfulness within us. If we are walking in harmony with the Holy Spirit and growing as disciples of Jesus, those spots should diminish in size. We should sin less and less while increasing more and more in holiness. Our goal as disciples of Jesus is to mature toward holiness and perfection (Matthew 5:48), thereby lessening the presence and influence of sin in our lives (see Figure 2).

FIGURE 2

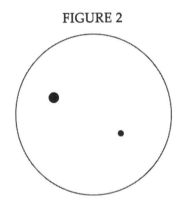

Less influence and fewer areas of sin in our lives

Bullies arise in the Church when people are not fully submitted to the lordship of Jesus Christ and are unwilling to obey the voice of the Spirit. There remains a great deal of unconfessed sin—of *self*—that wants to be in charge. Many people erroneously believe that all we need do is come to the altar, say a thirty-second prayer, and—*presto!*—we are a follower of Jesus. Nothing could be further from the truth! Such false teaching creates self-centered, consumerist church members who have not fully accepted Christ and who do not allow the Holy Spirit to transform them. Confessing and accepting Jesus is only the *beginning* step in a lifelong journey.

Hence, the sinful nature exerts itself repeatedly, drowning out the voice of the Spirit. Left unresolved, all that remains is our own personal agendas, bigotries, negativity and bitterness. These things—indeed our entire sinful nature—are fertile playgrounds for our real Enemy.

Know the real enemy

AT THE END of the 1940s, a cartoonist named Walt Kelly created a daily comic strip about the exploits of a possum named Pogo who lived in the Okefenokee Swamp. One line from the comic strip has become a well-known saying: "We have met the enemy, and he is us." Sounds like many of us in the Church.

As divisive, frustrating, mean and narrow-minded as some in our congregations may be, they are not the real enemy. To see them as the enemy is to commit two grievous errors. The first is that we dehumanize our brothers and sisters in Christ. Just as soldiers in battle tend to view the other side in the most derogatory and basest of ways—thereby making it easier to kill and to justify killing—we can fall into the trap of seeing bullies in the Church the same way. Prior to and during the 1994 genocide in Rwanda, the Hutu tribe labeled the Tutsi tribe as "cockroaches," thereby making it easier to denigrate and eventually massacre over 500,000 of them.

Second, when we see one another as villains and enemies we are fighting on the wrong front. Our time and energy is being targeted in the wrong direction. This only causes further division within the Body of Christ, and allows the true enemy to continue causing harm.

The enemy of the Church is Satan. His desire is to see the Church neutralized, broken down and ineffective. He sows dissention, spreads gossip and tries to distract us from our main goal. Satan does not want the gospel of Jesus Christ to advance.

Satan's oldest and best tactic is to use our sinful nature against us. We have all heard people say something like "Well, Satan really knows how to push my buttons." We are referring to those areas of weakness in our sinful nature, those places where we are more prone to sin. Satan subtly manipulates those areas of weaknesses, whether it is pride, greed or the need to be in control or to be right. He plays us against ourselves. We have indeed met the enemy.

Please do not misunderstand: I am not suggesting every grumpy person in the Church is possessed! It is not a matter of needing to call in an exorcist. Satan has not *invaded* the Edward Albridges of your congregation. The Great Serpent is merely poking certain tender and easily influenced places in us with a stick.

For example, if I struggle with greed then Satan can influence that. If I am in Christ, I am still responsible for turning away from greed. Yet it remains a sinful, unperfected aspect of my nature. It dwells within me as a pocket or spot of sin I wrestle with. I must rely daily on the grace of God in Christ and the indwelling Holy Spirit to help me overcome my greed. But Satan can influence my sinfulness. If the church wants to use money to help the poor, but my greed lies unchecked and unconfessed, Satan can push and prod so that I stand firmly against any such assistance.

The Serpent in the sanctuary

I HAVE OFTEN told my congregations that Satan is not looking for us to sign our name in blood on a piece of parchment, pledging our souls to him like Wolfgang von Goethe's *Faust*. He is not that theatrical in his plans. Satan would rather work from the shadows through our fallen human nature. Jesus said that Satan's objective is *"to steal and kill and destroy"* (John 10:10), and the Devil is brutally determined to do that in any way he can. Throughout history one of the most successful ways our Enemy has accomplished this goal is by pitting Christians against one another.

Paul was up to his neck in division in the Corinthian church. The Great Serpent had infiltrated their congregations very effectively. In fact, it was the issue of division and disunity (over a variety of social and theological concerns) that necessitated Paul's letters and visits.

In 1st Corinthians 1:10-16 we read,

> *I appeal to you, brothers and sisters, in the name of our Lord Jesus Christ, that all of you agree with one another in what you say and that there be no divisions among you, but that you be perfectly united in mind and thought. My brothers and sisters, some from Chloe's household have informed me that there are quarrels among you. What I mean is this: One of you says, "I follow Paul"; another, "I follow Apollos"; another, "I follow Cephas"; still another, "I follow Christ."*
>
> *Is Christ divided? Was Paul crucified for you? Were you baptized in the name of Paul? I thank God that I did not baptize any of you except Crispus and Gaius, so no one can say that you were baptized in my name. (Yes, I also baptized the household of Stephanas; beyond that, I don't remember if I baptized anyone else.)*

The first problem Paul addressed was a serious division over which apostle was the best, and who was the authoritative leader of the community. Division is one of Satan's primary tactics. He knows if he can get Christians divided over something, they will not have the time or energy to share the gospel and make disciples.

In Corinth, the congregation had degenerated into factions. One group claimed Paul as the rightful leader and father of their congregation. Paul was the apostle who had planted the Corinthian church, so this group was loyal to him. A second group claimed to follow Apollos, a gifted preacher and apostle who had visited the congregation (Acts 18:24-27). Most scholars believe Apollos was a much better speaker than Paul, and consequently a group arose that thought Apollos should be the senior pastor.

A third group pledged their apostolic allegiance to Cephas (Peter). It would seem that Peter likewise visited the church at one point. Being one of the original twelve disciples and an eyewitness to Jesus himself, it is not surprising there were those in Corinth who felt that Peter should be the one in charge. Finally, there were those who were just trying to follow Jesus. Perhaps they felt all the bickering about apostles was nerve-wracking and pointless. Perhaps they thought themselves more spiritual than the other groups ("Well, you are choosing to follow a mere man, but WE follow Jesus himself"). There can be no doubt Satan had stirred up quite a mess in the Corinthian church, preying upon the pride and arrogance of many in the congregation.

Satan hides out in our churches. The great reformer Martin Luther said, "Where God builds a church, the devil builds a chapel." I was leading a Bible study on the gospel of Mark once, and as we discussed the encounter with the demon-possessed man in the synagogue (Mark 1:21-28) one person asked, "How did the demon-possessed guy get into the synagogue to begin with?" With a laugh I replied that the Church is one of the best hiding places Satan has! The Evil One exists among our congregations because we are not as holy as we should be. We have unconfessed sin in our lives that Satan can influence. We have not truly surrendered to the lordship of Jesus Christ and allowed him to regenerate our hearts. Any or all of these could have been at play in Corinth.

The Corinthian believers were so divided over which apostle was better that they were ineffective in their witness and ministry. This is what Satan wants in every church. The longer we fight one another over issues of money or worship or committees, the fewer people we can effectively reach for Christ. In addition, those within our churches often fail to mature spiritually—or even begin to regress--because so much of their energy goes into fighting one another. Or worse yet, they disengage from the church completely so they do not have to deal with the drama every week.

When the bride of Christ is bullied by sinful attitudes and behaviors, it affects everything. We are not seeking God's glory nor are we being transformed more into the image of Christ. We want what works for us or what will keep our group in control ("I follow Paul"; "I follow Apollos"). We lose our focus on the mission and purpose of the Church, replacing it with agendas that seek to maximize and maintain our personal preferences. Worship, instead of being about God and for God, becomes about me and for me. Those with whom we may disagree—about anything from politics to the color of paint for the hallway—may slowly become "the opposition" or the "bad guys" in our minds. We cease to see them as brothers and sisters in Christ, and due to Satan's poisonous influence, we begin to draw lines of demarcation. If not recognized and handled quickly, we demonize the person across the aisle, gossiping about him or her, and doing our best to portray them in the worst possible light. And all the while Satan sits back and smiles wickedly.

The Serpent in the sanctuary does not care if Christians get together to worship or study the Bible—so long as those Christians are focused on themselves. If the worship or Bible study does not result in transformed hearts and lives, Satan is not worried. A powerless church is of no threat to Satan. In fact, it can actually do a lot of his work for him by presenting a poor witness, having a negative reputation, not reaching new people and not discipling those it does have.

CHAPTER 3
DEFENDING THE BRIDE OF CHRIST
FROM OUR SINFUL NATURE
AND THE INFLUENCE OF SATAN

"It is easier to cry against one thousand sins of others than to kill one of your own."

John Flavel

EVERY ONE OF us has the potential to be a bully in the church. As we saw in the previous chapter, within us lies a rebellious, sinful nature that constantly wars with God. No one is exempt; no one gets a free pass.

So how do we defend the church from our own sinful nature and the influence of Satan? After all, these two things represent the core of every single problem in the church (and the world for that matter). It seems like a monumental task to undertake. Thankfully, God has already done all the heavy lifting!

A death sentence

WHEN SIN ENTERED into God's good and perfect creation (Genesis 3), humanity was wrenched apart from God. A barrier was erected between Creator and created. Instead of complete union with God, humanity's sinfulness alienated us from the Father. On one side of the barrier is God—holy, just, righteous; on the other side is humanity—unholy, unjust and unrighteous. It is a no-win situation for us because as we have already said, there is absolutely nothing we can do to rectify this condition or remove the barrier.

Sin leads to death (Ezekiel 18:4; Romans 6:23; James 1:15). We are finite beings who must experience physical death, but sin also brings about spiritual death. Sin separates us from fellowship and intimacy with God. Under the dominion of the sinful nature we do not know or care about God. We live only to follow our own desires. We may consider ourselves "good" people who pay our taxes, tell the truth, and help little old ladies across the street. But the apostle Paul, quoting Psalms 14 and 53, said *there is no one who does good, not even one* (Romans 3:12). He followed that up with the sobering reality of Romans 3:23: *for all have sinned and fall short of the glory of God.* If this sin and separation is not resolved, we remain apart from our Creator for eternity.

The pardon

HOWEVER, THERE IS a pardon for the death sentence! God desires to be reconciled to his estranged creation (Romans 5:10; 2nd Corinthians 5:17-19; Ephesians 2:14-17). But because of our sinful nature we are incompatible. Our sinfulness cannot co-exist with God's perfect holiness. Yet God's love for his creation is so great and incalculable that he devised a way for us to be reunited with him. He does not require that we jump through hoops to get to him. Rather, God came down and made himself available to us in the person of Jesus Christ.

Here's where the heavy lifting comes in. Through Jesus, God provides the way for the sin barrier to be torn down. The voluntary sacrifice that Jesus made on the cross paid the penalty—death—that comes as a result of sin. While Jesus himself was without sin (Hebrews 4:15; 1 Peter 2:22), the apostle Paul wrote that *God made him who had no sin to be sin for us* (2nd Corinthians 5:21a). Jesus took upon himself the sins of the world, thereby *becoming* sin in the eyes of the Father. This was the reason that God abandoned Jesus on the cross (Matthew 27:46; Mark 15:34). The Father could not look upon the sin his Son had become. For the first and only time in all existence, the Trinity was severed. The three became two—Father and Holy Spirit—while the Son was alienated, becoming the fullness of all humanity's ugliness and rebellion.

The reason Jesus became sin for us was *so that in him we might become the righteousness of God* (2nd Corinthians 5:21b). By becoming our sin and paying the penalty that sin demands, Jesus effected our emancipation from sin's grasp. When we say "yes" to the saving grace of Jesus Christ, our sins are wiped away. The sin barrier is broken. All that we have done as a result of living by our sinful nature is removed. We are made new. We receive the righteousness of Jesus as our own, and we become the dwelling place of the Holy Spirit.

Coming to faith in Christ is like a two-for-one deal: not only do we receive new life and new birth in Jesus. We also receive the Holy Spirit. He takes up residence in every believer and supplies us with the power to reject temptation and turn from sin. This is how we gradually diminish and overcome our sinful nature: by maturing in our faith, by allowing Jesus to become greater in us, and by being obedient to the promptings of the Spirit.

We will struggle with temptation and sin throughout our lives. We remain fallen, imperfect beings, even with the life of Jesus in us. We still make mistakes, mess up and sin. However, walking in tandem with Jesus and the Spirit, we should grow in grace, love and holiness, thereby minimizing the influence our sinful nature has over us. If we allow our sinful nature to control us, we all have the potential to be a bully. This is unfortunately what we see happening in every church, to one degree or another.

Some bullies have never fully surrendered their lives to the lordship of Jesus Christ. They may have accepted the merits of his work on the cross. They may have confessed their belief in him. But there is no evidence—no "fruit" (Matthew 7:16-20, 12:33; Luke 3:8; John 15:4-16; Romans 7:4-5; Galatians 5:22)—that their lives have been changed. Such persons do not mature in their faith, so the sinful nature continues to have dominion over them.

Changing allegiance

IN ORDER TO defend the bride from our sinful nature, we must choose to confess and repent, *then* allow the Holy Spirit to work within us. Sounds simple, right?

Not so fast.

Confession and repentance are Christian buzzwords that we routinely toss around, but we fail to grasp their full meanings. Protestant churches treat confession as something that we trot out in the weekly pastoral prayer. Even if we come to the altar for prayer, or use the quiet of the Lord's Supper in which to confess, most often our confessions are rattled off like a grocery list: "Lord, I'm sorry for yelling at the kids this morning, and for not being truthful in the office the other day, and for my bad language when I'm mad, and for spending too much money online." While we may be recognizing those moments or areas in our lives where we could have been better, our tendency is to rush through our list so we can get to the next thing on the program.

Confession is not only about recognizing our sinfulness before God. The Greek word for confession, *homologèo* (homo-log-aye-oh), also means "to praise and celebrate." How often do we think of confession as a time for celebration? This is not a celebration of what we have done wrong, for that would be glorifying our sinful nature. The praise element comes when we realize that by God's rich mercy we can be forgiven and reconciled to him. There *should be* contrition (sorrow) of heart and spirit when we bring our sins before the Holy One. But with the assurance of forgiveness in Christ, we can turn to praise the One who makes that forgiveness possible.

Yet in order to truly be in Christ and to walk in harmony with him, we cannot stop at confession. One of the reasons the sinful nature reigns strongly in many Christians is because we have done little to nothing to change following our confession. We may confess our sins but if we do not also repent we have not finished the process.

The Greek word for repent, *metanoéō* (met-an-aye-oh), means "to regret," "to feel remorse for." We usually speak of it as turning away from sin or turning our back on sin. Regardless of the terminology, the concept is the same: to repent is to willfully move away from sin. Another definition for the Greek term is "to change allegiance."

Whenever we hear of an American citizen who has joined a terrorist organization we say they have changed allegiance. They have switched from one set of values, beliefs and practices to a different set. Biblical repentance means that we change our allegiance—we move from the sin we have committed to a different orientation. Following his baptism and wilderness temptations, Mark 1:14-15 says, "*...Jesus went into Galilee, proclaiming the good news of God. "The time has come," he said. 'The kingdom of God has come near. Repent and believe the good news!'"*

The good news was that *the kingdom of God has come near*. Jesus then instructed his listeners to repent and believe the good news. He wanted people to change their allegiance, and with a new kingdom orientation they were to believe. Believing was not merely giving intellectual assent to a set of propositions or doctrines, as we commonly think of belief. To believe in the biblical sense meant to act and behave in accordance with the values and principles of who or what was being accepted. Therefore, the message that Jesus brought to Israel was that the kingdom of God had arrived. In response, people needed to repent—change their allegiance—and believe—begin living in an alternate way.

Without true confession (including praise) and without real repentance—willfully choosing to behave in a new way, commensurate with the call of Christ—we are not subduing our sinful nature. We are making ourselves feel better, flattering ourselves that we have said all the right words and we can go on about our business. We need to bear in mind the words of teacher and pastor Andrew Murray: "Beware of the prayer for forgiveness becoming a formality. Only that which is sincerely confessed is really forgiven."

What is next?

ACCEPTING THE LORDSHIP of Jesus Christ is the first step in a lifelong journey. You are no more a mature Christian at that point than a toddler is ready to drive a car. Many people erroneously believe that saying "I accept Jesus into my heart" is all it takes.

When this is the case, there is hardly any transformation that takes place and almost no decision to take responsibility for spiritual growth. This explains why churches are filled with Christians whose spiritual growth is stunted due to apathy and a lack of biblical discipleship (we will talk more about this in a later chapter). Confessing and accepting the work of Christ in our lives, being "born again" and reconciled with the Father, is just the starting line. As the 1970 song by The Carpenters put it, "We've only just begun."

Once off the starting line we must be intentional about our growth in grace and holiness. It is YOUR responsibility to help make this happen. It is not the pastor's responsibility to grow you spiritually (although she or he is one agent of your growth). It is not the youth pastor's job to grow your children or grandchildren spiritually. I have seen too many Christians sit back and expect someone else to do all the work of discipleship for them. They want everything handed to them in convenient, bite-sized morsels that require no effort, no commitment and no change whatsoever on their part. They are childish, petulant and selfish because they take no responsibility for their own spiritual growth.

God has given us the Holy Spirit to aid in our journey of holiness, faith and discipleship. The Holy Spirit indwells every believer who confesses the name of Jesus and accepts his life and lordship (Romans 5:5, 8:9; Ephesians 1:13; 1 John 4:13). With the presence of the Spirit in the regenerated believer, God gives us access to the same power that raised Jesus from the dead. It is the job of the Holy Spirit to help us grow in our faith and spiritual understanding. The Spirit warns us of temptation and convicts us when we sin and fall away from God. We become more Christ-like with the aid of the Holy Spirit (John 16:8, 13-15; Romans 8:13-16; 2nd Corinthians 3:17). He is our spiritual source of energy.

I was delivering the children's message in worship one morning and I showed them a flashlight. When I turned the flashlight on nothing happened. I let them see that the flashlight had no batteries. I explained that the Holy Spirit is to the Christian what the batteries are to the flashlight: a power source. No batteries, no power.

"What can I do to make the flashlight work?" I asked the children.

"Put the batteries in it!" a chorus of voices replied.

I pulled the batteries from my pocket, placed them in the flashlight, and showed it to the children again. "Well, why isn't it working?" I asked. "I put the batteries in, just like you told me to."

Again the chorus of voices: "YOU HAVE TO TURN IT ON!"

Unfortunately, there are many Christians who have the "batteries in their flashlight" but never turn the flashlight on. They are sitting atop an immeasurable source of divine power, but for whatever reason refuse to take advantage of it. Even though the Spirit fills us *we choose* whether or not we cooperate with him. God will never force himself on anyone. He waits to be invited, welcomed and loved. The batteries cannot force the flashlight to activate. The button must be pushed in order for the flashlight to accomplish its intended function. We have the "battery" of the Holy Spirit; it is up to us to flip the switch on.

If we allow the Spirit to lead, teach, convict and mature us, a natural result is that we begin to sin less. As we have already noted, we will never be completely free of our sin nature until we are glorified in eternity. But if we truly hunger after God, and desire more communion with Jesus Christ, those times of sin will diminish. Sin becomes the exception, not the norm.

Walking with Jesus requires diligence and discipline—two things we are not terribly keen on in our instantaneous, streaming society. God expects us to do our part just as he does his. It is up to us to avail ourselves of the spiritual disciplines that will help us mature: worship, the sacraments, the study of God's Word, prayer and accountability. These are our weapons in the battle against our sinful nature. They are God's provision for us. Coupled with the Holy Spirit, we have all we need to walk in holiness, live in grace and better reflect the image of Christ.

But what if?

WHAT DO WE do if someone in the church is not walking with the Spirit? What if they are not sorry for the things they have said or done in the church? What if they continue to stir up trouble and be disruptive to the unity and mission of the Body?

Sadly, not everyone truly wants to accept the responsibilities of Christian discipleship. Many want the benefits of Christ's work without the commitment. Thomas à Kempis, the thirteenth-century Catholic theologian, said, "Jesus has many lovers of His heavenly kingdom, but few bearers of His Cross. He has many seekers of consolation, but few of tribulation. He finds many companions at His feasting, but few at His fasting. All desire to rejoice with Him; few are willing to endure anything for Him. Many follow Jesus as far as the breaking of the bread, but few to the drinking of the cup of His Passion. Many reverence His miracles, but few will follow the shame of His Cross. Many love Jesus as long as no adversities befall them. Many praise and bless Him so long as they receive some consolation from Him."[4]

We cannot make anyone else confess or repent. We cannot make anyone else apologize or ask forgiveness. Those choices belong to each of us alone. For sin to be diminished in the church, it must begin with me. And I must pray that God will use the changes in me to help bring about changes in others.

* * * * * *

"There is no neutral ground in the universe; every square inch, every split second, is claimed by God and counter-claimed by Satan."

C. S. Lewis

---

[4] Thomas à Kempis, *The Imitation of Christ* (Brewster: Paraclete Press, 1997), pp. 77-78.

Your congregation likely has an Ed Albridge or two. Due to an immature faith, a history of overbearing control or plain old stubbornness, they are bullying your church with their demands and threats. Trying to reason with them has not softened their position. They do not act like a disciple of Jesus should. Ed Albridge and those like him need our prayers for soft hearts, open minds and spiritual receptivity to God's Word. Satan is feasting on the sinful nature and must be confronted with the weapons of spiritual warfare.

If you want to defend your church from its bullies, you had better be prepared to go to war. *Spiritual* war. Satan is constantly working to pull people away from a relationship with Jesus. The Enemy runs rampant in most churches to one degree or another. In many cases he has become entrenched in a church's structure, traditions and culture—creating strongholds of power and influence.

In one church I helped with a turnaround, Satan had established just this kind of stronghold. He had been among that congregation for a number of years: a small number of women had almost absolute control over the church. Many of the men had abdicated their spiritual responsibility of leadership, and Satan influenced the need for power and control among the group of women. Nothing happened in that church which was not approved by at least one of those ladies. And if one of them was against something they were all against it.

Satan's eviction notice

AS I BEGAN to preach and teach on the biblical mission and purpose of the church, and as we began to make changes to help the church refocus itself externally, this group of women became increasingly angry. They spread rumors and even went so far as to telephone other church members and ask them *not* to attend worship. They were determined to undermine the vision God had for that congregation. Family members of anyone who supported the future vision were criticized and ostracized.

Eventually, after a lengthy conflict the majority of the congregation stood up to those ladies. Through a series of ugly events the congregation came to see the true hearts of the women. The majority—including close relatives of some of the controlling women—let it be known they would no longer tolerate their church being bullied. When that happened, breakthrough occurred.

About a year later I was in the office one day and a lady (who had been one of the key supporters of God's plan for that church) asked me a question. "Do you know when the turnaround started in this church?"

I thought about it for a moment. "Was it when I started conducting the leadership visioning process to see where God wanted to take us?"

"No," she replied.

"Was it when you and everyone else stood up to the bullies and took your church back?"

She shook her head. "No, it wasn't any of that. The turnaround began the day you walked into that sanctuary and started anointing the pews, the altar, the pulpit, the doors and windows. When you did that and claimed the authority God has given you, you handed Satan his eviction notice!"

Not long after arriving at that church I took some oil and went through the sanctuary anointing everything, confessing the Holy Spirit's presence and power in that place. I anointed doorframes and declared that no evil spirits were to come through those portals. I did the same with the windows. I claimed victory over the pews, calling upon God to touch and change the hearts and lives of those who sat in them. I anointed the pulpit where God's Word went forth, the choir loft, the organ and piano—just about everything I could reach was anointed with the sign of the cross.

The reason for this was simple: I knew that everything happening in that church had a negative spiritual source. The troublesome ladies were not bad or evil. They were not the true enemy. As the pastor, I knew I had a responsibility to use the authority God had given me. To go in and just continue "business as usual" would only have perpetuated an ineffective and dysfunctional church. I did not believe God put me in that church to walk it to its death. So the first thing that needed to happen was for Satan to be reminded who the church truly belonged to: Jesus Christ.

Authority

THE BIBLE MAKES clear there is a war happening in the invisible realm (Daniel 10:12-14; Matthew 16:18; 2nd Corinthians 11:13-15; Ephesians 6:10-17; Hebrews 2:14; 1 Peter 5:8; 1 John 3:8-9; Revelation 12:7-12). It is known as *spiritual warfare*. There are forces of darkness, evil and wickedness aligned against God. It is a battle for the souls of humanity.

However, contrary to popular thought, God and Satan are not evenly matched. They are not like two chess masters trying to outmaneuver the other. God is supremely all-powerful; Satan is not. God is all-knowing. Not so with the Devil. These are not equally matched titans locked in eternal combat. Satan is ultimately a defeated foe (Colossians 2:15), although for the time being he has limited power (Revelation 12:7-9, 12).

As disciples of Jesus Christ, empowered by the same Holy Spirit and under the same missional directive as Jesus, we have the ability to take authority (Luke 10:19) over Satan's schemes. We exercise a shared authority, claiming in the name of Jesus Christ that evil cannot and will not remain in our churches. That authority is part of the image of God within us.

John Wesley, the founder of the Methodist movement, understood the image of God in us to include what he termed the "political image." This, Wesley believed, is the capacity we have as human beings to be stewards over all that God has entrusted to us. We exercise a limited authority so that we might reflect God's love and grace back into creation. God "loans" us some of his power so that we may govern and steward all the things he has placed into our care. It is our God-given responsibility to oversee and care for those things that are within our spheres of influence.

Satan does not want you or me to exercise this divine authority. He laid claim to it when Adam and Eve sinned in the garden, thereby abdicating their responsibility of stewardship. Separated from their perfect communion with God, the first man and woman metaphorically turned their backs on the authority that had been granted to them to rule in God's stead (Genesis 1:28).

Nature abhors a vacuum, as they say, and it was no different in this case. With God's authority abandoned by its original recipients, Satan stepped in and claimed it for his own. This is why Jesus says, *"I will not say much more to you, for **the prince of this world** is coming"* (John 14:30, emphasis mine), and why Paul would write, *The **god of this age** has blinded the minds of unbelievers* (2nd Corinthians 4:4, emphasis mine). 1 John 5:19 also tells us...*that **the whole world is under the control of the evil one*** (emphasis mine). Satan exercises his limited dominion over our world, working his evil influence into everything around us, contributing to the brokenness brought on by our sinfulness.

Whenever Christians gather to worship and pray they are pushing back the darkness in their area. The more they worship and pray the more darkness is pushed back. And the more darkness that is pushed back, the angrier Satan becomes. He begins to throw everything he has at us—individually and as the church—because he knows that lives can be transformed and people can be saved. Satan does not want us to pray or worship. He does not want us to read the Bible. He does not care if we sit in a pew for sixty years as long as we do not allow God's power to change us and use us. In fact, some of Satan's most effective agents sit stone-faced in worship services every week, looking for something to complain about.

However, the bride of Christ is not without resources. All those who are walking in fellowship and obedience with Jesus have the God-given authority originally bestowed on Adam and Eve. When we are made new by accepting Jesus, the political image in us is repaired. It is not perfected (since we are still prone to sin), but we have enough of it restored so we can exercise it on behalf of God for his creation.

In addition, we have the stated authority of Jesus himself, shared with us for the fulfillment of his mission in the world: *Then Jesus came to them and said,*

> *"All authority in heaven and on earth has been given to me. Therefore go and make disciples of all nations, baptizing them in the name of the Father and of the Son and of the Holy Spirit, and teaching them to obey everything I have commanded you. And surely I am with you always, to the very end of the age."*

> (Matthew 28:18-20)

Since all authority resides in Jesus, and since he has commissioned us to *go,* he has bestowed some of his authority upon us to make disciples, baptize and teach. Likewise, Luke 10:19 records Jesus conferring some of his authority on his disciples: *"I have given you authority to trample on snakes and scorpions and to overcome all the power of the enemy; nothing will harm you."*

Therefore, in order to defend the bride of Christ from being bullied by Satan's influence we must reclaim our biblical authority and exercise it over our Enemy.

Pastor, the church you are serving is Christ's bride in that location. She deserves the best opportunity to grow, multiply and bring glory to God. If you are facing a bully (or any other issues that stem from a negative spiritual source), it is *your responsibility* to use the authority Christ has granted you. Do not sit back and allow Satan to manipulate, influence and dominate your flock! Use the Word of God to pray for deliverance, to cast out the demonic spirits, to assert your role as spiritual leader in that place. Christ is the Head of the church, and you are the woman or man to whom he has entrusted his bride.

If you are a member of a bullied congregation, remember that according to the priesthood of all believers you are a priest before God and each other. As a follower of Christ you have the spiritual authority to bind on earth and in heaven, and to loose on earth and in heaven (Matthew 16:19). Talk with your pastor and church leaders. Make a covenant to cover them in prayer (because as leaders they will be one of Satan's first and favorite targets), and to pray authoritatively against Satan's work in your church. Also be sure to have godly prayer partners who will covenant to bear you up regularly in prayer. As soon as you begin taking the battle to Satan he will take shots right back at you.

Battle plans

HERE ARE SOME things you will need to keep in mind as you prepare to exercise Christ's authority and engage the Enemy in spiritual warfare.

(1) Deal with your own sins first. You *cannot* exercise authority over Satan until you have first dealt with your own sins. If you try to engage in spiritual warfare with unconfessed or intentional sin in your life, Satan will eat your lunch! Find a godly friend in whom you can confide, confess to and pray with. Take proactive steps to avoid the temptations that lead to sin. No, you do not have to be perfect before you can pray against Satan, but you had better be very sure you are right with God before you do. Otherwise, your prayers will be ineffective and you will be placing yourself in a spiritually vulnerable position.

(2) Surround yourself with faithful prayer warriors. Spiritual warfare is not a solo act. You should have people lifting you up in prayer regularly. For example, if you know that you are going to anoint the pews in your church on Tuesday at 10:00 AM, let your prayer warriors know so they can be interceding on your behalf during that time. Satan is going to paint a big red target on you, your family and church leaders so you need plenty of spiritual backup.

(3) Be well grounded in the Word of God. You do not have to be a PhD candidate in Biblical Theology to engage in spiritual warfare, but you should have a growing knowledge and application of the Bible in your life. The Word of God is foundational for defeating the plans of the Enemy. See Appendix 1 for specific passages regarding Satan and spiritual warfare.

(4) Be prepared for backlash and spiritual attacks. As soon as you begin to exercise the authority you have in Christ, demonic forces *will* take notice. Remember that they have likely been a threat for quite a while so they will not back off easily. One of Satan's favorite tactics is to try and take down the spiritual leader(s) of a church (Mark 14:7). He will use family, friends, circumstances, church members, finances—anything and everything—to do this. Also bear in mind that some in your congregation who are being led by their sinful nature will resist what you are seeking to do. Satan will influence and manipulate their sinful nature to use them as obstacles along the way.

(5) Be humble. Remember that the true power comes from God through the Holy Spirit. The authority we seek to exercise is not found or manufactured in ourselves. Do not become arrogant or conceited about your role in spiritual warfare. Satan can, will and does take advantage of our hubris. We become ineffective in spiritual warfare the moment we think ourselves effective.

(6) Practice spiritual discernment. Not everything that happens in the church is the work of Satan or his demons. That patch of mold appearing in the parlor is probably because the wall is damp, not because Satan is gunning for the Ladies' Knitting Society that meets there every month. If you go looking for demons behind every pew chances are good you will find one every time, even if one does not exist. As the old saying goes, "When all you have is a hammer everything looks like a nail." Do not be a spiritual hammer finding demon nails everywhere you look.

(7) Know your weapons and stick to them. A hammer is a valuable tool. It is designed to drive and pull nails. A gun is a powerful weapon. It is designed to injure and kill. It is not wise to use a gun to drive a nail, and you would look rather silly trying to kill a deer with a hammer. In the same way, God has given us very specific weapons to use in spiritual warfare.

The situation in the Corinthian church necessitated Paul writing a follow-up letter to the congregation. In 2nd Corinthians 10:3-5 he stated,

> *For though we live in the world, we do not wage war as the world does. The weapons we fight with are not the weapons of the world. On the contrary, they have divine power to demolish strongholds. We demolish arguments and every pretension that sets itself up against the knowledge of God, and we take captive every thought to make it obedient to Christ.*

Our weapons in spiritual warfare are prayer, the Bible and the Holy Spirit. The moment we deviate from these weapons and begin trying to fight on human terms (i.e., from our sinful nature), we have played right into Satan's hands. We cannot and will not be effective with any other weapons.

(8) Don't be afraid to let people leave. Pastors are notorious for wanting to please everybody, even though we know it is impossible. And no one wants to see people leave the church. However, if Satan has embedded himself deeply within your church it is quite possible that, during the course of the spiritual battle, some of the controllers and negative attitudes will leave the church. *Let them.* If their hearts are not right with the Lord, if they are there for the wrong reasons, and if they refuse to engage in fulfilling the mission of the church, you are better off without them. But know they will likely leave a path of destruction in their wake, pulling impressionable members along with them.

Church consultant Bill Easum says, "...spiritual things bring out either the best or the worst in people. Some people are going to get madder than Hell and do unbelievably bad things before it is all over."[5]

It will be uncomfortable, difficult and stressful, but it is necessary for your church to move forward. If those persons have a change of heart and repent, welcome them back with open arms. But if they refuse to cooperate and continue to stir up trouble, do not feel guilty about showing them the door. Until their hearts are right with God they will be a stumbling block for the growth and mission of the church.

(9) It will cost you something. Warfare always has its costs and spiritual warfare is no different. It may cost you sleepless nights, an upset stomach or panic attacks. It could cost you your job. It is *vital* that you have a solid support network of family and friends around you. Your family will experience the consequences of spiritual warfare as Satan targets them in an effort to get to you. Your family will need to be strong, pray together and communicate effectively. If you are single or do not have family in your immediate area, ally yourself with godly brothers and sisters in Christ who can strengthen and support you.

(10) Persevere. Satan will not be displaced quickly or easily. This battle will require that you remain vigilant, prayerful and committed to defending your church from Satan's influence. Remember: anything worth having is worth fighting for. The longer Satan has gone unopposed in the church, the longer it will take to break his strongholds. But do not give up, because *the one who is in you is greater than the one who is in the world* (1 John 4:4).

* * * * * *

There is an Ed Albridge or two in every congregation. Ed may be frustrating, overbearing and petty but he is not the real enemy. Nor is Ed "possessed" by demonic forces. The Prince of Darkness has taken advantage of Ed's lack of repentance and his sinful nature

---

5 Bill Easum, *A Second Resurrection: Leading Your Congregation to New Life* (Nashville: Abingdon Press, 2007), p. 71. Used by permission. All rights reserved.

in order to use him as a tool to threaten and intimidate the church. While we may get discouraged and want to give up, we must remember that the church is the bride of Christ. She is the betrothed of her Beloved. The Lord has plans for her, and as he told Peter in Matthew 16:18, *"and on this rock I will build my church, and the gates of Hades will not overcome it."*

No matter how long Satan has been in your church—no matter how hard he fights—Jesus will not let his bride be ruled by Satan. Jesus has already given his life for the Church. Satan cannot overcome that.

Clergy and laity: study the Scriptures. Pray together against the common foe. Use oil to anoint areas and items in your church, and confess the presence and power of the Holy Spirit over them. Do not sit back and allow evil forces to dominate your worship or outreach or meetings. Take charge! Take the fight to Satan. Let him know that the redeemed of the Lord will rise up and reclaim the holiness and majesty of the Church!

CHAPTER 4
IDENTITY CRISIS
OR
"I FORGOT WHAT I CAME INTO THE ROOM FOR"

The bride of Christ is bullied
by our own spiritual dementia

"To forget one's purpose is the commonest form of stupidity."

Friedrich Nietzsche

IT IS HAPPENING to me more frequently. I walk through the house to do something or get something, only to discover that I forgot what I went to do or get. It happens to all of us as we get older. This does not mean we are going senile. We may have other things on our mind. Our wires might be getting crossed at the moment. We may be tired or overly emotional.

In a December 2011 issue of *Scientific American,* authors Charles B. Brenner and Jeffrey M. Zacks reported on a study conducted by the University of Notre Dame that found a link between walking through a doorway and forgetfulness. Participants displayed slower and less accurate responses to a series of questions when walking through a doorway into another room than when they walked the same distance across a single room.

"The doorway effect," say the authors, "suggests that there's more to remembering than just what you paid attention to, when it happened, and how hard you tried. Instead, some forms of memory seem to be optimized to keep information ready-to-hand until its shelf life expires, and then purge that information in favor of new stuff."[6]

The shelf life for many of our thoughts must be exceptionally brief since we routinely forget small things. But from now on, instead of announcing that we just had a "senior moment" when we forget why we went into the kitchen, we can just blame it on the doorway!

Memory is important. It links our past with the present. Since our brains cannot hold all the information we learn throughout the course of our lives, only selective things are stored in our long-term memory. This is a good thing in today's world, where we are inundated with more information in twenty-four hours than the eighteenth-century person had access to in a month. It is important what we remember and why.

Do you remember when?

I CAN REMEMBER the first time I saw *Star Wars* back in 1977 but I cannot remember a single formula I learned in algebra. I can remember the thrill of hearing my son laugh for the very first time but I cannot remember what classes I took my junior year of college. I can remember the awe and humility I felt as I worshiped in a house church with persecuted Christians but I cannot remember what I had for dinner last Tuesday.

People, places, events, sounds and smells stored in our long-term memory are linked to important moments in our lives. We can remember the heartache of losing someone to death because it is a major, life-changing event. But trying to conjure up memories of the periodic table of elements or what the weather was like on Thanksgiving five years ago does not stay with us. Things of that

---

[6] Charles B. Brenner and Jeffrey M. Zacks, *Why Walking Through a Doorway Makes You Forget*, http://www.scientificamerican.com/article.cfm?id=why-walking-through-doorway-makes-you-forget.

nature did not have a significant impact on our lives. What sticks with us are the things that have touched us in special ways.

This is true in the church as well. The long-term memory of churchgoers centers around the nostalgia of former days. Significant moments have made an impact on us that causes them to remain in our in our long-term memory. You may have heard or said something like:

- "Do you remember when we used to have thirty people in the choir every Sunday morning, and sometimes as many as fifty for Christmas and Easter cantatas?"
- "Remember when Pastor Wallace's Bible study on Wednesday night was full?"
- "I can remember when the Willing Workers Sunday school class had to bring in extra chairs back when Mr. Greeling was the teacher."
- "Do you remember when the new sanctuary was built and how the money just came rolling in for it?"
- "Yes, Mr. Davenport always came through with extra money when the budget was tight. It's a shame he's passed away."
- "We never used to have a problem getting people to volunteer to be Flower Coordinator."

Nostalgia selectively keys in on favorite persons or circumstances, conveniently ignoring or forgetting times of struggle, ineffectiveness and disunity. By doing so, nostalgia creates a golden era when everything worked, everyone got along, and there were no problems. Unfortunately, no extended periods of time like that actually existed. Nostalgia paints a preferred past and this deceptive image becomes the standard by which the present and future are judged.

Nostalgia affects older members the most due to their longevity and commitment to the local church. They can see anything new or different as a threat to the preservation of what little remains of the church's former glory. Many believe that if the church just got back to what it used to be, the problems of today would be resolved. If families just made church attendance a priority like they used to do, we would have a full sanctuary every week. If people honored their commitments to the church with more faithfulness, we would be able to accomplish more. If stores and businesses were all closed on Sundays like they used to be, more people would come to church.

It is true that fifty, sixty or seventy years ago the church held a more prominent and respected place in society. The Christian faith had a monopoly in our western world. Today things are radically different. Whether we like it or not, we are part of a globalized, interconnected world that simultaneously isolates us from one another. We live in a time of unprecedented progress. It is understandable that many in the church would like to escape back to simpler times.

However, this is not only impractical; it is impossible. Yet nostalgia for an idealized past remains a real threat to the Church. I knew a man who truly believed that if the church just returned to the way things used to be all of the church's problems would disappear.

I knew a lady who believed that "the day the music died" (the aviation accident in February 1959 that claimed the lives of rock & rollers Ritchie Valens, Buddy Holly, and J.P. "The Big Bopper" Richardson) marked the beginning of the decline of western civilization. From the perspective of this man and woman, everything that has happened since Eisenhower, Elvis Presley and the assassination of JFK has been undeniable proof that the world is going to hell. Nostalgia prevents us from hearing the cries of the world around us. It keeps us yearning for something long gone instead of working for something better now.

Spiritual dementia

NOSTALGIA IS A form of what I call *spiritual dementia*. Spiritual dementia is a subtle bully that keeps the bride of Christ from achieving her full purpose. It robs the church of its memory and mission. We remember bits and pieces but in essence we forget *who* we are and *whose* we are. And since spiritual dementia develops over time it is difficult to notice until it is quite advanced.

Spiritual dementia causes churches to limp ineffectively along because they have forgotten their purpose. They no longer have a vibrant mission. They exist only to serve those who attend, to keep the doors open and the bills paid. They no longer have any real identity.

Medical dementia is the loss of brain function due to certain diseases. Dementia impairs memory, thinking, language, judgment and behavior. Spiritual dementia does the same thing to the Church. It causes the church to lose its unique identity as the Body of Christ in the local community. The church forgets why it is here.

Other traits of brain function are also impacted by spiritual dementia. Thinking in the church slowly decays. People are not encouraged to ask questions, to probe, to doubt or to think outside of dogmatic or denominational lines. Thinking becomes calcified into very narrow categories such as "us vs. them" or claiming only one style of worship is acceptable.

Language suffers as the bride of Christ is bullied by spiritual dementia. Preferred buzzwords and theological terms become the litmus test of who truly believes. Words in committee meetings or the parking lot become more negative, critical and judgmental. Only certain styles of preaching are deemed acceptable.

And let us not forget body language. The majority of communication between people is non-verbal. This is true for churches as well. Members rarely, if ever, notice what the body language of their church is saying. But a visitor can quickly tell what the church is communicating!

Everything we do communicates and everything about the Church communicates something. When the Church is bullied, verbal and non-verbal language is internally focused. Members can be overheard complaining about someone who has parked in their spot or is sitting in their pew. Worship is dry, unmoving and a concession to apathy. Little effort is put forth to provide convenient parking, bright children's facilities, visible signage or expedient times for meetings or events. The language of the body cries out that only those inside the building truly matter. If your men's or women's group longs for new and younger participants, but refuses to change their meeting time from Thursdays at 2:00 PM, do not be surprised that you have no younger attendees.

Churches that are bullied by spiritual dementia are often judgmental. As with the decay of memory, churches become increasingly judgmental about the world and the people in it. It is not unusual to find churches that avoid entire populations or people groups because they "aren't like us." Professor and author George G. Hunter III notes, "In many Christian settings, being separate from the world is now assumed to be normal Christianity, and complaining about the awful natives and how they behave and live is the indoor sport of choice."[7] These churches are quick to point out the sins of others while ignoring their own.

Churches under the influence of spiritual dementia have a habit of forgetting who is in charge. The Bible tells us that Jesus alone is the Head of the church (Ephesians 1:22, 4:15, 5:23; Colossians 1:18, 2:19). Pastors and spiritual leaders have been placed in the church under the authority of Christ to serve as regents and stewards of the flock. While the pastor, priest or elder is required to make many decisions and to be the leader, he or she should be fully submissive to the Head. Since the church is the Body of Christ, it is his kingdom agenda that guides and propels us, not the agendas of those who want power and control.

Finally, spiritual dementia affects the church's behavior. Instead of living out the mission of Jesus to the world around them, intimidated churches reveal self-centered, narcissistic behaviors. Attention to missions and outreach are all but forgotten. Hospitality

---

[7] George G. Hunter III, *Radical Outreach: The Recovery of Apostolic Ministry & Evangelism* (Nashville: Abingdon Press, 2003), pp. 205. Used by permission. All rights reserved.

will be perfunctory if extended at all. Only those things that directly benefit the existing members are deemed worthy of funding. More enthusiasm is generated for making apple butter or quilts than for making disciples. Such churches may occupy a physical space in the community but no longer have any significant spiritual presence.

When I knew that I was moving to pastor another church, I went to the town where it was located to set up bank accounts, look at the parsonage and get an initial feel for the area. While going about my errands I asked random people, "What can you tell me about _____ Church?" I wanted to know what sort of reputation the church had in the community. I repeatedly received two answers.

Some people knew it as the church that had a distinct building, unlike any other in the community. But more disheartening was the response "I really don't know." This particular church was one of the oldest in the area. Yet hardly anyone in the community knew anything about it. Over the years the church had lost its identity. Spiritual dementia had set in.

There is one very significant difference between spiritual dementia and medical dementia: We have a say in whether or not we have spiritual dementia. Someone suffering from medical dementia does not have that luxury. If our church is bullied by spiritual dementia, we *can* do something about that. We can take proactive steps to recapture our lost memory, identity and mission. We can devote more effort to prayer. We can submit ourselves to an intense study of God's Word as it relates to the Church. And we can place ourselves and our church back under the full Lordship of Jesus.

The *missio Dei*

GOD IS A missionary God. The *missio Dei*—Latin for "the mission of God"—is to go to the hurting, needy and lost with the good news that the kingdom of God is here. God sent Jesus into our world to show us what his love looked like, sounded like and acted like. God became *incarnate* in the person of Jesus.

Jesus was the ultimate missionary. He willingly left the glories of eternity to become like us—a human being trapped in skin and time—in order to lead us back to the Father. To be like Jesus is to incarnate the gospel in our words and actions. As God sent his Son, so the Son sends the Church into the world. Therefore, every church, without exception, exists to be missional. We are the incarnational presence of Jesus in the world.

Churches bullied by spiritual dementia have forgotten their mission and purpose. They think and act as if their job is to populate Heaven, which it is not. The *missio Dei* means working to bring about the kingdom of God here on earth—to incarnate the love of God in Christ so that others are drawn into a right relationship with the Father. Heaven is the promised destination but it is not the goal. Heaven is the icing on the cake.

When we focus on Heaven merely as a goal to achieve or as a more palatable way of dodging Hell, we miss the point. God wants to redeem the world and *everything* in it—puppies and politics, cultures and creativity, ecosystems and egos. In order to accomplish this he invites the Church to join him in that great redemptive work. It is not just about going to Heaven to be with Jesus when we die. To focus only on avoiding Hell and claiming Heaven is to cheapen the mission of Christ, to emasculate the Church and the gospel, and to imply that God does not care about anything in the physical world (there is the false dualism we discussed in Chapter 1).

When spiritual dementia overtakes a church, the *missio Dei* is cast aside. The church is easily pushed around by a host of other agendas: personal, corporate or denominational. We allow our mission to be determined by the loudest voices, the most money or what brings the least inconvenience, rather than by what Jesus, the Holy Spirit and the Word of God tells us. Spiritual dementia shifts our focus from fulfilling the commands of Christ to maintaining and preserving the institution.

As we have seen, early believers had no extravagant buildings or fancy robes, no paid clergy or performing choirs. These things arose in the wake of Constantine's interest in Christianity. As the emperor blended elements of the Roman political and civil arenas with the Christian faith, the church became more institutional and inflexible. It began to take after its patron, the empire. Structures and institutions certainly have their place but they can never become more important than the cause and mission of Christ.

Do not forget to remember

WE MIGHT BE tempted to think that spiritual dementia is a new phenomenon among God's people. This is not the case. Throughout the Old Testament Yahweh continually called the people of Israel to remember all he had done for them: his deliverance, favor, mercy and compassion. They had a recurring problem with forgetting.

The first time God commanded his chosen people to remember was in Exodus 20:8: *Remember the Sabbath day by keeping it holy.* In Deuteronomy 4:9-10, before the people crossed the Jordan to claim the land promised to Abraham, Moses instructed them,

> *"Only be careful, and watch yourselves closely so that **you do not forget** the things your eyes have seen or let them fade from your heart as long as you live. Teach them to your children and to their children after them. **Remember** the day you stood before the Lord your God at Horeb, when he said to me, 'Assemble the people before me to hear my words so that they may learn to revere me as long as they live in the land and may teach them to their children.'"*

(emphasis mine)

God knew that as the people took possession of the Promised Land they would encounter a variety of new faiths and gods. They had spent forty years wandering aimlessly in the desert due to their previous failure to trust Yahweh (Numbers 13:1–14:35; Deuteronomy 1:19-40). In that time they had forgotten—surprise, surprise—the gods of Egypt they had known before the exodus. Now they would be faced with new religious beliefs and practices.

They were instructed to remember the covenant they had made with God (Deuteronomy 4:31) and to remain humble after they had settled in their new land:

> *"When the Lord your God brings you into the land he swore to your fathers, to Abraham, Isaac, and Jacob, to give you—a land with large, flourishing cities you did not build, houses filled with all kinds of good things you did not provide, wells you did not dig, and vineyards and olive groves you did not plant—then when you eat and are satisfied, be careful **that you do not forget** the Lord, who brought you out of Egypt, out of the land of slavery."*

(Deuteronomy 6:10-12, emphasis mine)

Do not forget to remember.

Moses' final message to the people, recorded in Deuteronomy, contains eighteen admonitions to remember and not forget. Unfortunately, the people did not heed the words of Moses or the commands of Yahweh. By the time they were comfortably settled in their new land they repeatedly forgot God and pursued their own sinful ways (Judges 3:7; 8:34). This rebelliousness and hard-heartedness continued throughout Israel's history (2 Kings 17:38; Jeremiah 2:32, 3:21, 18:15; Ezekiel 22:12; Hosea 13:6). The wisdom literature of the Bible likewise recognizes the people's forgetfulness (Psalm 78:10-12, 103:2, 106:7; Ecclesiastes 12:1).

When things are going well our tendency is to forget the works of God. Success, arrogance and self-sufficiency seduce us into believing that *we* have accomplished or achieved or overcome on our own. God recedes to the margins of our consciousness.

I knew a lady who experienced a series of hardships and setbacks in her life. When I met her she was about as low as she could possibly go. In the months that followed, as our church reached out and helped her, she started to attend worship. Slowly but surely she began to get back on her feet. As this happened I noticed her attendance and participation declined. Whenever I saw her and talked with her she always had plenty of reasons why she had not been involved.

Everything was fine for a few months and then she faced some additional setbacks. Things started to spin out of control in her life once again and it was not long before she was back in church. I watched this pattern repeat itself over and over. When everything in her life was going smoothly we rarely, if ever, saw her. But let trouble strike and she was back. I could not help thinking how this was a microcosm of the entire story of the book of Judges and another symptom of spiritual dementia.

A friend of mine once said we all get caught up in the highs and lows of our lives, and when that happens it is not difficult to forget about the teachings of Christ and the true purpose of the Church. It is far too easy for us to mow down someone in our quest to gain something else for ourselves. When Sunday morning rolls around it is also too easy and convenient to rationalize our words and behaviors from the past week, and to find ways to justify them. Due to our fallen human nature and constant battle with sin, we may even completely forget the ugliness we have committed by focusing only on the good qualities we dream up for ourselves.

Gettin' above your raisin's

I WAS BORN and raised in the South and live there still. One of the expressions you hear from time to time in this part of the country is that someone has "gotten above their raisin's." It means the person has forgotten their humble beginnings. The person has become wealthy, powerful or famous and has allowed the success to go to their head. We say they have forgotten their roots and who helped them along the way. They have the "big head."

Paul had a church full of Christians in Corinth who had "gotten above their raisin's." They had a serious case of spiritual dementia. Beginning in 1st Corinthians 1:17, Paul presented the eloquent case of God's foolishness as revealed in the cross in comparison to the "wisdom" of the world.

Greco-Roman culture highly valued wisdom and these first-generation Christians were enamored with it. Paul pointed out that God used something foolish—like preaching about the cross—to bring salvation to those who believed. *Jews demand signs and Greeks look for wisdom, but we preach Christ crucified: a stumbling block to Jews and foolishness to Gentiles, but to those whom God has called, both Jews and Greeks, Christ the power of God and the wisdom of God. For the foolishness of God is wiser than human wisdom, and the weakness of God is stronger than human strength* (1st Corinthians 1:22-25).

Due to this infatuation with wisdom the Corinthian believers had forgotten one very important point: they were not as hot as they thought they were. It was necessary for Paul to bring them back down to earth. They had forgotten their roots and who they had been before Christ.

Paul wrote in 1st Corinthians 1:26-31,

> *Brothers and sisters, think of what you were when you were called. Not many of you were wise by human standards; not many were influential; not many were of noble birth. But God chose the foolish things of the world to shame the wise; God chose the weak things of the world to shame the strong. God chose the lowly things of this world and the despised things—and the things that are not —to nullify the things that are, so that no one may boast before him. It is because of him that you are in Christ Jesus, who has become for us wisdom from God—that is, our righteousness, holiness and redemption. Therefore, as it is written: "Let the one who boasts boast in the Lord."*

The Corinthians thought they had attained the pinnacle of their spiritual quest. They thought they knew it all. Just as can happen with us, the Corinthian believers forgot what God's grace had done for them. Their redemption and salvation were not due to any worldly wisdom, as they presumed, but only through the merits of Christ's sacrifice for them.

Spiritual dementia leads us to forget that being called and chosen by God—as Israel was in the Old Testament—does not give us special privileges or entitlements. Being called and chosen by God comes with great responsibility and obligation. The Corinthians failed to remember that. We fail to remember that when spiritual dementia bullies us to demand preferential treatment, personal convenience and consumer privilege over the mission of Christ.

We have lost our mind

AS WE HAVE said, spiritual dementia causes us to forget *who* we are and *whose* we are. We lose our identity as the church and we can forget that we belong to Christ. The stress of our daily lives, the rate of change around us and the media messages that constantly bombard us—all these and more can cause us to lose track of who we are in Christ.

One of the greatest gifts we have received as the redeemed people of God is the mind of Christ. Unfortunately, spiritual dementia causes us to forget this very precious gift.

In 1st Corinthians 2, Paul continued his argument about God's divine wisdom and the foolishness of the cross. Paul pointed out how his own preaching was not with fancy words and dramatic flourishes, like those used by the professional orators of his day. Instead, Paul claimed that it was through his weaknesses that God's power was made known. It was the work of the Holy Spirit that brought the Corinthians to salvation, not the wildly popular rhetorical skills of paid speakers. Nor was it the politically parsed speech of rulers and leaders. None of the princes, kings or emperors could recognize God's wisdom in Jesus Christ. Paul quoted from Isaiah 64:4 to illustrate that human wisdom is a pale wisp compared to what God knows:

However, as it is written: "What no eye has seen, what no ear has heard, and what no human mind has conceived"—the things God has prepared for those who love him—these are the things God has revealed to us by his Spirit.

(1st Corinthians 2:9-10a)

Some things just have to be seen to be believed. I discovered this one summer when my family visited Grand Canyon National Park in Arizona. It was our first physical view of the canyon. Pictures and words cannot do justice to the magnificent, awe-inspiring panorama (see, I just tried to do it...) that is the Grand Canyon. It is one thing to see it on a YouTube video or as a photo print hanging on a wall; it is another thing to stand on the edge and see it spread out beneath you.

That is what Paul was getting at by quoting Isaiah. We can think and pretend and convince ourselves we know and understand God. But the truth is we do not have the slightest clue. We cannot begin to imagine, in the most creatively fertile imaginations on the planet, what God's plans are. To do so would be like a blind man attempting to describe a picture of the Grand Canyon.

However, Paul went on to tell the Corinthians that since they were in Christ and had received the Holy Spirit, they possessed "the mind of Christ." As they were spiritually awakened to new life, the Spirit of God gave them insight into the spiritual things of God.

For who knows a person's thoughts except their own spirit within them? In the same way no one knows the thoughts of God except the Spirit of God. What we have received is not the spirit of the world, but the Spirit who is from God, so that we may understand what God has freely given us. This is what we speak, not in words taught us by human wisdom but in words taught by the Spirit, explaining spiritual realities with Spirit-taught words

(1st Corinthians 2:10b-13)

To be reborn through Christ is to receive a spiritual understanding of what God has accomplished in the incarnation, life, death and resurrection of Jesus. And this, Paul said, did not come from human effort or intellectual awareness. It was a gift so that the follower of Christ can grasp God's plan of redemption and salvation, and can live out their role in that grand story. Those who do not have the Spirit—who have not surrendered themselves to the lordship of Christ—cannot understand such foolishness. They cannot grasp how God has accomplished his plan.

Then Paul says this: *But we have the mind of Christ* (1st Corinthians 2:16).

The Christian possesses the very mind of Christ. Now this does not mean we are omniscient (all-knowing). Nobody knows everything despite what some people may try to get you to believe! Rather, having the mind of Christ means having unity, just as perfect unity exists between the three persons of the Trinity. It means having discernment and compassion. It means knowing the *missio Dei* and that we share in the same mission. To have the mind of Christ means self-sacrifice, surrender and service.

Paul wrote to the believers in Philippi and urged them to remember they possessed the mind of Christ and what that meant for them:

> *In your relationships with one another, have the same mindset as Christ Jesus: Who, being in very nature God, did not consider equality with God something to be used to his own advantage; rather, he made himself nothing by taking the very nature of a servant, being made in human likeness. And being found in appearance as a man, he humbled himself by becoming obedient to death—even death on a cross!*
>
> (Philippians 2:5-8)

To have the mind of Christ is to be humble, to become a servant of all, to be obedient, to lay down one's life for Christ and one another.

When spiritual dementia is the bully, we forget that we have the mind of Christ. We do not focus on unity but on what will most benefit us. We do not exercise discernment and compassion wanes. Our understanding of the *missio Dei* becomes twisted and self-centered. Surrender, service and self-sacrifice; humility, obedience and a willingness to die to self are lost. In essence, we have lost our mind.

Our fallen human nature tries to replace the mind of Christ so that we get our way. The church falters and fails because it is guided by faulty memories, nostalgia, sinful attitudes and personal preference. Perhaps we have a faint recollection that the church should be more than it is, that it should accomplish more than it has, and that it should mean more than it does—but there is no willingness to make the hard changes necessary to get back where we belong.

Perhaps it is time once again to consider the words of Abraham Lincoln in his Proclamation for a National Day of Fasting, Humiliation, and Prayer, from April 1863: "We have been the recipients of the choicest bounties of heaven. We have been preserved, these many years, in peace and prosperity. We have grown in numbers, wealth and power, as no other nation has ever grown.

"But we have forgotten God. We have forgotten the gracious hand which preserved us in peace and multiplied and enriched and strengthened us; and we have vainly imagined, in the deceitfulness of our hearts that all these blessings were produced by some superior wisdom and virtue of our own.

"Intoxicated with unbroken success, we have become too self-sufficient to feel the necessity of redeeming and preserving grace, too proud to pray to God that made us! It behooves us, then to humble ourselves before the offended Power, to confess our national sins, and to pray for clemency and forgiveness."

To do this would go a long way toward defending the bride from spiritual dementia and renewing the mind of Christ within us.

CHAPTER 5
DEFENDING THE BRIDE OF CHRIST FROM SPIRITUAL DEMENTIA

"It does not do to dwell on dreams and forget to live."

J.K. Rowling

Humility. Confession. Repentance.

These are the three actions Abraham Lincoln prescribed for the nation in the speech that closed the previous chapter. It is a good place to start. You can never go wrong with humility, confession and repentance.

But there are additional actions we need to consider. I believe that God has given us an intellect, wisdom and experiences to utilize. He will do his part but he also expects us to use the resources he has provided. We have to cooperate with his grace and plan.

In order to protect the church from spiritual dementia, we need to examine four R's that will bring us back to our biblical mission and purpose. The fours R's are *Recognize, Revisit, Reclaim* and *Revitalize.* If we engage in these actions we can restore the mind of Christ in our churches. Let us take a look at each in turn.

The first R: *Recognize*

JUST AS AN addict has to acknowledge his or her dependency as the first step toward recovery, the church must likewise **recognize** it has a problem with spiritual dementia. We must be honest with ourselves about our church. While we may not want to look too closely at the warts and wrinkles, it is crucial we do so in order to move forward. The following suggestions can help your church recognize its predicament.

First, begin internally. Take some time to assess different aspects of your church. For example, how are people greeted when

75

they arrive at the church? Are there greeters and volunteers to help people find their way around? Or is the greeting merely perfunctory? Someone might say, "Well, we don't have very many people in our church so we don't have greeters." You may not have greeters in the formal sense, but that is not an excuse to skimp on genuine hospitality. Every church member should be an usher and greeter, regardless of whether they officially serve in those capacities or not.

Other things to recognize and take note of: is the worship service or other activity (Vacation Bible School, an outreach event, etc.) easy to follow for visitors? Are there parts of the service that need explaining before being carried out? You would be surprised how many lifelong church members know little to nothing about the reason behind some elements of weekly worship. Do not assume that everyone knows what a Chrismon is, or why your denomination uses wine or grape juice during the Lord's Supper. Taking an extra moment to explain the little things goes a long way toward making visitors feel more connected, as well as helping everyone to remember.

Is there adequate signage in and around your building? Mrs. Giffenbopper knows where the Senior Saints Sunday school class meets, but visitors do not. Can the nursery, children's areas and restrooms be found easily? Do not make the mistake of assuming your guests will just find them.

Speaking of the nursery, spend some time evaluating this important part of your building. Were the toys considered out of date back in 1973? Are cribs and tables safe, clean and inviting? Is the room brightly painted? Are drawers and cabinets clearly marked? If your church uses beepers or monitors, make sure the batteries work before handing them out. If your church takes the time, effort and resources to provide a positive nursery experience, visitors *will* take notice.

I have heard it said that there are two locations in the church that have the greatest influence on whether a first-time visitor returns. It is not the sanctuary no matter how venerable or modern. It is not the spiffy church offices. It is not the welcome center, the Sunday school classroom or the fellowship hall. The two areas that leave the greatest impact on visitors are the nursery and the restrooms. Some people will decide if they want to return to your church based upon their impression of these two areas.

In one church I served, I gathered the trustees and several other church leaders together to do a building walk-through. I gave each person a clipboard, paper and pen, and assigned them different sections of the building. I asked them to think and act as if they were first-time visitors and make notes on what they observed in their assigned areas. (If you can get actual first-time visitors or those unfamiliar with your church to do this, so much the better.) Everyone came back and made a master list of points that were identified so they could begin to be addressed by the trustees. And sure enough, there were some things that people had gotten used to over the years and no longer saw them as issues.

Look at everything from a different perspective. We get comfortable in our routines and become accustomed to ignoring small problems. We know that the men's room door sticks and has to be pushed hard, or that the fluorescent light in the corner of the fellowship hall is broken. We take these things for granted since we have become used to them. But visitors will notice them right away and can quickly form the impression that the church does not care about the little things.

You might choose to enlist the help of non-members, as their input will be blunt and honest. Sometimes pastors and church leaders bring in "mystery visitors"—like stores use mystery shoppers—to observe what happens and then provide valuable feedback.

* * * * * *

Second, *listen* carefully to what goes on around you. As we said in the last chapter, churches suffering from spiritual dementia often use language that only insiders understand. People speak in terms that have meaning only within a small circle of members. The language of worship is often stilted, dull, unexplained or confusing.

Atrophied thinking reveals itself in such favorite phrases as "But we've never done it that way before," and "We have church every Sunday—all people need to do is walk through the doors to find us." New ideas for ministry and outreach are discouraged, fought over and sometimes censored outright. A judgmental attitude exists toward those who are "not like us" and is often ingrained within the congregation in small cliques. I knew one church that offered two worship services on Sunday morning. People attended their preferred service time and style but when new members were received through the second service, the majority in the first service showed no interest in meeting the new people.

Listen to what happens in administrative meetings. Is most time and energy spent on pacifying the complainers and rehashing old arguments? Do committee members dread having to attend? In such settings it becomes easy to hear and see the effects of spiritual dementia as people push their preferred agendas that often have to do with nostalgia or maintaining the status quo.

* * * * * *

Third, go external. Are parking spaces for visitors convenient to the building and clearly marked? Is the exterior of the building inviting or do the weeds have a monopoly on the sidewalk and edges of the building? Is there trash lying about? Are external signs clear enough to direct people to the specific places they are looking for (e.g., the nursery, sanctuary, visitor parking, etc.)?

As you move farther away from your building, most churches have some sort of signage along the main road through town. Take a look at yours. Is it faded, bent or worse yet, missing? Was Eisenhower in the White House the last time it saw a fresh coat of paint?

Next, ask about your church around the community. When you are out walking the dog, picking up a gallon of milk or renewing your driver's license, ask what people know about your church, and listen closely to their replies. You might want to ask questions such as:

- What do you think is significant or different about the church?
- Have you ever visited there? If so, what was it like for you?
- What is the church known for in the community?
- If the church disappeared, what would the community miss the most?
- What sort of reputation do the people of the church have?

If your church is suffering from spiritual dementia many of these questions may likely be answered with a shrug, or with predominately negative impressions. Churches with misplaced identities have often lost their connection to the local community as well. Such churches are seen as offering spiritual services only to the members but have no meaningful impact beyond their own doors.

Not everyone will accept the fact that anything is wrong with their church. They have grown blind to the harsh realities, content to live in their own little self-serving bubble. Regrettably, such members will likely never change their minds or come around. We are called to love them and serve them as best we can, but not be threatened or hindered by them in the work God has set before us.

Even the strongest person has difficulty admitting they have a problem. Admitting that our church has a problem and is not effective is also difficult. But if we bring ourselves to honestly and critically reflect on who we are and what we are called to do, it becomes apparent our churches need work. Recognizing this means we are deeply concerned that our church is not all it can be or that God wants it to be.

The second R: *Revisit*

WE KNOW THAT churches bullied by spiritual dementia often fixate on better days in the past. Those gilded times normally revolve around a beloved pastor, a time of great growth in the congregation or when now-deceased members still made up the core of the church. In order to jettison this nostalgia it is important to **revisit** that past.

This may sound counterintuitive since an idealized past is what is holding many churches back. But in order to move forward a congregation will respond better if their history is recognized and celebrated. The purpose of this is to emphasize the church's legacy and accomplishments while at the same time weaving in ideas and vision for the future.

Many churches have an annual homecoming Sunday when members are invited to return from near and far. Families sometimes schedule their reunions around such events. In addition, churches have special celebrations when they reach a significant milestone, such as a fiftieth or one-hundredth anniversary. These are optimal times to revisit the past.

But what if your church does not have a major milestone on the horizon? What if your congregation has not held a homecoming in forever? Well, there is nothing to prevent your leadership from *planning* a homecoming event! Or you may choose to schedule a series of special worship services and invite former pastors (or other previous staff) to preach, administer the sacraments, lead worship or teach.

In revisiting the past, be sure to tell the stories of how the women's society, men's prayer breakfast or the Senior Saints Sunday school class began. Highlight the contributions of members who played important roles in those ministries. Remember the high points of the church's past. Maybe it was when Pastor Wallace's Bible study was running over with attendees or when the money for the new sanctuary came in abundance. Maybe it was the Easter morning when seven families were baptized and joined the church, or when the members pulled together to help out the family who had immigrated to the area. Every church has a history of high points; these are often the very things that people use to browbeat the church in the present. Recognize them, celebrate them and keep emphasizing the new vision God has for the congregation.

These times of celebration and looking ahead are also opportunities to terminate any ministries of the church that are no longer effective. Many churches continue ministries and activities long past their expiration date because (a) it is a link to the past, or (b) because "someone from Mrs. Giffenbopper's family would get upset if we stopped having the men's prayer breakfast, since it was her grandfather who started it." If a ministry or activity no longer fulfills a need or is perpetuated simply for the sake of continuity, then it is time to lay it to rest.

When it is determined that a ministry or activity has run its course, plan a time to recognize and celebrate all that it has accomplished. Again, this can be done as part of worship or as a stand-alone service. Retire the ministry gracefully, with respect and honor to all those who made it successful. Emphasize how that ministry has set the stage for the next thing God has in store (Isaiah 43:18-19), and what the future vision is for that legacy.

Another idea is to use part of a worship service—or an entire service if you prefer—to recognize deceased members. Every year the different conferences of my tribe, the United Methodist Church, gather to hear reports, take care of administrative business, worship, fellowship and celebrate what God is doing in our midst. One part of each annual conference (as they are called) is the Service of Remembrance. It is a worship service commemorating the legacies of pastors or spouses who have died during the previous year. It is a time of tribute, memory and closure.

If the church has a written charter from the time it was established, read it aloud in the special service. The reasons why the church was originally founded are likely still valid reasons for its continued existence today. By pointing out how the present and future are a direct continuation of the past, many members can open up to change and be less affected by spiritual dementia.

It takes some delicate balancing to revisit the past and offer up the future at the same time. Too much of the past merely reinforces the idea that "the good old days" were much better; too much of the future will cause people to retreat even further into the womb of nostalgia. We do not revisit the past to bemoan how bad things are now, but to draw inspiration and hope from what has gone before.

* * * * * *

Joshua 4:1-7 says,

> *When the whole nation had finished crossing the Jordan, the Lord said to Joshua, "Choose twelve men from among the people, one from each tribe, and tell them to take up twelve stones from the middle of the Jordan, from right where the priests are standing, and carry them over with you and put them down at the place where you stay tonight."*

> *So Joshua called together the twelve men he had appointed from the Israelites, one from each tribe, and said to them, "Go over before the ark of the Lord your God into the middle of the Jordan. Each of you is to take up a stone on his shoulder, according to the number of the tribes of the Israelites, to serve as a sign among you. In the future, when your children ask you, 'What do these stones mean?' tell them that the flow of the Jordan was cut off before the ark of the covenant of the Lord. When it crossed the Jordan, the waters of the Jordan were cut off. These stones are to be a memorial to the people of Israel forever."*

God wanted a permanent memorial to mark the crossing of the Jordan and Israel's entrance into the Promised Land. The mound of stones was a point of connection with the past—an exceptional moment in the history of God's chosen people. When future generations asked their elders about the stones, the story of God's covenant promise to Abraham could be revisited. It does not say the people were supposed to sit around the stones, venerate the stones, keep the stones from weathering or make a regular pilgrimage to the stones. Those rocks were a connection with the past, a visual reminder of a remarkable milestone. But they were not the goal.

The Lord had greater plans for Israel—and indeed for all creation—than just setting up a pile of rocks as an historical marker. He had a future for them (Jeremiah 29:11) that was greater than anything that had come before. But they would never have achieved those things if they remained zeroed in on the stones. Our churches need to revisit the successes and blessings of the past as a way of emphasizing God's faithfulness for the future. But we cannot allow ourselves to be consumed by those times. They should point us toward the next thing God has in store for us.

The third R: *Reclaim*

PEOPLE SUFFERING FROM medical dementia can help offset its effects by cognitive stimulation. They can practice problem-solving skills with memory aids that assist in improving brain performance. The bride of Christ can likewise focus on things that will help defend her from the bully of spiritual dementia. By doing so, we **reclaim** our main mission and purpose.

Most Christians have a general idea what the church is about. They associate it with weekly worship services, weddings and funerals, potluck dinners and committee meetings. It is amazing the number of professed believers who have little to no biblical understanding of what the church is. That is one reason I began this book with an overview of the church.

If today's church is to fulfill its missional mandate she must reclaim a biblical *ecclesiology* (the study of the church), and jettison all the superfluous baggage that holds her back. Christ's church is about revealing and offering an alternative, grace-filled community—a physical representation of God's kingdom here on earth. We are to be about the business of making disciples, not balancing budgets or maintaining the institution.

To do this, churches need to invest time in studying the *missio Dei* and exploring God's plan and purpose for the church. Pastors: preach a sermon series or conduct a Bible study in Acts, highlighting important elements of the church's life together: prayer, the sharing of resources and aid to the poor, accountability and discipleship, worship and missions. There are small group resources and Sunday school curriculum available that can help enlighten and educate. The more believers are exposed to and understand God's biblical design for the church the better we are able to reclaim that design within our own congregations.

Another option is to spend some time studying the renewal movements that have taken place throughout the history of the church. In nearly every age there have been individuals or groups who sought to renew the church by returning to the basics of apostolic Christianity. It would benefit us immensely to reflect on the rise and influence of Christian monasticism in the 400s and 500s AD. There is much we can learn from persons such as Catherine of Siena and the great reformer Martin Luther, as well as from the Methodist movement in the eighteenth century and the Azusa Street revival of the early twentieth century.

The Church must constantly have the prodding of renewal by its side. Otherwise, she becomes stale, disconnected and ineffective. Voices for renewal are necessary in order to keep the church biblically grounded and outwardly focused. To escape from spiritual dementia is to reclaim our legacy of renewal—to be the voices that press for transformation, to prophetically call the church back from its self-absorbed condition.

It is during this phase that the pastor, staff and church leaders will want to point out areas where spiritual dementia has caused the church to go astray. Discuss such things as the language used within the church. Use sermons and teaching opportunities to highlight how judgmental attitudes and behaviors impact the perceptions of those outside the church. Help members understand the importance of biblical hospitality.

In reclaiming the true mission and purpose of the church, prayer must be a fundamental component. Many churches have strong prayer ministries that can undergird efforts to overcome spiritual dementia.

Other churches place little practical emphasis on prayer. There are the perfunctory prayers before a meeting or during worship but there is no fervor or deep commitment to prayer. If we are serious about putting an end to bullying, prayer will once again need to be the heartbeat of every local congregation. We only need to look in Acts to see the emphasis the first believers placed on prayer.

Bear in mind, as we have previously noted, that Jesus Christ is the Head of the Church. Pastors are entrusted with leadership and oversight but Jesus is supreme. If he is not in charge, and if the Body does not respond to his commands, nothing else will matter until there is corporate confession and repentance. Just as individual Christians can claim Jesus as "Savior" but dodge around Jesus as "Lord," so too can the Church. Pastor, if Jesus is not the full and complete Head of your church, make that your first priority. Until he holds the place of primacy in every aspect, the church will continue to struggle and be largely ineffective.

If you are not getting your direction from him it is time to back up and set things right. It is not your vision or ideas or creativity — excellent though they may be — that will lead your church forward. It is only Christ the Head and the Holy Spirit who will do that. If you are trying to run the show for your own power or control, or trying to advance it by sheer force of will or charisma, *stop it now.* You will burn out and become disillusioned, frustrated and weakened in your leadership. Remember: Satan wants to take *you* out of the picture. He can do that by encouraging you to rely on your own strength and giftedness.

If you have been trying to make things happen on your own — if Jesus is not allowed to function as the Head of his own Body — then drop everything, find a nice quiet place and wait before the Lord. Confess your sins. Renounce your reliance upon your own skills, knowledge or experience. Throw yourself into the arms of Jesus and let him lead his own Body.

The fourth R: *Revitalize*

THE FINAL 'R' stands for **revitalize**. This is an ongoing process and as such, requires ongoing recognition and emphasis. Unlike the previous steps this one will not have a specific starting and ending point. Pulling the church out of spiritual dementia requires a consistent focus on what is happening now and in the future. You may have recognized and celebrated the past but as you move forward it is necessary to let the church know where you are going, and to accentuate God's preferred future.

There are numerous books available on the subject of vision and you are encouraged to explore some of them (see Appendix 3). Vision casting is beyond the scope of this book; however, it is important to realize that the church must have direction as it moves ahead. This is the time to share what God has placed on your heart regarding the future. That vision will be a combination of your thoughts and ideas, the inspiration of the Holy Spirit, and God's Word.

If you ask, God will give you his vision for your church. You may have to wait upon him for a while, since he prefers working on his timetable rather than ours! But if you are faithful, prayerful and obedient, God will show you his vision for the congregation. It will be up to you to articulate and promote that vision. Again, there are excellent leadership resources available to aid you in that process.

Church members: ask your pastor what the vision is for your church. He or she should be able to tell you. If not, I encourage all church members to force their pastor to take some time off for the purpose of visioning! Send your pastor on a weekend retreat equipped with a pen, some paper and a Bible. Arrange for a guest speaker in her absence and for other leaders to conduct worship.

This is not a vacation for your pastor. *It is important spiritual work.* Pastors need time to pray—and most importantly, *to listen* to

God. The demands of ministry—coupled with their own families, health and life circumstances—keep many pastoral leaders from spending adequate time in prayer. If your church needs vision, release your pastor to seek the Lord's heart for it.

* * * * * *

During the revitalization process, you will want to get a couple of small "wins" under your belt early on. Have some achievable goals that you can build momentum on. Maybe you have a goal of increasing your worship attendance by five percent over the next three months. When you achieve that goal, let the congregation know it has been accomplished. Your goals might be getting more children involved, restarting the choir, launching a new ministry or any number of other things. Goals will be different for each church in each context. The idea is to have some tangible successes you can point to that will show your forward progress. When people can actually see things happening, it generates enthusiasm and dampens some of the negativity. Plus, success builds momentum, which is essential.

One simple way to highlight these "wins" is to incorporate personal testimonies into the worship services. These need not be the "how-I-met-Jesus" testimony but should focus on what God is doing in the church now. People may wish to acknowledge growth in their Sunday school class, new faces in worship or new opportunities for outreach.

Some may want to speak about what God is doing in their own spiritual journeys, or among their family and friends. Someone may want (and need) to thank God publicly for successful surgery and recuperation. Another may want to praise God for landing a job or getting out of debt. In one church I served we opened the floor each Sunday morning for people to name any joys or concerns they had. One elderly lady often commented how much she valued being in worship and how much she loved the people around her. It was a heartfelt *thank you* to God and to the church. I believe the Holy

Spirit worked through her expressions of gratitude to encourage others in their spiritual journeys.

Reality orientation therapy

ONE APPROACH SOMETIMES used for dealing with medical dementia is called *reality orientation therapy*. This process is designed to improve cognitive performance by helping reduce feelings of mental disorientation, memory loss and confusion. You have seen evidence of reality orientation therapy in long-term care facilities for the elderly: all those clocks, calendars and announcement boards (identifying the month, day and year). Patients and residents may often be seated at or near windows so they can see the weather outside.

This helps create an environment where perceptions of immediate surroundings are directed toward the reality of the external world. They serve to keep the mind alert, hopefully improving intellect, language skills and cognition. Churches seeking to escape from spiritual dementia can utilize their own version of reality orientation therapy.

Today's world—with its relentless changes, mindless television programming and non-stop news cycles—is often overwhelming and difficult for older church members to comprehend. Truthfully, we all have problems keeping up with technology and the rate of change around us. It is easy to want to close the door and keep it all at bay. Aging generations find it increasingly difficult to keep up or to even want to make the effort. A withdrawal into the memories and nostalgia of younger days is understandable.

Our people will function better if they have some understanding of the changes in the world around us, where those changes come from and why. In essence, we need to orient our people to the reality that surrounds them. We need to help them understand how the waters of the "cultural sea" we swim in have changed. We need reality orientation therapy. I have found that people appreciate even a basic understanding of how and why our society has experienced such tremendous cultural upheavals in the past few decades. If nothing else it provides them a better footing for understanding their children or grandchildren.

You might consider a class or two—perhaps during the Sunday school hour—that look at such things as

- Modernism: its effect on society and the church. What is it, where did it come from and how has it affected our thinking, behaviors and worldview?
- Postmodernism—the reaction to modernism and its effect on society and the church. What is it, where did it come from and how is it affecting the thinking and worldviews of emerging generations?
- Relativism—the place of absolute truth in today's world. Why does truth seem to be such a fluid, individualized thing?
- Individualism—the supremacy of the one over or against the whole. The United States is a nation of rugged individualists and the church is deeply infected with a me-first attitude. How do we embrace the individual and her/his unique identity while collectively being part of the Body of Christ?

These are just a few of the subjects that can help people orient to a shifting world and complex society. Yes, this requires pastors, staff and church leaders to do their homework, or be able to bring in qualified persons to address such topics. But the more people know about the transitions that occur around them the better they can cope.

It is also important to emphasize that God remains sovereign even in the chaos of our evolving society. None of these changes have caught him off guard. He has not been napping while these things have occurred, nor do they hinder what he wants to do. It does, however, require that the church adapt to its new environment and find creative, God-honoring ways of fulfilling the *missio Dei*.

This does not mean the church compromises its faith, beliefs, doctrines or the essence of the gospel. We cannot because if we do we have nothing unique to offer a hurting world. But we must find ways to contextualize our churches to reach the lost and make disciples in this new day and age. God still desires to be reconciled to the lost and it remains the church's first order of business to help make that happen.

For many people the church is an oasis of tranquility in a desert of technological innovation, social disruption and the incessant siren call of the media. The church offers—if only for an hour or two—a way to step away from all that mess and slow down. To relax. To breathe. There is nothing wrong with that. We all need it from time to time.

The problem arises when we choose to exist in that self-contained oasis of security and comfort. God has not called us to disengage from the world. Instead, he has equipped us to enter and engage that world for those who remain outside his grace. Spiritual dementia enfolds a church when members prefer the oasis to the rest of the world.

We have the mind of Christ. There is nothing the Church cannot accomplish in the power of the Holy Spirit, with fervent prayer and surrendered lives. Spiritual dementia can be counteracted. We do not have to limp along, wistfully pining for former days of glory. The Spirit yearns to be loosed in our churches to accomplish what only he can do. *You* have an important role to play in allowing that to happen.

What lies ahead for your church can be greater, more powerful and more amazing than anything that has come before. The glorious future that the founders of your church once envisioned still waits. Recognize. Revisit. Reclaim. And revitalize.

CHAPTER 6
I'LL TAKE UP MY CROSS, BUT IT BETTER NOT GIVE ME SPLINTERS!

The bride of Christ is bullied by a lack of biblical discipleship

"The most tragic thing in the suffering of Christ was not the cross, but the sleeping disciples."

Erkki Melartin

LEGEND SAYS THAT twin brothers Romulus and Remus founded the city of Rome. They were born to a vestal virgin named Rhea Silver and the god Mars. It had been prophesied that the twins would depose their murderous and conniving uncle, Amulius. To prevent this Amulius had the twins abandoned on the Tiber River. They were discovered by a she-wolf who suckled the children until a kindly shepherd took the infants in. When Romulus and Remus were grown they decided to establish a city, but in an argument Romulus killed his brother. Thus Rome bears the survivor's name. Or so the story goes.

As is the case in many heroic stories of antiquity, Romulus and Remus were foundlings—that is, they were abandoned at an early age. The practice of abandoning infants at birth has been known among societies throughout history, including the Romans, Greeks, and Etruscans.

Children were often abandoned in the wilderness if they were born with a physical handicap that would hinder growth or development. Poverty-stricken parents often had little choice but to abandon a child they could not feed or raise.

Girls were abandoned with greater frequency due to the high cost of raising daughters (dowries, weddings, etc.), or simply as a way to selectively choose which gender grew to adulthood.

The horror and brutality of this makes us cringe but the sobering reality is that child abandonment continues today. We hear news reports of an infant found in a dumpster or an alley. As the story develops we are relieved when the foundling has been adopted. Even among the societies of antiquity, infants were more often than not abandoned near high-traffic areas. In this way children might be found and taken in by those who could take responsibility for them.

The church is to find the lost, bring them into the kingdom, and take responsibility for training them in the faith. Unfortunately, one of the bullies we face is a lack of biblical discipleship. We rarely provide adequate, ongoing training in what it means—and what it costs—to follow Jesus. For many generations we have failed to make true disciples, opting instead for converts or members. We have left new or young believers to fend for themselves, creating spiritual foundlings who cannot grow as God intended.

A-C-T-S

WHAT EXACTLY IS biblical discipleship? What does it look like? A brief overview will help us better understand what it is the church has surrendered in exchange for accommodation and expediency.

The Greek word translated as "disciple" is *mathetes* (mah-thay-tez). It means follower, learner, pupil. A disciple is one who willingly follows another in order to learn from and imitate him. We are familiar with the fact that Jesus chose twelve men to be his key disciples. He had other followers, including women, but the Twelve were the ones he specifically designated *apostles* (Luke 6:13). Robert Webber, author of *Ancient-Future Evangelism: Making Your Church a Faith-Forming Community*, says: "The work of the church in forming the spiritual life of the new disciple is to *train the new*

Christian in the practice of living in the pattern of the death and resurrection of Jesus Christ."[8]

The Twelve were called away from their normal, ordinary lives in order to follow Jesus, learn from him and imitate him. As we study the gospels we find several non-negotiable elements of the discipleship process. Not surprisingly, these elements still apply.

You may be familiar with the A-C-T-S prayer model. It is an acronym that some people use to help guide their prayers. Each letter represents an important attribute and prompt for prayer. "A" is for adoration. "C" is for confession. "T" is for thanksgiving. And "S" is for supplication. Those who use this model find a rhythm for their prayers and a convenient way to assure the most important aspects of prayer are addressed.

I propose we also use the A-C-T-S model to help us focus on four key elements of biblical discipleship. This way we can remember the vital components of discipleship that we find in the gospels. The A-C-T-S model for biblical discipleship is as follows:

A → **Accountability**

C → **Commitment**

T → **Time**

S → **Service**

Accountability is a willingness to be held answerable or responsible for our actions. In terms of the Christian faith it means being in a relationship of honesty and vulnerability with others in order to mature as followers of Christ. Accountability is not a tool for judgment or a weapon of fear. It is not about elevating oneself above others by pointing out their faults or failures.

We see evidence of accountability when the disciples return from their first "ministry tour" in Mark 6:30: *The apostles gathered*

---

[8] Robert Webber, *Ancient-Future Evangelism: Making Your Church a Faith-Forming Community* (Grand Rapids: Baker Books, 2003), p. 89. Used by permission. All rights reserved.

around Jesus and reported to him all they had done and taught. They debriefed and discussed their experiences. Jesus held them accountable for what he sent them out to do.

Likewise, since the disciples were given the secrets of the kingdom of God (Luke 8:10), they were held accountable for what they knew and understood: *Whoever has will be given more; whoever does not have, even what they think they have will be taken from them* (Luke 8:18). Jesus always holds his followers accountable for what he has revealed to us. Do you realize that you are accountable for what you hear from God's Word each week? As the pastor, priest or teacher expounds the Scriptures we are responsible for putting into practice what we hear.

Jesus also taught accountability in the Church (Matthew 18:15-17), and the apostle Paul reinforced the need for believer-to-believer support and honesty (1st Corinthians 5-6; Galatians 6:1-2; Ephesians 4:25, 32).

Accountability requires a humble, teachable spirit—one that is willing to submit to the guidance, challenge and encouragement of other believers. In order to have true accountability we must be honest and vulnerable, allowing others into every aspect of our lives. This is not for the purpose of gossip, judgment or condemnation. It is so we can *sharpen one another* (Proverbs 27:17), that we might attain *to the whole measure of the fullness of Christ* (Ephesians 4:13b).

While studying in seminary I was part of a men's discipleship group. We met weekly and held one another accountable for our spiritual maturity and growth in grace. We shared our temptations, our failures and mistakes, our joys and triumphs. Each meeting included times of laughter, prayer, reflection, hope, encouragement and honesty. Brutal honesty!

Following each man's time of sharing the group leader would ask, "Have you lied about anything you've told us?" It was a final check before moving on to the next person, a way of recognizing that we have a tendency to gloss over our sins and shortcomings, or to embellish how we want others to see us.

Being part of that group taught me a lot about biblical discipleship. It is not easy. It is not quick. It is not always convenient or comfortable. To be an authentic follower of Jesus—to live and walk in ever-increasing holiness each day—requires that we do things we may be reluctant to do on a regular basis. Thus, the Church is home to many who believe in Jesus but are not following Jesus according to biblical standards.

The "C" stands for **commitment**. Biblical discipleship demands a high level of dedication. Jesus calls us to a serious commitment of love and sacrifice. To be a true disciple we must love God first and foremost, and love others as ourselves (Matthew 22:37-40). This is what is referred to as the Great Commandment. And as we seek to love others we will take seriously the Great Commission to go into the world and make new disciples (Matthew 28:19-20). If we love God but ignore other people, we become like the Pharisees of the gospels. If we do not love God but love other people, we may be good philanthropists or humanitarians, but we are not followers of Jesus.

The commitment to biblical discipleship requires sacrifice. On multiple occasions Jesus made it plain that following him would not be easy. In fact, we discover him "weeding people out" at times, intentionally stating the demands and cost of being with him (Matthew 10; Mark 10:17-22; Luke 9:57-62; 14:25-35; John 6:25-66). Many people during his day were unwilling to make the necessary sacrifices. Many remain unwilling today.

To be a disciple of Christ is to imitate him in all ways—especially in self-sacrifice. We are called to lay down our lives on behalf of others. We are expected to go without and do without in order to help others see and know Jesus. A disciple mimics his or her master. Disciples seek to replicate, as closely as possible, every word and action of their teacher.

At one point during my childhood my parents thought I was developing a foot problem. One day they noticed I was limping, favoring my right foot over my left. There was no pain or obvious injury. I was taken to the doctor and examined but nothing came to light. What was most peculiar was that my limp came and went. Sometimes I had it; most of the time I did not.

Then one day it all came together for my parents. We were at my grandparents' house and my grandfather was walking across the backyard to check on his rose bushes. I was trailing along behind him—and my parents saw my limp reappear. It was the exact same limp my grandfather had, the result of his childhood bout of polio. Because of my great love for my grandfather I wanted to be just like him, even down to his unique limp. I was doing everything I could to imitate him. This is the commitment that followers of Jesus are expected to give.

The "T" in our discipleship acronym stands for **time**. To be a disciple of Jesus, and to be a discipler of others, demands an intentional investment of time. In Mark 3:13-15 we find something significant that is often overlooked:

> *Jesus went up on a mountainside and called to him those he wanted, and they came to him. He appointed twelve **that they might be with him** and that he might send them out to preach and to have authority to drive out demons.*

> (emphasis mine)

Before the Twelve engaged in any act of ministry they were called to *be with* Jesus. That is, they were to spend time with him. They were to invest their lives in him. To walk the path of authentic biblical discipleship is to devote time to Jesus. And guess what? One hour a week in worship, or two hours if you also toss in Sunday school, does not cut it.

Jesus invested three years in training the Twelve. They spent all their time together. Those men not only witnessed all that is recorded in the four gospels, but all the "in between" stuff: nights around the campfire, walking along the road, early breakfasts and late dinners, laughter. First they were called to follow; then they were called to be with Jesus. Only after watching, learning, questioning and experiencing the Word-made-flesh were they ready to imitate the life of their Master.

Finally, the "S" in A-C-T-S stands for **service**. To be a true disciple according to biblical standards is to be a servant to all. Jesus captured the essence of this when he said, *For even the Son of Man did not come to be served, but to serve, and to give his life as a ransom for many* (Mark 10:45).

He *displayed* the essence of it when

> *"...he got up from the meal, took off his outer clothing, and wrapped a towel around his waist. After that, he poured water into a basin and began to wash his disciples' feet, drying them with the towel that was wrapped around him."*
>
> (John 13:4-5)

In order to ensure the disciples did not miss the staggering significance of his actions, Jesus told them,

> *"You call me 'Teacher' and 'Lord,' and rightly so, for that is what I am. Now that I, your Lord and Teacher, have washed your feet, you also should wash one another's feet. I have set you an example that you should do as I have done for you."*
>
> (John 13:13-15)

This part really is as simple and straightforward as it sounds. What Jesus did for us we are to do for others. That is it. Jesus was not using metaphors or allegorical language. There are no hidden codes or secret explanations. Jesus took on the role of a servant. So should we. Yet most of the time we do not do it.

To follow Jesus is to serve all those we come in contact with. Sometimes this may be as simple as a smile while holding the door open for someone. At other times it may require us to take a large step outside our comfort zones. It is in serving others that the purest expression of Christ's love is made real.

My wife served on a mission team to India in 2005. One day they drove past a bridge and underneath was a group of women washing clothes on the bank of a murky, sluggish river. When their team leader asked about the women, the local pastor who was serving as their translator said those women were the lowest caste in Indian society. They were the undesirables, those whom no one else would associate with.

The pastor said that one day he was talking with a well-to-do friend and the subject of the bridge came up. The friend said, "I've seen people going down to the riverbank with food and clothes. I know they're people from your church. I know they're Christians. No one else would dare to be seen around those people. Only the Christians are willing to go to them and help them." That is authentic discipleship in action.

Jesus left no room for doubt or equivocating when it came to the requirement to serve others. He said that anyone who claims to love him would show that love by obeying his commands (John 14:23). They would not live as those in power do, abusing their authority (Luke 22:25-26). Nowhere was the expectation of service to others more clear-cut than in Matthew 25, where the righteous and unrighteous receive their eternal reward based on what they did — or did not do — for the helpless and most vulnerable.

If A-C-T-S represents vital, non-negotiable aspects of what it means to be a disciple of Jesus Christ, how is it that there is such a scarcity of real disciples in today's Church? Why has a lack of biblical discipleship become a bully that threatens our witness and effectiveness? We can continue to use the A-C-T-S model to provide some answers.

The other A-C-T-S

"The man who has nothing more than a kind of Sunday religion — whose Christianity is like his Sunday clothes put on once a week, and then laid aside — such a man cannot, of course, be expected to care about growth in grace."

J. C. Ryle

WE CAN CONTINUE to use the A-C-T-S acrostic to get a better look at how the Church is threatened by a lack of discipleship. However, this time around it will be the *anti*-A-C-T-S. It shows us four key qualities of undiscipled Christians. A lack of biblical discipleship produces...

A → **Apathy**

C → **Control**

T → **Takers**

S → **Shallowness**

Apathy can be found in every church to one degree or another. In churches with no significant discipleship process, however, the complacency is more pronounced. There is little to no interest in missions or outreach. Weekly worship tends to be lifeless and flat although this does not seem to be a concern for those attending. Church events that do not directly benefit the members are written off or ignored. More emotion is generated when discussing the color of paint or a misprint in the bulletin than in winning the lost.

Apathetic Christians are unwilling to take responsibility for anything in the church unless it can generate more power or influence for them. They drift in and out each week, contributing nothing to the advancement of the kingdom of God, but always expecting their demands and entitlements be honored. They evidence no desire to mature in their faith and take no initiative to do so. Although they may attend Sunday school and worship regularly there is no visible life transformation. They simply occupy the same space each week. Such people may hold the honor of being the oldest member, or part of the founding family, but they remain spiritual infants. They have not grown beyond their initial confession of Christ.

I used to wonder how that could be possible. How could someone who has attended church faithfully for decades be complacent about the things of God? I (naively) thought the member with the greatest longevity would be one of the most mature. Sadly, this is often not the case.

The reason is that for many years the church has taken a satanic shortcut when it comes to discipleship. Instead of emphasizing the crucial nature of discipleship—and maintaining high expectations for members to be discipled—the church has taken the approach that people will just "pick up what they need to know" as they go along. The thinking goes that if they just attend Sunday school and worship then they are being discipled. We do not have to look far to see the error of this.

Sunday school is not designed for discipleship. It was created as an educational model for poor children in industrialized England who could not afford to attend school, or who had to work during the week. The Sunday school was a place for underprivileged children to learn how to read and write using the Bible. Today's Sunday school is still predominately educational with a strong fellowship component included. Some classes may engage in mission projects or provide benevolence assistance but that is not their primary function. They exist to share information from and about the Bible.

Nor is worship designed for discipleship. Worship is for the gathered body of believers to celebrate and re-enact the saving work of God in Jesus Christ, empowered by the Holy Spirit. It is for the public proclamation of the Scriptures, for the administration of the sacraments and for the edification of the faithful. Some growth and maturation as a follower of Jesus can and does occur in Sunday school and worship. But when this happens it is usually in very small increments over long periods of time. "A worship service (show) can supplement the discipleship process," says pastor and author Jim Putman, "but it cannot create disciples alone. Discipleship demands intentionality and relationship—by which each person is invested in specifically. This cannot happen in a worship service."[9]

However, in order to avoid the hard work of making disciples the Church has focused on making members. The assumption is that once people become church members they will magically acquire what they need to grow in grace. It is like the student who puts a textbook under her pillow in the hope she will absorb the knowledge she needs through osmosis. The church is guilty of relying on osmosis instead of making disciples. Without encouragement, prodding and strong expectations, people will not be motivated to grow in their faith. We will always settle for the path of least resistance. Therefore, whenever the church takes this shortcut we make apathetic spiritual foundlings.

The "C" stands for *control*. In churches where discipleship has been downplayed or ignored, battles for control are regular occurrences. The drama generally plays out with one group of members (a committee, class or family) maintaining a death grip on positions of authority in the church. They assure that others in their clique are kept in key decision-making positions. In this way they are able to control the church's finances and, by extension, its ministries and mission. You can bet there is a lack of biblical discipleship if the same extremely vocal people (with longevity, wealth or family connections on their side) have an overriding say in how money is spent, staff is hired, worship is conducted or the building is used.

Due to our sinful nature we all have the potential to grab for more and more power. And if we do have authority and control

---

9 Jim Putman. Taken from Real-Life Discipleship: Building Churches That Make Disciples, p. 23. Copyright © 2010 by NavPress. Used by permission of NavPress. All rights reserved. Represented by Tyndale House Publishers, Inc.

over others none of us are immune to the temptation of abusing our power. But Christ-followers who are maturing in their faith and being held accountable by others are keenly aware that Jesus Christ is in charge. He calls the shots. It is the responsibility of the Church to carry out his commands just as it is the responsibility of our physical bodies to carry out the commands given by our brains.

Sometimes the pastor is the dominant controller in the church. As pastors, we are to be discipled just like anyone else. We are not exempt because we wear a collar or have the word *Reverend* before our name. It is vital that pastors—and all key church leaders—be striving to mature in the faith daily. We cannot take our people somewhere we are not going. We cannot show them something we ourselves are not seeing.

Pastors can bully churches by insisting they have a hand in everything that happens. They can also intimidate staff or committees in order to see their own personal agendas furthered. And many pastors are guilty of not relinquishing ministry to the people, opting to do everything themselves, thereby exerting unhealthy control and robbing people of the opportunity to use their gifts in ministry.

Authentic disciples recognize and understand that Christ calls us to humility, unity and obedience. Whatever power or control is entrusted to us as clergy or laity is "on loan" from God. We are stewards of God's authority on the finance committee or deacon board or trustees. We are to work in unison with one another and the Holy Spirit to accomplish the will of God.

The "T" stands for *takers*. These believers are always the recipients, never the givers. They are constant consumers who offer little to the church in return. Takers want everything done for them. They want everything to focus on them.

The Dead Sea receives its water from the Jordan River. This is the only major source of flowing water that feeds the hypersaline lake. Once the Jordan empties into the Dead Sea it has nowhere to go. There are no rivers or streams to carry the water away so it sits and evaporates. Due to the high salt content of the water no fish can live in the Dead Sea. Its name is appropriate. It takes and takes and takes but never gives away. This is what undiscipled believers do. They are takers.

These believers often have an immature, selfish perspective about the church. They assume that because they give money they are entitled to everything without having to do anything. Some takers do not even give money yet still operate under the assumption that the pastor and the church are there for one reason: to fix every complaint and cater to every whim.

Because they have not been adequately discipled, takers do not understand—much less practice—humble service. Takers will not volunteer to help with any activity unless they are going to personally benefit. Their attitude is that the church exists to keep them happy and comfortable. Due to our culture of instant gratification, takers demand things be convenient, to their liking and with no expectation to do anything beyond sitting in the pew. They want maximum benefit for minimal effort.

The "S" in our A-C-T-S acrostic stands for *shallowness*. Undiscipled believers exhibit shallowness in their thinking, speech and actions. As we have already noted, everything revolves around their wants and wishes. There is a distinct lack of biblical understanding, even though these people may have heard thousands of sermons, sat in years' worth of Sunday school classes and attended countless hours of Bible study. They may have accumulated a lot of knowledge but it has never resulted in a changed heart and life. The Church in the United States today does not suffer from a lack of knowledge. It suffers from a lack of depth.

Shallowness prevents undiscipled believers from stepping out in faith, serving others, supporting missions or volunteering. They are unable to see beyond their immature demands so naturally there is little concern for those in need around them. They have not learned that to follow Jesus is to lose one's life, to take up the cross, to accept the role of servant. No doubt they have *heard* this many times in their church careers. But it never penetrates to the heart.

When a church suffers from a lack of biblical discipleship there is no accountability for words and actions that do harm among the Body. There is no vision. There is little outreach other than the requisite adopting-a-family-at-Christmas, nor is there any forward movement for the church. Pastors and church leaders are pestered and bullied to acquiesce to the demands of a few. Without a solid foundation of biblical discipleship, the church degenerates into a private and exclusive social club that props up hypocrisy and vanity.

Lust and litigation

I LOVE HOW the Bible does not shy away from depictions of our fallen human nature. It does not hide or sugarcoat the human condition. I find hope and encouragement from people like Jacob, David and Peter. If they could walk with God despite their failures and sins, then I have a chance, too. I am in good company! But it is not just individuals (or even families) who are shown in all their unvarnished complexity. So is the church in the New Testament. I find hope and encouragement here as well. If a church like Corinth could walk with God (1:5-7; 5:7; 12:27; 14:12) despite their laundry list of issues, then our churches have hope too.

It is easy for us to say the church in Corinth lacked spiritual discipleship. As we noted in the Introduction, this was a congregation of first-generation believers. There were Jewish Christians and Gentile Christians, and all of them were new to this "following Jesus" thing. They were trying to find their way with a new worldview, while still existing in the world they had been familiar with all their lives. Sounds like us, doesn't it?

In 1st Corinthians five and six, Paul addressed two moral concerns that had become—quite literally—the talk of the town: sex and lawsuits. Lust and litigation. By confronting these two problems Paul gave us insight into the necessity of biblical discipleship and how it works.

Ancient Corinth was a rambunctious, gritty town. It was Las Vegas, Bangkok, and Amsterdam all rolled into one. The sex trade was one of the city's thriving, lucrative enterprises. It was common for men to visit the temple prostitutes of the various gods. In some cases, depending on the deity, it was required.

Paul received word that the culture's openness and lackadaisical attitude toward sexual promiscuity had infiltrated the church, and to a very nasty degree. *It is actually reported that there is sexual immorality among you, and of a kind that even pagans do not tolerate: A man is sleeping with his father's wife* (5:1). Yikes! Even the pagans were shocked by some of the goings-on in the Corinthian church.

Paul went on to chastise the church for allowing such sin to continue, and also for the fact they were taking pride in it (5:2)! While we might be tempted to go easy on them because they were new Christians just finding their spiritual feet, Paul was not.

> *For my part, even though I am not physically present, I am with you in spirit. As one who is present with you in this way, I have already passed judgment in the name of our Lord Jesus on the one who has been doing this. So when you are assembled and I am with you in spirit, and the power of our Lord Jesus is present, hand this man over to Satan for the destruction of the flesh, so that his spirit may be saved on the day of the Lord.*

(1st Corinthians 5:3-5)

According to Paul, it was vital to the survival of the congregation that the sinful man be expelled from the church. His actions—and the tolerance of the congregation—were a serious detriment to their witness. The church was not just another temple in Corinth. Jesus Christ was not just another deity to fawn before. The church in Corinth was the physical manifestation of Jesus, his hands and feet to those lost in darkness. Paul would not tolerate the bride of Christ being bullied by a lack of spiritual understanding.

The issue of sexual immorality also surfaced in the second half of chapter six, where Paul made it clear that one's body was a temple of the Holy Spirit. Men were not to visit the temple prostitutes because their bodies belonged to their wives (if they were married, 7:4). If they were single, they were to remain celibate until such a time as they did choose to marry. Paul even went so far as to say,

> *Do you not know that your bodies are members of Christ himself? Shall I then take the members of Christ and unite them with a prostitute? Never! Do you not know that he who unites himself with a prostitute is one with her in body?*

> (1st Corinthians 6:15-16)

Regardless of the sexual permissiveness in the surrounding culture, Christians were to respect their bodies and conduct themselves in an altogether different way. They were to stand apart, to be different, to be holy.

Then there was the issue of lawsuits.

> *If any of you has a dispute with another, do you dare to take it before the ungodly for judgment instead of before the Lord's people? Or do you not know that the Lord's people will judge the world? And if you are to judge the world, are you not competent to judge trivial cases?*

> *...Therefore, if you have disputes about such matters, do you ask for a ruling from those whose way of life is scorned in the church? I say this to shame you. Is it possible that there is nobody among you wise enough to judge a dispute between believers? But instead, one brother takes another to court— and this in front of unbelievers!*

> (1st Corinthians 6:1-2, 4-6)

The disputes within the church were not just over philosophical or theological issues but also had to do with personal rights and possessions (6:7). Believers were going to court against one another. Once again Paul was deeply concerned about how this affected the witness of the church.

These two matters highlight the necessity of biblical discipleship and that without it we easily slip sideways into sinful attitudes or behaviors. It is too easy to allow our human nature to get the best of us and compromise the witness, not only of ourselves, but of our churches as well.

We acknowledge the Corinthian church was in its infancy and therefore it had no systematic understanding of what it meant to be discipled. That was part of what Paul was teaching in his letters. He took their problems and turned them into teaching opportunities. When it came to concerns about sex and marriage he discipled them in how these intimate relationships were to be viewed and practiced under the lordship of Christ. Theologically, he taught that their individual bodies were temples of the Holy Spirit (3:16), that the parts of their bodies were parts of Christ himself (6:15) and that the Church was made up of many different people and gifts (12:12-27).

With this education Paul sought to enlighten them to a new way of thinking and behaving. The Corinthian Christians had changed their allegiance and Paul had to help them learn what that meant. Everything from relationships to economics, from citizenship to worship, was directly affected by this new allegiance to Jesus. They needed to learn exactly how and why being a Christian was different from anything else they had ever experienced. If we think about it, authentic biblical discipleship today should do the same thing. Our change of allegiance should be accompanied by sustained, ongoing training in how to live out this new life we have chosen.

If the Corinthians continued to act like the society around them the church would become a laughingstock. It would be irrelevant in no time. The culture would see no difference between being a follower of Jesus and being a follower of Apollo or Artemis or

Caesar. It was vital that new Christians across the Mediterranean world learn what it meant to be *mathetes*—disciples, learners—of Jesus Christ. That is one reason why the letters of Paul, Peter, John and other apostles were circulated among churches.

The Church in today's world must likewise reclaim this understanding and practice. Without it, people will be unable to see any difference between followers of Jesus and followers of the numerous gods available today.

CHAPTER 7
DEFENDING THE BRIDE OF CHRIST FROM A LACK OF BIBLICAL DISCIPLESHIP

"Believing without discipleship isn't believing,it's agreeing to a set of facts about a religious figure."

Bill Hull

LET US GO ahead and get the grim unpleasantness out of the way right now: we have all been—or are—involved in churches that have seen people come to faith in Christ yet are left undiscipled. We rejoiced when they professed their faith and we are delighted to have them in our congregations. But in most instances we just left them to figure things out on their own. After all, that is the testimony of many of us.

The anti-A-C-T-S occurs in every church because we emphasize membership more than discipleship. It is much easier to make someone a church member than it is to make him or her a disciple. Just get them in the door, make them a member and our denominational paperwork looks better. We can brag about how many church members we have. Well, it is time we started talking about disciples instead of members.

Jesus had a plan when it came to discipleship. He utilized a four-step process that invited people to higher (or if you prefer, deeper) levels of commitment and communion with him. In order to defend the bride of Christ from a lack of biblical discipleship we need to return to that process. This is true for the first-time believer who just came to faith and it is true for those who faithfully fill our churches each week, most of whom have never been properly discipled. Many have stalled in their spiritual growth. They remain dedicated believers and church members but they are missing out on the deeper joy, maturity and intimacy that come with ongoing sanctification.

We can visualize the plan of Jesus by using the stair step progression shown in Figure 3:

FIGURE 3

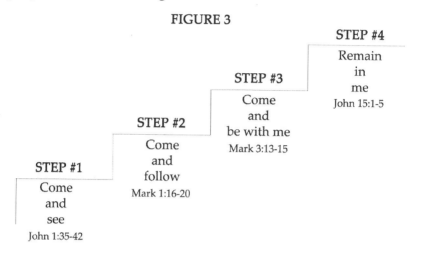

Step #1: Come and see[10]

WE HAVE ALL been shopping with someone and when we find something we want them to see, what do we say?

"Come here, I've got something to show you."

We ask them to come and see. We have discovered something we believe the other person will be interested in. "Come and see" is the first invitation Jesus extended to those he wanted to follow him. As an invitation it is easy, open-ended and non-threatening.

In New Testament times, rabbis gathered disciples around them who would carry on their teachings. Each disciple sought to duplicate within himself the person, character and lifestyle of the

---

[10] Bill Hull, *The Disciple-Making Church: Leading A Body Of Believers On the Journey Of Faith* (Grand Rapids: Baker Books, 2010), pp. 28-30. I am greatly indebted to Mr. Hull for the four steps of this discipleship plan and for his permission to use them here.

rabbi. We might think of it as an apprenticeship (more on this shortly).

John the Baptist acquired disciples of his own. However, when he pointed out Jesus, two of those disciples started after Jesus.

> *Turning around, Jesus saw them following and asked, "What do you want?"*
>
> *They said, "Rabbi" [which means "Teacher"], "where are you staying?"*
>
> *"Come," he replied, "and you will see."*
>
> (John 1:38-39)

There was the invitation. Come and see.

What was Jesus actually saying with this invitation? Was he really proud of the hotel room he had for the duration of his stay near the Jordan River? Did he want these two disciples to "oooh and aahhh" over the nice pad he had to crash in? Not at all.

Jesus invited them to come and spend time with him. They were being offered the opportunity to hang out with Jesus for a little while and to see how he lived. Jesus wanted them to experience first-hand what he did and how he conducted himself. In the vernacular of the automotive industry, the two disciples were taking Jesus for a test drive.

Many of us came to faith in Christ this way. Someone invited us to a worship service, a youth event, a revival, a potluck dinner or some other church function. There was no obligation other than simply being there. It gave us a chance to look, listen and experience the culture and atmosphere of the church. Some of you are members of a church right now because you felt welcomed, supported, and important when you responded to the invitation to "come and see."

Using the verb *come* means we have to get up and move away from something. We have to leave something behind in order to move to something else. To come when someone calls is to respond in obedience. It can be frustrating when your friend does not come and see the thing you have found in the store. She chose to ignore the invitation because she did not want to leave what she was doing.

One of the inquisitive followers of John the Baptist was a fisherman named Andrew (John 1:40). He responded to the invitation from Jesus. Andrew and an unnamed friend left behind the familiarity they had grown accustomed to as followers of John the Baptist.

When we use the verb *see* we are inviting people to look intentionally at who we are and what we are doing. To see is to open the eyes and look directly, to focus your attention on.

Sometimes when we are in the store with our friend we may respond to their request to come and see. We wander over to them but we only give a cursory glance at what they have to show us. We may look but we do not actually see. "Yeah, that's neat," we say without ever really taking the time to look closely. When Jesus extended the invitation to "come and see" he invited those men to enter his life. They had the opportunity to be in a very basic relationship with him and to watch carefully and intently what was happening.

We do not know what they saw in those few brief hours but it changed everything.

> *Andrew, Simon Peter's brother, was one of the two who heard what John had said and who had followed Jesus. The first thing Andrew did was to find his brother Simon and tell him, "We have found the Messiah" [that is, the Christ]. And he brought him to Jesus.*

> (John 1:40-42)

Reclaiming a commitment to biblical discipleship in the Church means that we extend the invitation for people to "come and see."

This requires us to be open and authentic in our churches. In today's world people are hungry for what is real. They appreciate vulnerability, honesty and sincerity. This does not mean our churches must be problem-free before extending the invitation (good luck with that!). It means we are to make every effort to be true, positive and forthright about who we are.

We are to invite people into our lives and our churches to assess for themselves the validity of our claims. Do we live what we say? Is our hospitality as friendly as we claim? Are we truly concerned about the plight of the poor and needy around us? How do we treat children and youth? Does Jesus inform and transform our decision-making or do we just make decisions based on what we want?

The pathway to discipleship begins with a simple invitation. We do not have to force, push, cajole or put on airs. Ours is to invite and to live the way of Jesus. People will make up their own minds. Some may respond to our invitation, check us out and decide "No, thank you." Others will respond and begin to see the life of Jesus, and the presence of the Holy Spirit, at work among us.

Step #2: Come and follow

WITH EACH STEP in the discipleship process Jesus calls us to a higher level of commitment and communion. The second step he used in training his disciples was "come and follow." We see this in Mark 1:16-20:

> *As Jesus walked beside the Sea of Galilee, he saw Simon and his brother Andrew casting a net into the lake, for they were fishermen. "Come, follow me," Jesus said, "and I will send you out to fish for people." At once they left their nets and followed him. When he had gone a little farther, he saw James son of Zebedee and his brother John in a boat, preparing their nets. Without delay he called them, and they left their father Zebedee in the boat with the hired men and followed him.*

In the gospel of John, Jesus invited Andrew to "come and see." Andrew in turn rounded up his brother, Simon, to show him the

Messiah. Next we find Jesus strolling along the shoreline where he ran into Andrew and Simon again. This time he invited them to "come and follow."

As we know, the invitation to "come and see" is safe and open-ended. Andrew and his friend could take their time, and come and go as they wanted. There were no strings attached with that first invitation. However, with "come and follow," the commitment was immediately taken up a notch. Jesus invited Simon, Andrew, James and John to begin living the way he did.

Initially they were given the opportunity to observe and ask questions. They had the flexibility to stay as long as they wanted and even to decide *against* any kind of deeper commitment. But with the invitation to "come and follow," the four fishermen were being asked to step up and decide. It was time to "go big or go home."

The very first mission team I participated on was to the island of Andros in the Bahamas. A friend and I went along with a youth choir. They were going to conduct vacation bible school as well as sing in some of the local churches.

One day after we finished our work I saw some of the youths climbing up an embankment and disappearing over the top. I could hear whoops and cries of excitement so I decided to investigate. I crested the ridge and discovered the youths near the edge of a cliff overlooking the ocean. As I approached I saw one of the boys run and jump off the cliff! He hung in mid-air for a split second and then dropped to the warm waters below. I joined the group and they told me they were taking turns leaping off the cliff.

"Aw, that sounds *cool!*" I exclaimed. I walked to the edge and peered over. Sure enough, there was the boy who had just jumped, paddling back to the shore. One of the other adult leaders was down in the water as a spotter. I commented that it looked like fun and that I had always wanted to try something like that.

"*Are* you going to try it, Todd?" one of the youths asked.

114

Nearly a dozen faces looked intently at me. It was time to go big or go home. After a moment's hesitation I said, "Yeah, I'll do it." Handing my glasses to one of the youths, I crept to the very edge. Thankfully, I am near-sighted so I could not see all the details of what lay beneath me. It was all just a blue blur.

I jumped. Please feel free to insert your mother's favorite comment here: "If all your friends jumped off a cliff, would you do it, too?" Actually, Mom, yes I wou—err, *did*.

I came face-to-face with the choice of whether I would stand on the cliff talking about jumping—or whether I would commit to the next step and actually jump. Peter, Andrew, James and John came face-to-face with a choice: stay where they were or follow Jesus.

I do not remember the thoughts that went through my mind as I leapt off the cliff and plummeted to the waters below. I think they went something like "*AAAAAAHHHHHHHH!!*"

—SPLASH!!!—

"Hey, I didn't die!"

In order to make that jump I had to surrender things. I had to let go of something if I wanted to take hold of the next thing. I said goodbye to the security of *terra firma* under my feet. (Some might say I also said goodbye to my common sense!) We do not mature as disciples of Jesus Christ without letting go of some things. What was beneficial and necessary at one step in our spiritual journey may have to be relinquished in order to move to the next place God wants us.

Peter, Andrew, James and John surrendered their family business, some of their relationships—even some family connections—in order to accept Jesus' invitation to a deeper life.

When we read the gospels we are constantly confronted with the masses that surrounded Jesus. Wherever he went during his earthly ministry there were mobs of people: crowds needing food, crowds wanting miracles, crowds along the seashore, crowds in the house. We might say all these were responding at some level to "come and see." They were given the opportunity to watch and listen, to find out more about who Jesus was. But Jesus does not leave us in the "come and see" stage. He challenges us to take the next step—to make an actual commitment to follow him.

In John 6:54-56, Jesus told the crowd around him, *"Whoever eats my flesh and drinks my blood has eternal life, and I will raise them up at the last day. For my flesh is real food and my blood is real drink. Whoever eats my flesh and drinks my blood remains in me, and I in them."*

John goes on to record,

> *On hearing it, many of his disciples said, "This is a hard teaching. Who can accept it?" (6:60), and From this time many of his disciples turned back and no longer followed him. "You do not want to leave too, do you?" Jesus asked the Twelve.*

> (John 6:66-67)

Many who followed Jesus were simply after a handout, a performance or were looking to satisfy their curiosity. If we study the gospels closely, whenever Jesus started to attract a large crowd he soon gave a challenging teaching like the one in John 6. But there were others:

- *Now when Jesus saw the crowds, he went up on a mountainside and sat down. His disciples came to him, and he began to teach them* (Matthew 5:1-2). This teaching took the form of the Sermon on the Mount with such difficult things as love your enemy, do not worry, and lusting in your heart is the equivalent to lusting in the flesh.
- In Mark 4, Jesus spoke to the crowds in parables about sowing seed and putting a lit lamp under a basket. He told his disciples that if people wanted to put forth the effort they could grasp the meaning of his parables.
- In Luke 11, when the crowds demanded a sign from Jesus, he responded by talking about "the sign of Jonah" and the judgment coming upon that generation. The

threat of being stuck in a big fish or facing a final reckoning was not the way to guarantee a successful membership drive.

- In John 8, Jesus told them they did not know God as their Father but were instead of the devil because they would not accept him.

Herein lies what may be the crux of the lack of biblical discipleship in our churches. We may respond to "come and see," but when we realize that Jesus demands more of us we drift back to the edges of the crowd. Or we may even stop following altogether. I believe Jesus continues to stand before many in the Church, pleading with them to "come and follow." But they are not willing to make the commitment. They have heard about the dedication required, the discipline, the changes necessary—and they want no part of it. They will hang around in the crowd, perhaps wearing a Christian label, but never showing the reality of Jesus in their lives.

* * * * * *

Throughout history craftsmen and artisans have employed apprentices. An apprentice was someone (usually a young person) who was committed to learning a particular trade or skill under the tutelage of a professional.

For example, a father in the Middle Ages would take his son to the local stonemason, blacksmith or carpenter. He would declare his son a candidate for apprenticeship. After a brief period of observation by the craftsman, if the boy had potential, the stonemason, blacksmith or carpenter would agree to take the boy on as an apprentice. The boy's father would pay a sum of money to cover the cost of apprenticeship, which included room and board with the craftsman.

When Jesus invites us to "come and follow," it is like the boy being accepted as an apprentice. It involves a new set of commitments and responsibilities. There is no longer the option of coming and going as we please. There are now some definite strings attached. We have taken an oath of allegiance that we will walk in the footsteps of Jesus.

Yet most of our churches include believers who are unwilling to make a deeper commitment. They are content to drift around the periphery. Churches bullied by a lack of biblical discipleship often have far too many Christians of the "come and see" variety but not very many who "come and follow."

Step #3: Come and be with me

THE RANKS OF true disciples become thinner with this step. Jesus calls us to "come and be with me." We are invited to know Jesus more intimately. It is at this stage where the presence and person of Jesus decidedly transforms us because we are in close, constant proximity to him.

Let us return to our previous example of an apprentice. As we said, if the craftsman found potential in the boy he would agree to accept the lad as an apprentice (the equivalent of "come and follow" in the discipleship process). Once everything was agreed upon the boy went to live with the craftsman. This was a permanent arrangement until the young man had completed his training. With the exception of holidays, festivals or extenuating circumstances, the boy lived with the master craftsman. Part of the commitment of an apprentice was spending the majority of his time in close proximity to the teacher.

The apprentice watched his mentor at work and he worked alongside his mentor. In addition, the boy also learned about the life of his master. The apprentice shared meals with the craftsman's family, slept under their roof and was like an extended part of the family. He learned to *live* like the master craftsman. The third level of commitment for the follower of Jesus is to watch Jesus at work, to work alongside of him and live like him.

Prior to attending seminary I worked as a graphic artist and as a part-time disc jockey for a small radio station. When starting out in both jobs I told my supervisors that I liked to learn by watching someone do a particular task, and then trying to do it myself while they observed. Many people prefer to learn this way: You do it. Let me watch. Let me do it. You watch.

To learn that way means being with the person who is training you. You observe what they do; they observe what you do. And when there are mistakes the teacher is there to point them out. That is the approach Jesus used with the original Twelve and it is what he offers us with "come and be with me."

As we know from Mark 3:13-15, Jesus selected twelve men to be his closest disciples. Before they did anything else their first task was to be with Jesus. The Twelve were to spend all their time with Jesus. This was not just a weekend getaway. Like the master craftsman and his apprentice, these dozen men had to make even stronger commitments, entailing even greater sacrifices.

The disciples were going to become itinerant vagabonds. They accepted a commitment that found them frightened in a boat on a stormy sea (Matthew 8:23-27), harassed by the religious leaders (Mark 7:1-2), homeless (Luke 9:57-58) and hanging out in a Samaritan village (John 4:40). Such was the price to know and be with Jesus. Whatever comforts they may have been used to were gone (think of the luxuries Matthew, the tax collector, had likely enjoyed). Everything about their lives—family, work, friends and religion—changed because they had been invited to be with Jesus constantly.

Unfortunately, many Christians hit the brakes at this point in the discipleship process. They respond to the invitation to "come and see." They may even respond to the invitation to "come and follow." But then they realize this third step involves giving up what they cherish most in order to draw closer to Jesus. This is the obstacle that many stumble over and never move beyond.

Matthew, Mark, and Luke all record an encounter Jesus had with a young man of considerable wealth. When he questioned Jesus about what he needed to do in order to have eternal life, Jesus instructed him, *"Go and sell all your possessions and give the money to the poor, and you will have treasure in heaven. Then come, follow me"* (Mark 10:21; cf. Matthew 19:21, Luke 18:22).

The young man paused for a moment, the conflict no doubt evident on his face. The trio of gospel writers all record two key points. The first is that the young man *went away sad.* The second point was the reason for the first: *because he had great wealth.*

The young man had obviously replied to the invitation to "come and see." He had replied to the invitation of his Jewish faith to "come and follow," for we know he was a deeply spiritual man due to his commitment to keeping the commandments. But when the invitation was extended to come and be with Jesus, he could not let go of his wealth. So he rejected the invitation. His obstacle to a deeper relationship with Jesus was his material possessions and the status he received from them. It remains a problem for many Christians today.

When Jesus issues the call to "come and be with me," he is asking for his followers to know him the way a child does a parent and vice versa. We do not want our children to analyze us or just figure out how we work. For proper health and development, children need close, direct interaction with parents. It is vital they know us personally and intimately. Studies have repeatedly shown how children are negatively affected when deprived of close personal contact with parents, especially in the formative years of life. It is an act of cruelty and neglect if parents do not provide intimate contact for their young children.

It is not enough to know that Jesus healed the sick, fed the hungry or died on a cross. Non-Christians can tell you these things about Jesus. Our knowledge must go deeper than that. Disciples should possess a greater depth of intimacy with Jesus. The time spent in the presence of our Master should be as obvious as it was for Peter and John in the fourth chapter of Acts.

The two apostles were hauled before the Jewish high court for teaching about Jesus. Peter, filled with the Spirit, launched into a powerful declaration about the power of Jesus. Then in 4:21 it says:

The members of the council were amazed when they saw the boldness of Peter and John, for they could see that they were ordinary men with no special training in the Scriptures. They also recognized them as men who had been with Jesus.

It was apparent to everyone gathered in the room that Peter and John had spent considerable time in close personal contact with Jesus. The way they spoke, the way they carried themselves, the way they lived—all pointed to the fact they not only had been with Jesus, but they knew him deeply and personally as well.

If we are to rescue the bride of Christ from a lack of biblical discipleship, we are going to have to take the next step in our commitment. We cannot turn back when we get to step three. The time we spend with Jesus must increase. Too many respond to Christ's call like the rich young man and too few respond like Peter and John. We should not be surprised that our churches include those who cannot be recognized as having been with Jesus.

Step #4: Remain in me

FOLLOWING THE RESURRECTION and ascension of Jesus, the book of Acts tells us that the followers of Jesus were about 120 in number (1:15). Think about that for a moment. After three continuous years of ministry, countless teachings and multiple miracles, all Jesus could claim was a following of "about" 120 people. By today's standards of success we would say that Jesus had not been very effective.

A pastor, preacher, teacher and leader like Jesus should have had thousands of followers. At least that is how we think today. We assess a church or pastor or ministry based on how many numbers they have. But as we have seen, Jesus was not interested in gathering huge numbers. He *was* interested in gathering disciples who were fully committed to his mission.

I have always said that Jesus can do more with a group of thirty Spirit-filled, dedicated servants than he can with a church of 300 or 3,000 who just want to be seen, consume or control. It is not the number of people that make a difference. It is the number of people who willingly submit to the lordship of Jesus Christ, no matter the cost, that make a difference.

Such submission is found in the fourth and final step of the discipleship process. It is the invitation to "remain in me." In John 15:1-5 Jesus said,

> *"I am the true vine, and my Father is the gardener. He cuts off every branch in me that bears no fruit, while every branch that does bear fruit he prunes so that it will be even more fruitful. You are already clean because of the word I have spoken to you. Remain in me, as I also remain in you. No branch can bear fruit by itself; it must remain in the vine. Neither can you bear fruit unless you remain in me.*
>
> *"I am the vine; you are the branches. If you remain in me and I in you, you will bear much fruit; apart from me you can do nothing."*

Jesus turned up the heat on his disciples one final time. He asked them to take what may arguably be the hardest step of all, the one that would place them into the very heart of the Father himself.

The Greek word translated here as "remain" or "abide" is a figurative expression of someone who does not leave the place in which he finds himself. He has settled in for the long haul, putting down roots. John used this term throughout his gospel—eleven times in chapter 15 alone—to denote an inward, ongoing, personal communion with God. This meant more than simply continuing to believe in Jesus. It meant a progressive, intimate union with him.

We might think of it this way: when we visit the optometrist to have our eyes examined we are given a test in which our eyes are forced to cross. We look through a set of lenses and the doctor asks us to focus on a line of letters on the opposite wall. As she adjusts the controls to make our eyes cross, we are asked to tell her when we see two rows of letters. Then we have to say when the two rows merge back into one. The invitation to "remain in me" is like the two going back into one. We become synonymous with the person of Jesus. When people see us they are seeing Jesus.

If we respond to the invitation to remain connected to Jesus we will produce fruit. In other words, the more we surrender ourselves and walk in harmony with Jesus the more God is able to use us to touch lives and change the world.

Three types of believers are inferred in the John 15 passage: those who bear *no fruit* (15:2a), those who bear *some fruit* (15:2b), and those who bear *much fruit* (15:5). The maturing disciple is part of this last group.

Most references to John 15:2 talk about God "cutting off" the unfruitful branch. This can easily be misinterpreted to suggest that if you do not win someone to Jesus you will be cut off. That is not what is meant here. This passage is not talking about losing our salvation or losing God's grace. It is about remaining, abiding—being fully grounded in our relationship with Jesus—so that he can use us for his purposes on earth.

The Greek word translated as "cut off" or "removed" is *airo* (aye-ro). It also means *to lift up* or *to pick up*—as in "Please pick up the cat" or "Let's lift up our hands in praise." Given this understanding the text can be read *"I am the true vine, and my Father is the gardener. He **lifts up** every branch in me that bears no fruit..."*

This is one aspect of the work of a vinedresser or gardener: to lift up the branches that have drooped down and to expose them to the sun once again so they may be fruitful. Instead of reading this text as a threat or guilt-trip, perhaps we would do better to understand it as God's tender, loving attention to those branches which are capable of producing fruit, but which need to be picked up, nurtured and placed back in the light.

The second group inferred in this passage is the branches that produce some fruit: "...while every branch that does bear fruit he prunes so that it will be even more fruitful."

God's pruning is about making clean again. The branches that are fruit bearing are to be periodically stripped of superfluous wood or leaves so they can continue to serve their purpose. We often experience such pruning or cleansing when we go on a spiritual retreat, attend a conference or engage in heartfelt worship. God renews and restores our hopes and spirits; he grants us rest and renewed energy to continue bearing fruit.

When we respond to the invitation to "remain in me" we are submitting ourselves to be a fruit-bearing branch connected to the vine of Jesus Christ. We are committing to a deeper immersion in the Word of God. We vow to make ourselves available to serve others and be used however God sees fit.

* * * * * *

We all need discipleship in every season of life and at every stage of our spiritual journey. The new believer needs to absorb the basics of the faith. More mature followers need to continually strive for the next step in holiness and perfection. Biblical discipleship is crucial for equipping the saints for the work of ministry (Ephesians 4:12), for training and developing new leaders, and for providing accountability, encouragement and opportunities for service.

It has been said that proper discipleship involves three elements. First, *we all need a Barnabas* **beside us**. We need someone who is at the same place we are spiritually, someone who can walk with us at the same pace.

Second, we all need a Timothy **below us**. Paul invested in the life and spiritual growth of young Timothy. We likewise should have someone younger than us or newer in the faith that we are mentoring.

And third, *we all need a Paul* **above us**. Every one of us should be in a relationship with an older, more mature believer. They do for us what we do for Timothy: they mentor and guide us as we seek to develop our faith more deeply.

Highlight these points!

IF YOU ARE the type of person who likes to highlight things that stand out to you, pop the cap on that highlighter. There are three final points we need to consider before moving on.

First, biblical discipleship in the church must begin with the pastor. As with everything else, the pastor (and leadership staff) sets the tone for the congregation. Groups and organizations take on the qualities and characteristics of their leaders. If the pastor is excited, enthusiastic and continually supportive of biblical discipleship, the church will eventually reflect that. It will not happen overnight. It will take time for an emphasis on biblical discipleship to take hold.

On the aforementioned mission trip to Andros each team member was responsible for steering the boat on our journey to the island. During my turn at the wheel I discovered something very important: it takes time for the rudder to respond to the wheel. Since none of us were experienced sailors, our initial tendency when steering was to overcompensate when we did not see immediate results on the compass. We learned that we had to adjust the wheel, wait for the rudder to respond and then check the heading on the compass. This had to be done in small increments. We could not just grab the wheel and spin it like a maritime "Wheel of Fortune." And the larger the ship, the longer it takes for the rudder to respond to changes at the wheel. It takes longer to see a course correction even though one is "in the works."

Pastors, staff and key lay leaders can help make the transition to a church focused on authentic biblical discipleship. It will come about through gradual changes, some perhaps almost microscopic. But over time the patience and commitment can pay off with a congregation that understands and values true discipleship. It is our responsibility as church leaders to see that discipleship is not glossed over, given lip service or ignored. We must be vigilant and intentional.

Church leaders also need to be in discipling relationships. It is easier for the pastor to encourage discipleship when someone else is mentoring him or her. It does no good to emphasize discipleship if those in leadership are unwilling to engage in the process. *Every* Christian needs to be discipled and to be discipling others.

Second, every church needs a process of assimilation. There should be an organized system for new believers, new members and existing members to access the discipleship process.

When someone comes to faith in Christ in your church, what structures are in place to help them learn and grow? Is there a formal process new believers go through—a "basics of Christianity" class—partnering them with a more mature church member? Is there a pastor's introductory class or something similar? If not, we are abandoning new believers when they are most spiritually vulnerable.

What sort of system is in place for new members to be discipled? The lovely couple that just moved into the area may have transferred their membership from their previous church, but we should have a way to incorporate them into the discipleship process. Is there a small group they can plug in to or a new members' class they can attend?

We are often hesitant to ask those who transfer their membership to go through a new member class. We do not want to offend them (so our reasoning goes) by implying they do not know the basics of the faith or anything about the church. Plus, we are afraid that if we require them to be in a disciple-mentor relationship they may choose not to join at all. Most churches are so hungry for new faces or thicker membership rolls that we completely skip any discussion of discipleship.

Yes, that lovely couple may have been deeply involved in their previous church and they may have a solid understanding of the faith. Nevertheless, there is always more we can learn. There are always new heights to which God wants to take us. At its simplest, a system of integration serves to introduce new members to the unique culture, history and practices of the church they are joining.

Existing church members also need a process whereby they can progress in their spiritual maturity. Sunday school and worship can provide a small percentage of this, but as we have said that is not their primary purpose. Those who have been part of the local church for years need small groups dedicated to discipleship. They need one-on-one, disciple-mentor relationships. If they are truly progressing in their faith and maturity they will recognize—and embrace—opportunities for discipleship that are geared toward them.

Third, some people do not want to be discipled. Even though discipleship has been spoken about in countless sermons and Bible lessons, some people simply want nothing to do with it. They do not want other people "poking around in their business." The cost of truly following Jesus, and of being committed to ongoing spiritual maturity, requires more than some are willing to give. No matter how much it is emphasized there are those who will turn their nose up at the idea.

Pastors, do not spend your valuable time trying to change their minds. If such people are unwilling to allow the Holy Spirit to work within them you will simply be wasting your energy. Focus instead on emphasizing, modeling and encouraging discipleship. You will not win those who have hardened their hearts. Only the Lord can change them and then only if such persons allow it. An authentic follower of Christ has learned that discipleship is not optional. It is mandatory.

CHAPTER 8
MAUSOLEUM, MUSEUM, OR MOVEMENT?

The bride of Christ is bullied by man-made traditions

"Tradition is a guide and not a jailer."

W. Somerset Maugham

WHEN I WAS growing up our family had a Christmas Eve tradition. Following the candlelight worship service at church, Dad, Mom, and I went across town to my grandparents' house. Once there my grandparents opened their Christmas presents, usually with a little help from me. We shared the chocolates my grandfather inevitably received and enjoyed being together. On Christmas morning my grandparents came to our house. I cannot remember a Christmas morning when they were not already sitting in the living room by the time I got up and dashed in to see what awaited me under the tree.

That was our holiday routine throughout my childhood and youth. This tradition developed because my dad often had to work on Christmas Day. He was allowed to go in a little later than normal so our Christmas mornings happened around 6:00 or 6:30 AM. Dad could be part of the activities before leaving for work. It was easier to visit the grandparents on Christmas Eve so they could be there the next morning. Even when Dad was no longer required to work as many holidays we still maintained the tradition. We had gotten accustomed to it.

A tradition is a shared belief, value or action that binds people and communities together. They are passed down from one generation to another. They can be customs that are unique to a family—such as my family's Christmas schedule. Schools and other organizations have traditions such as the annual seventh grade trip to the state capital or the Girl Scout cookie sales. Some traditions are national, such as fireworks on the Fourth of July or singing the National Anthem before a sporting event. Traditions represent and reflect the essence and values of an entire population, tribe or group. They often carry great symbolic significance.

Traditions give us a tangible link to our past, to those things we want to honor and pass on to future generations. Some of our most meaningful memories derive from traditions such as wedding anniversaries, birthdays, going to Grandma's at Thanksgiving, or the annual summer trip to the cabin.

Churches likewise have their traditions. It might be the manner in which a baptism is performed, the robes the choir wears, which week Vacation Bible School is held or how meetings are conducted.

But what happens when church traditions become more important than sharing the gospel? What happens when the traditions we cherish prevent the church from fulfilling its mission and purpose?

We have a bully. The church is threatened by its own traditions.

Passover and hand washing

THERE ARE A few traditions mentioned in the Hebrew Scriptures. In 2 Chronicles 35:25, a tradition began in the wake of the death of King Josiah of Judah:

> Jeremiah composed laments for Josiah, and to this day all the male and female singers commemorate Josiah in the laments. These became a tradition in Israel and are written in the Laments.

Josiah was responsible for significant spiritual reform in Judah during his reign. Unlike many of his predecessors, Josiah's heart was committed to God. He destroyed the places of false worship, and when the Book of the Law was discovered, Josiah read it aloud and renewed Israel's covenant with God. For many years after his death it was traditional to praise the deeds of Josiah and remember what he had done for his people.

The Old Testament prophet Micah referred to *the statutes [traditions] of Omri and all the practices of Ahab's house* (6:16). Micah prophesied against Israel, accusing them of keeping the traditions that were instituted by wicked King Omri and his predecessor, Ahab. Because the people had embraced the foul practices and sinful ways of those leaders, God brought judgment against Israel.

Perhaps one of the oddest traditions mentioned in the Hebrew Scriptures refers to the daughter of Jephthah, found in Judges 11. Jephthah led Israel—a very loose confederation of tribes at that point in their history—in battle against the Ammonites. Following his victory, Jephthah made a rash vow to sacrifice the first thing that came out of his house when he returned home. Unfortunately, it was his daughter who came out to meet him.

She requested two months to be with her friends and mourn the fact she would never be married or bear children. There is much debate as to whether Jephthah fulfilled his vow and sacrificed his daughter, or if she lived a spinsterish existence in the mountains for the rest of her life. Regardless, at the conclusion of the story the writer said, *From this comes the Israelite tradition that each year the young women of Israel go out for four days to commemorate the daughter of Jephthah the Gileadite* (v. 40).

Perhaps the best-known tradition from the Old Testament is the Passover. Inaugurated to remember Israel's slavery in Egypt and God's subsequent deliverance, it is a tradition that endures to this day. The Passover celebration is filled with symbolism. The candles, the wine, the food and the stories shared around the table all point to the faithfulness of God and to his special relationship with Israel. It is a tradition that binds all Jews together no matter where they are. The Christian practice of Holy Communion, the central tradition of the Church, comes directly from the Passover.

In the New Testament, two of Paul's letters briefly mention traditions, although in very general ways. In 1st Corinthians 11:2,

Paul praised the church...*for remembering me in everything and for holding to the traditions just as I passed them on to you.*

We have no idea what traditions Paul referred to, but within the context of the chapter the apostle addressed issues of propriety in worship. Perhaps he referred to worship practices specific to that congregation, or traditions observed in all the churches—such as prayer, the Lord's Supper or receiving an offering for those in need.

In Colossians 2:8, Paul cautioned the believers,

> *...see to it that no one takes you captive through hollow and deceptive philosophy, which depends on human tradition and the elemental spiritual forces of this world rather than on Christ.*

False teachers and charlatans with impressive oratory skills threatened the churches of the Mediterranean basin. Paul reminded the Colossian church that the vaunted wisdom of those frauds was not based in Christ but on man-made traditions.

Nowhere in the New Testament do man-made traditions come under fire more fiercely than in the gospels. Mark 7:1-5 records an incident between Jesus and the religious leaders:

> *The Pharisees and some of the teachers of the law who had come from Jerusalem gathered around Jesus and saw some of his disciples eating food with hands that were defiled, that is, unwashed. [The Pharisees and all the Jews do not eat unless they give their hands a ceremonial washing, holding to the tradition of the elders. When they come from the marketplace they do not eat unless they wash. And they observe many other traditions, such as the washing of cups, pitchers, and kettles.] So the Pharisees and teachers of the law asked Jesus, "Why don't your disciples live according to the tradition of the elders instead of eating their food with defiled hands?"*

To understand this complaint we need to go back to Exodus 30:17-21. Aaron, the priest, and his sons were required to wash their hands and feet in a bronze washbasin when they entered the Tabernacle. They also washed before approaching the altar to offer sacrifices. God told Moses, *"This is a permanent law for Aaron and his descendants, to be observed from generation to generation"* (v. 21).

The ritual of washing was prescribed solely for the priestly class of Israel. It was not a universal law for everyone to observe. However, the Pharisees wanted to maintain the purity and holiness of coming before the Lord, and they felt everyone should honor God the way they did. They washed; therefore, *everyone* should wash.

If the Pharisees wanted to maintain purity through ceremonial washing that was fine. The problem was the condemnation they heaped on those who did not. The Pharisees viewed such persons as sinners, unclean, not fully committed to God. They took a rule designed for a specific group and applied it to every single person, hence their complaint against Jesus and his disciples. (Mark went even further, noting the Pharisees' penchant for washing nearly everything and observing many other traditions.)

Jesus responded sharply to the Pharisees' complaint:

> *"You have let go of the commands of God and are holding on to human traditions."*

And he continued,

> *"You have a fine way of setting aside the commands of God in order to observe your own traditions! For Moses said, 'Honor your father and mother,' and, 'Anyone who curses their father or mother is to be put to death.' But you say that if anyone declares that what might have been used to help their father or mother is Corban [that is, devoted to God]—then you no longer let them do anything for their father or mother. Thus you nullify the word of God by your tradition that you have handed down. And you do many things like that."*
>
> (Mark 7:8-13)

Ouch!

Jesus pulled no punches here. He accused the Pharisees of honoring their own man-made traditions instead of adhering to the written commands of God. He accused them of dishonoring their parents by claiming "Corban."

Corban was a sacred vow (that could not be broken), which allowed for material assets to be gifted to the Temple. By doing this, the Pharisees dedicated resources to the Temple that should have gone to support their families. In addition, the act of claiming Corban was an opportunity to flaunt their piety before others. They looked good publicly—"My, what devout and generous men those Pharisees are!"—but behind closed doors they neglected their own families. Jesus said they invalidated the fifth commandment in order to maintain their man-made tradition.

Our human rules and observances can often eclipse God's law and his grace. We can become so fixated on observing every rule or tradition that we miss the main purpose of the Church. When the maintenance of our church traditions supersedes people experiencing the grace of God we have a serious problem on our hands. It leads to our churches becoming mausoleums or museums rather than divinely empowered movements.

What's in the box?

CHURCH TRADITIONS VARY from one congregation to another. Our traditions help us share values and history. They help us stay connected and grounded in tough times. Traditions help us remember even as we look ahead.

Each generation must redefine the practices of the Christian faith to fit their cultural context. This does not mean each generation gets to pick and choose what they like in the Bible, or which historic doctrines they will follow. But it does mean that as each new generation faces challenges and opportunities they must find ways to confess, share and live out their faith. Some of the things that worked for my parents' and grandparents' generations did not always work for mine. And what works for my generation will likely not work for my sons' generation. The Christian faith is constantly fluid around an unchanging core. God is always revealing himself anew in every age and culture. Some of our Church traditions, such as the Lord's Supper and praying together, go all the way back to the church in Acts. Others have been added over the years in attempts to actualize the faith for a given place or point in time.

Previous generations were raised in the waning days of Christendom. This meant that if one was born in a Christian area or nation, it was automatically assumed he or she was a Christian. Attendance at worship and Sunday school, serving on various committees, and protecting the morals and doctrines of the church were strongly emphasized. They were the standard by which Christian faithfulness was judged. As a result, over time people came to associate following Jesus with sitting and listening to a sermon. Or chairing the administrative council. Or making sure no one moved the altar furniture.

Certain sets of beliefs and practices became ingrained in each local church. One generation passed these rules on to succeeding generations:

☹   You do not run in the church.

☹   Choir practice is always on Wednesday nights.

☹   Do not go to the movies.

☹   We only help people who help themselves.

☹   It is not worship if it does not take place in a church sanctuary.

Being faithful to Jesus had little to nothing to do with feeding the hungry, showing hospitality to strangers, taking care of the outcast, advocating for the poor or working for peace and justice. Little was made of sacrifice and surrender for the betterment of others. Instead, what was passed from one generation to the next were morality, rules and man-made traditions.

Imagine the oldest members of your church handing you a beautifully wrapped box. The box represents the essence, history and practice of the Christian faith. Removing the lid and looking inside, you discover the foundational doctrines of the faith: a covenant God who longs to be in a personal relationship with his creation; the sinfulness that separates us from God and one another; the atonement of Jesus Christ on the cross; his bodily resurrection; the promise of his eventual return; and many others.

Also inside the box are our sacramental practices, our history (both as a local congregation and as part of the Church universal), the confessional affirmations and creeds, the teachings of Jesus and the apostles, the revelation of God to humanity in the Holy Scriptures. Many of the items in the box are unique. They cannot be diluted or replaced without stripping the Christian faith of its essence.

The oldest members of your church place this incredible box into your hands. They are anxious to see that all they have built and supported is taken care of. They were expected to honor the contents of the box as they received it and have taught others to do the same. They were guided by the commitment to protect and preserve the institutional faith they inherited.

But if we look carefully we begin to see that some of the things in the box did not come from Jesus or the historical Church. In fact, some of the box's contents may even be contrary to the life and instructions of Jesus. They are things that the local church and its members have included as part of their expression of the faith. Congregants have received comfort and peace from these things. They represent aspects of their personal and corporate faith that have been meaningful across the years. The problem arises when the line between historic Christian tradition and local church tradition is blurred, when man-made traditions outweigh the foundational traditions.

In the practice and expression of our faith we come to equate our man-made traditions with the foundational traditions of the church. We mistakenly assume that having the Christmas Eve candlelight service at 10:00 PM is the only time it can be held. If someone suggests we move it to 7:00 PM in order to be more accessible for families with young children, people get upset. Accusations are hurled that "nobody cares about the old people anymore" or that the pastor or the worship committee is "destroying our church with all these changes."

The time a worship service is held is not part of the historic traditions of the Church. It reflects cultural needs and practices. Yet a man-made tradition like the time of a Christmas Eve service can take on untouchable, semi-divine qualities.

Death by tradition

MANY CHURCHES DECLINE and die because they are unwilling to differentiate between foundational Christian tradition and man-made tradition. Both are jumbled together in their box and as far as they are concerned, making sure the pulpit is never moved is just as inviolable as the sacrament of baptism. Such churches generally fall into two categories. They are either mausoleums or museums. They are reverent, well-maintained dead spaces in the community or they are a place where the past is on display.

Christianity is a *movement*. We are the active, living presence of Jesus Christ in the world. We are to be moving forward, changing, offering the grace and welcome of God's kingdom to all. If we are a mausoleum where the dead rest quietly (yes, think about your typical worship service) or a museum to what used to be, we are guilty of diminishing our relevance, presence and power. We are to blame for turning the body of Christ into a corpse.

I knew a church where some of the congregation had a desire to reach out to children. The congregation, like their building, was aging rapidly. The children and grandchildren of the remaining members were not present in the congregation. The church knew it needed to reconnect with the children of the neighborhood if it wanted to survive.

It was suggested that several of the rooms on the second floor of the educational building be redone to serve as a children's ministry area. The majority of the congregation never went to the second floor any longer because they could not navigate the stairs. It had been years since many of them had been up there.

At the top of the stairs was a large room that held a small adult Sunday school class of middle-aged attendees. This classroom was the largest on the floor and it was suggested it could become the main children's gathering area. Smaller rooms across the hall could be used for music, worship or crafts. In order to make this happen the adult class would need to trade rooms and move a few doors down the hall.

It never happened.

The adult classroom was known as the "Mr. Deceased-Church-Member's Room." There was even a small picture of this saint on the wall. This individual taught Sunday school there for many years.

When the suggestion was first made there was immediate resistance from some of the congregants about turning "Mr. Deceased-Church-Member's Room" into a children's area. Never mind the fact that the adult class only had a handful of participants occupying a space that could have held five times as many. Never mind that Mr. Deceased-Church-Member had always been supportive of children's ministry while he was alive. Because two of the members of the Sunday school class had influential names, the idea of an upstairs children's ministry area never materialized. They were unwilling to let go of their traditional Sunday morning class space in order to reach their community. There was no new influx of children and their families, all because the church was bullied by the fact that "this has always been Mr. Deceased-Church-Member's classroom, and it wouldn't be proper to turn it over to children."

In preparing for this chapter I posted the following question on my Facebook page: "For all my church-going friends: What are some man-made traditions in the church you have seen fought over or elevated to near-divine status?" My page blew up with responses!

One pastoral colleague told of a church that almost split because the new worship committee chair decided that gold bows on the church's doors at Christmas would be better than red bows. Using red bows had become part of the holiday decorating tradition. This same colleague also told me about a church that suffered from a long-standing disagreement over their cemetery policy. My friend said, "They were too busy fighting over a field of dead people instead of trying to reach the living ones across the street!"

Another friend told of a Sunday school class that refused to change their start time from 9:30 AM to 9:45. Every Sunday at 9:30 they would shut the door to their classroom and not let anyone else in. It was traditional that Sunday school—at least for that particular class—started at half-past nine. No exceptions.

One aspect of man-made tradition revolves around items donated to the church in memory of someone. It does not matter if it is a pulpit Bible (that has not been read from in decades), a table or lamp, a picture of Jesus or an entire room—to suggest doing anything with such items is guaranteed to stir up a hornet's nest. One church leader was informed, "You can't remove those books from this room because they were placed there in memory of my grandmother."

Our bull-headed determination to cling to outdated, man-made traditions is a factor in the ongoing decline of our churches. It is difficult to attract younger generations because (a) they do not understand the majority of our man-made traditions, and (b) they do not understand our defiant refusal to let them go—or at least ease them somewhat—especially when they hinder the mission and purpose of the church.

Squabbling over a hymnal given in memory of Great Aunt Giffenbopper or refusing to allow a room to be used for ministry makes little sense to those who visit our congregations. They quickly see the disconnect between what we profess and what we actually do. We may claim allegiance to Jesus and his mission in the world but when we stymie attempts to rearrange the worship space or to install a new nursery, we reveal that only our personal preferences and entitlements matter.

To eat or not to eat, that is the question

ONE THING WE can say about the church in Corinth is that it probably had few man-made traditions. The church simply had not been around long enough to have lifetime members demanding their own preferences. Nor did they have any church buildings to idolize and bicker about. However, Paul had been asked, either by letter or in person (1st Corinthians 1:11), about a practice in Corinth that was something of a community-wide religious tradition. It had the potential to negatively impact the faith of weaker believers.

Lack of food was a recurring problem throughout the Roman Empire. Famines were common. As the population of the Empire grew with the conquest of new lands, food resources were spread even thinner, especially for the poor. One responsibility of any government is to see that people have access to adequate food. The practice of *panem et circenses* — "bread and circuses" — was a way for politicians to win popular support by providing free bread and entertainment for the masses.

Meat was an item that the majority had little access to. The wealthy and elite enjoyed meat as part of their diet but most people subsisted on a diet of grains, vegetables and fruit. The one time when meat was more accessible was following the sacrifice at a local temple. The unused parts of the animal were taken to the marketplace and sold, or the temple prepared them and held religious feasts. This was often the only time the lower urban classes got meat. It was therefore something of a tradition for people to attend a temple feast.

The issue presented to Paul was whether or not a Christian should eat the meat that had been offered in sacrifice to an idol. Was eating free meat at a temple morally and spiritually acceptable for this new thing called "Church"? What did buying sacrificial meat mean for the lifestyle of a Christian? Paul responded:

> So then, about eating food sacrificed to idols: We know that "An idol is nothing at all in the world" and that "There is no God but one." For even if there are so-called gods, whether in heaven or on earth (as indeed there are many "gods" and many "lords"), yet for us there is but one God, the Father, from whom all things came and for whom we live; and there is but one Lord, Jesus Christ, through whom all things came and through whom we live.

(1st Corinthians 8:4-6)

The message Paul received from Corinth included two phrases in current use among the believers: "An idol is nothing at all in the world" and "There is no God but one." Some in the church recognized that a temple idol was nothing more than wood, stone or metal. It was not real; it possessed no powers. It was just a symbol. For them, to eat food that had been sacrificed to an idol did not mean they believed in or worshiped whichever deity was represented.

The Corinthian believers also acknowledged the basic tenant of monothcism: there is only one God. For them, believing in God and following Jesus Christ were not antithetical to enjoying a bit of free meat at a temple feast. They knew it was just meat and their spiritual lives were not impacted one way or the other if they ate it. Paul acknowledged as much: *But food does not bring us near to God; we are no worse if we do not eat, and no better if we do* (v. 8).

However, Paul quickly pointed out: *But not everyone possesses this knowledge. Some people are still so accustomed to idols that when they eat sacrificial food they think of it as having been sacrificed to a god, and since their conscience is weak, it is defiled* (v. 7).

What concerned Paul was *the well-being of other believers* in the church. Some knew the meat provided by temples did not make them a follower of another god. But what if other Christians saw their brothers and sisters eating sacrificial meat? What if other Christians were not as spiritually mature and thought that eating such meat went against Christ? Would the actions of the more mature or discerning believers not cause confusion--perhaps even temptation—for those who were not as mature?

Yes, Paul told them. Their actions did have a significant impact on fellow Christians:

Be careful, however, that the exercise of your rights does not become a stumbling block to the weak. For if someone with a weak conscience sees you, with all your knowledge, eating in an idol's temple, won't that person be emboldened to eat what is sacrificed to idols? So this weak brother or sister, for whom Christ died, is destroyed by your knowledge.

(1st Corinthians 8:9-11)

If they saw the knowledgeable, wiser and more mature believers partaking in meat that had been offered in sacrifice, those weaker in their faith might stumble. The weaker might think, "Hey, it must be okay if Temerius is doing it. He's a really strong leader in the church."

Yet if the weaker brother went ahead and ate, his conscience may trouble him. His vulnerable faith could be jeopardized.

When you sin against them in this way and wound their weak conscience, you sin against Christ. Therefore, if what I eat causes my brother or sister to fall into sin, I will never eat meat again, so that I will not cause them to fall.

(1st Corinthians 8:12-13)

Paul deliberately chose to forego eating meat if he thought doing so might cause another Christian to sin. This does not mean Paul was a vegan, as some have suggested. He may very well have been. The point here is not what sort of dietary lifestyle Paul chose for himself. The point was that Paul made his decision based on the effect it might have on his Christian witness.

This is a point that needs greater attention in our churches. Man-made traditions satisfy the individual or small cliques within the church. While the tradition may be innocuous by itself, the way it is defended or venerated creates a negative witness. Churches bullied by man-made traditions do not stop to think about what their preferences and traditions do to others. They do not pause to consider whether their tradition may cause someone weaker in the faith to stumble, fall or perhaps give up on church altogether.

Often the attitude is "I've been a member of this church all my life. I'm not going to start changing things around just for a few new people." When such attitudes are present, we should not be surprised that our churches resemble mausoleums or museums rather than a true movement of the Holy Spirit.

CHAPTER 9
DEFENDING THE BRIDE OF CHRIST FROM MAN-MADE TRADITIONS

"People should think things out fresh and not just accept conventional terms and the conventional way of doing things."

Richard Buckminster Fuller

ON MARCH 13, 2013, the Roman Catholic Church welcomed its 266th pope, Jorge Mario Bergoglio, to the Holy See. He made history by being the first non-European pope of the modern era, the first pope to come from Latin America, and the first Jesuit to be elected. Three days later Bergoglio made history again by taking the papal name of Francis, the first pope to ever do so.

Following his election the pope appeared on the balcony at the Vatican before a throng packed into St. Peter's Square, just as his predecessors had done for centuries. Traditionally, the pope's first public act is to bless the assembled crowd. However, Bergoglio broke with the established tradition.

Writers Chelsea J. Carter, Hada Messia, and Richard Allen Greene, reporting for CNN.com, said: "Rather than bless the crowd first, he asked them to pray for him.

"'Let us say this prayer, your prayer for me, in silence,' he told the cheering crowd.

"The willingness by Francis to dispense with tradition was interpreted by a Vatican spokesman as a sign he will be willing to chart his own path in other ways."[11]

---

11 Carter, Chelsea J., Messia, Hada and Greene, Richard Allen. *Pope Francis, the pontiff of firsts, breaks with tradition*, http://www.cnn.com/2013/03/13/world/Europe/vatican-pope-selection

The Vatican spokesman did not know how right he was. On Maundy Thursday, only fifteen days after his election, Pope Francis knelt before a dozen young people at a Rome detention facility and washed their feet. Included in that group were two women and several Muslims.

Previous popes commemorated this solemn act on the feet of twelve high-ranking priests, representing the original twelve disciples of Jesus. The foot washing was traditionally held in the Basilica of St. John in Lateran, surrounded by all the pageantry and ceremony of the Roman Catholic Church. But in keeping with his emphasis on humility and simplicity, Pope Francis enacted the ritual in a jail, with twelve young offenders as representative disciples. I think it was a moment that made Jesus proud.

Since becoming pope, Francis has regularly refused the preferential treatment that accompanies the role. When he was introduced on the day of his election he refused to stand on an elevated platform, preferring to stand shoulder-to-shoulder with his assembled cardinals. He wears less ornate vestments than his predecessors. His residence is a Vatican guesthouse, not the papal apartments in the Apostolic Palace. He has paid his own hotel bills and rides the bus instead of using his special car. There can be no doubt that Pope Francis is forging a new path for the Church.

His approach rankled many Catholic traditionalists, however. By washing women's feet some feared the pope could be preparing to allow the ordination of women. Those who preferred the opulence of the Church were concerned about Francis' emphasis upon the poor and needy. Not even the pope is immune to criticism when it comes to upsetting tradition.

Some will say, "Yeah, but he's the Pope. He can do whatever he wants."

Yes, he can. But Francis' tradition-shattering actions were not merely because he could. It was not because he wanted the publicity or because he thought it would be a nice thing to do. Francis broke with established tradition in order to communicate that something new was taking place. He sent a message that his pontificate would not be business as usual.

By breaking from entrenched ritual and practice, Pope Francis alerted the Catholic Church—and the world—that some things about the Christian faith are negotiable. There are some things that should be preserved and some that can be let go. Francis understands that a return to the humble and sacrificial example of Jesus speaks louder and clearer than centuries of man-made traditions.

If the head of the Vatican city-state and leader of the world's 1.2 billion Catholics can break away from some traditional practices, there is no reason our local churches cannot do the same. We do not have to be bullied by man-made traditions. It is time to open up that beautiful box handed to us by our elders and determine what is and is not negotiable.

Defining the differences

THERE ARE ASPECTS of the Christian faith that have endured since the book of Acts. We continue to meet regularly for worship (Acts 2:46) and to baptize new believers (Acts 2:38). We learn and grow spiritually. We fellowship, pray and celebrate the Lord's Supper (Acts 2:42, 46) across the globe. Churches serve the needy (Acts 6:1-6), share the good news of the gospel (Acts 3:11-26) and reflect and represent the reign of God's kingdom (Acts 4:32-35).

The dual nature of Christ, the atoning work of the cross, the origin and role of the Holy Spirit, the place of the Old Testament within the Christian faith and original sin are just some of the examples of doctrines that have been handed down across the centuries. We may disagree with some parts of our theological heritage but if we deny the divinity of Christ, his sacrificial death or bodily resurrection, then we can no longer call ourselves Christian. Some of our historic traditions and beliefs are simply not up for "pick and choose" status.

Within the gilded box preserved by our ancestors is this collection of the basic tenants of Christianity. They are non-negotiable. You cannot jettison these beliefs without divesting Christianity of its uniqueness. We have these doctrines today because in the first few centuries of the church's existence, attempts were made to do just that. Church councils met to assess and systematize the theological beliefs that form the essence of Christianity as we know it today. Many of the traditional doctrines and creeds we follow originated during that time—as responses to challenges from Gnostics and pagans.

Yet also within our box are many traditions that *are* subject to change, restructure or even abandonment. It is up to each church to identify—and differentiate between—those things that have historically formed the core beliefs of Christianity, and those things that have developed as a result of local church culture and practice.

For example, have you or anyone you know experienced church conflict over the choir? Or how about the debate on whether the pastor should wear a robe or not? We have seen or heard nasty skirmishes over the church building. These are three examples of man-made traditions or practices that have no grounding in the New Testament. Choirs, clerical robes and church buildings all arose as Christianity and the Roman Empire became more intimate bedfellows.

Choirs were used to serenade important government officials, victorious generals or the deities of Rome. Clergy robes developed as a way of setting clerical leaders apart, just as scholars in the academic world were set apart by their vestments. The church did not begin gathering in specialized buildings until the fourth century AD. There is no biblical connection for any of these three traditions, yet Christians across the years have battled one another over them.

Would we be less Christian if pastors and priests stopped wearing robes? Of course not. Would our faith be in jeopardy if we did not have choirs on Sunday morning? No. Would we stop being the church if we lost our church building? Not at all. In fact, we might find ourselves becoming *more like* the early church in its power and attraction if we had fewer buildings. We will look at this in more detail in the next chapter.

Do choirs, robes and buildings help us? Sure they do. But they are also negotiable. We could function just as easily—and in some cases more freely—if we did not have them. We can get by if we do not have a bulletin each week or if someone does not decorate the altar. We cannot survive if we compromise on the atoning death of Jesus Christ or cast aside the teachings of the apostles.

In defining the difference between man-made traditions and historic Christian traditions we must assess the role and purpose of each one. Historic Christian tradition seeks to provide a sense of unity around the irreplaceable. We all agree that remembering and celebrating Holy Communion is a non-negotiable aspect of the faith. That is a tradition that has endured since Jesus inaugurated it hours before his crucifixion. We cannot and must not lose it or compromise on it.

However, the man-made traditions that surround our remembrance and celebration of Holy Communion should not be that rigid. If we say, for example, that the only right and proper way to receive the Lord's Supper is by kneeling at an altar rail then we have established a man-made tradition with no basis in Scripture or church history. We have elevated our personal preference or local church practice to the level of non-negotiable. We have effectively communicated that if you are physically unable to kneel you are not partaking in the right way. This is the exact attitude Jesus confronted in the Pharisees.

As we know, the Pharisees took a small component of the Law—ritual washing, designed for priests—and applied it to everyone with a broad brush. And if everyone did not follow the prescribed ritual (as defined in intricate detail by the Pharisees) they were thought to be less devout. The Pharisees were guilty of elevating the practice over the purpose.

Our churches can communicate negative impressions when we allow ourselves to be bullied by man-made traditions. We can imply that only those "in the know" can understand a particular tradition or practice. This creates a sense of superiority and exclusivity. "You'd have to have been born and raised here to understand the background of this," might be a common statement.

Those who are "in the know" are often the keepers of the traditions, a situation that can foster unhealthy control issues. In one church I visited there was a lady who decorated the altar every week. She did an excellent job. When I suggested that other gifted people in the congregation might be able to help out, share the responsibility and bring different expressions of beauty to worship, I was told bluntly that she did not need—or want—any help.

Decorating the altar was something her mother had done for years prior to her death. The woman had taken over the responsibility and she enjoyed doing it. She went on to tell me that she kept all the altar decorations at her home so they would not be available to anyone else (even if she were to allow someone else to do the decorating). She was the "keeper of the tradition" of decorating the altar. This gave her a sense of power and control, and effectively neutralized any chance for others to share their gifts in that manner.

Man-made traditions can also hinder the growth of the church. What if a new couple had visited that lady's church and wanted to share their gift of design in worship? What if God wanted to use them to bring something new and different to the worship experience? Once they found out that the keeper of the tradition was not interested in helping train others they would have migrated to another church. Keepers of local church traditions have a vested interest in not seeing their church grow because growth means new people, and new people always want to help out and do things differently!

Our preferential traditions also remove the focus from Jesus. Instead of joyful, exuberant worship on Sunday morning, more attention is directed toward the fact that the pastor did not wear a coat and tie. The presence of Jesus takes a back seat to the fact there is a new hymn listed in the bulletin. The Holy Spirit is bound and gagged because we are still upset about a group that was allowed to use the building the night before.

If a tradition aids us in connecting with God more deeply, if it is open and flexible enough to navigate societal changes, if it grounds us solidly in the faith of the historic church—then it should remain in our beautiful box. On the other hand, if a tradition alienates people from God, will not adapt to fit changing circumstances, or is maintained merely because "we've always done it that way," it may be time to rethink its place in our box.

Now about those hymns...

HAVE YOU EVER noticed that the New Testament does not give us a prescribed order of worship? We are told repeatedly that the early church met in the temple courts or in private homes to worship. Yet nowhere are we told exactly *what* they did or *how* they did it.

The reason is because worship must be contextualized for every community and culture. To some degree the worship at the church in Antioch was different than worship at the church in Rome. Just like today the worship of a church in Nebraska will be different than the worship of a church in Nigeria. God did not hand down a single monolithic order of worship because every church needs to reach its local community in relevant ways. The New Testament does not prescribe one universal way of worship.

So why do we assume that the way our church worships is the only right way? I have known people who firmly believe that if worship takes place anywhere but a church sanctuary it is not really worship. What does that communicate to those who attend a service in a family life center, school cafeteria, storefront or living room?

Is it "worship-lite" if it is held outside a church sanctuary? Can God only move and work within the confines of a building with stained glass? Of course not! Yet this is what we often communicate when our tradition (actually our personal preference) of only worshiping in a sanctuary is venerated.

The one thing that regularly gets overlooked in our vehement defense of man-made traditions is that every tradition started out as something new. And everything that was once new faced opposition as well. An excellent example of this is Sunday school.

Englishman Robert Raikes developed the idea of "Sunday school" as a way to teach poor children how to read and write. In the late 1700s, the Industrial Revolution drew thousands of people into the cities in search of work. Most did not have the money to send their children to school. Another obstacle to education was that children often worked six days a week, for sixteen or eighteen hours on end, in deplorable conditions. They simply had no opportunity to receive an education.

However, the children had Sundays off. Many often ended up roaming the streets or getting into trouble. Raikes was burdened with compassion to reach these children so he used the Bible to teach them how to read and write. He worked diligently to ensure the children received a rudimentary education, while at the same time teaching them morals and the Christian faith.

The Sunday school idea caught on and spread. But when it crossed the Atlantic Ocean to America there was tremendous opposition to it, *mostly from church leaders!* Sunday school was accused of everything from Sabbath breaking to indoctrinating impressionable children with political ideologies. Some of the most staunchly opposed even suggested one would go to hell for participating in Sunday school!

Yet today Sunday school is considered one of the traditional pillars of the church. Just make a casual reference to possibly doing away with Sunday school and listen to what erupts. It is adored by nearly everyone, sometimes even being viewed as a non-negotiable of the faith.

Worship music is another example. Every pastor and choir director has received at least one letter, e-mail or personal comment about the service music. Consider this note received by one pastor:

"What's wrong with the inspiring hymns with which we grew up? When I go to church, it is to worship God, not to be distracted with learning a new hymn. Last Sunday's was particularly unnerving. While the text was good, the tune was unsingable and the new harmonies were quite discordant."

This unsettled parishioner was not referring to the latest Hillsong UK or Chris Tomlin song. The letter was dated 1890 and the hymn being criticized was "What a Friend We Have in Jesus"!

Another letter, dated 1874, lambasted a new song that had been introduced the previous week:

"Was it the organist's idea or yours that our peaceful worship service was shattered by that new hymn last Sunday? The music was sacrilegious; something one would expect to hear in a den of iniquity, not a church! Don't expect me even to attempt to sing it next time!"

The hymn in question? "I Love to Tell the Story."

And finally, people always threaten to leave if their man-made traditions are not honored:

"Pastor, I am not a music scholar, but I feel I know appropriate church music when I hear it. Last Sunday's new hymn, if you call it that, sounded like a sentimental love ballad one might expect to hear crooned in a saloon. If you persist in exposing us to rubbish like this in God's house, don't be surprised if many of the faithful look for a new place to worship. The hymns we grew up with are all we need."

How many of our faithful congregants would imagine that in 1865 "Just As I Am" would cause such a ruckus?

Yet all three of these hymns are now considered traditional, beloved, and nearly sacrosanct. In fact, pastors and worship leaders hear all too frequently, "Why can't we go back to singing the old songs like 'I Love to Tell the Story' or 'What a Friend We Have in Jesus'?" What is thought of as traditional and untouchable today was not always so. Times change. Music changes. Ways of expressing worship to God in music changes. But when we demand only one type of music we effectively shut the door on genuine seekers, wrongfully assuming that our traditions are the only things that matter.

If you don't know, ASK!

I CONFESS THAT as a child I did not ask a lot of questions in school. Like most children I did not want to be thought of as dumb and picked on by my classmates. So I would sit silently at my desk, hoping someone else would ask my questions. Occasionally someone did; most of the time they did not. I ended up even more stressed than if I had just overcome my fears, raised my hand and asked.

As I grew and matured I discovered the value in asking questions. However, I never recall questioning my faith or the church as I was growing up. I suppose I took those things for granted or was just not spiritually mature enough to ask. Seminary taught me about asking questions. But I did not get serious about questioning some of our ecclesiastical traditions until I was on staff at a large church.

One Sunday morning after the senior pastor finished his sermon and we were beginning to sing the closing hymn, a teenage girl and her mother came to the altar. The senior pastor indicated for me to go down and speak with them. I knelt in front of them and asked how I could help.

"My daughter wants to accept Jesus Christ and become a Christian," the mother said with tears in her eyes.

I smiled and nodded—on the outside. On the inside I was thrown into a panic. Two thoughts whizzed through my mind: (1) *Do we have enough time to do this before the hymn is over*, and (2) *What do I do now?!* For a moment all my seminary training flew out the window. I was about to help this youth cross the threshold into the kingdom of God and all I could think about was how many verses were left in the hymn!

Collecting myself internally, I asked a few questions and we talked about the young lady's decision. We all joined hands and I had her repeat a prayer after me. We arose from the altar just as the hymn concluded. I returned to my place on the platform. The mother and daughter returned to their seats. The senior pastor gave the benediction and just like that it was all over.

But something was gnawing at me on the inside. I just helped a young lady become a Christian—but was a brief prayer at the altar all there was to it? She had confessed and accepted Jesus Christ as her Savior and Lord—yet there was no celebration, no joy. There was a perfunctory prayer—a process, a formula—so we could keep things moving along. After all, we would not want people to be late getting to the restaurants, would we?

For the first time I really began to question what it meant to be a follower of Christ. Did a thirty-second prayer and a pat on the back equal salvation? What about life transformation, discipleship and progressive sanctification? Yes, we could claim another profession of faith on our year-end reports. But conversion and rebirth was supposed to be so much more than what had happened. Never before had I been so driven to question so many things about my faith.

That incident launched me on a quest to understand more clearly what the Church was and was not, what being a Christian really meant, and how the faith had developed across the centuries. I began reading about the history and practices of the early Church.

I returned to the gospels and the book of Acts with renewed vigor and purpose. And I slowly began to see that much of what we do on Sundays, or even as Christians, bears little resemblance to what Jesus said and did.

As a result I learned to start asking "Why?" about everything in the church. It is a practice I continue to this day, especially when I am appointed to a new church. I have found this one question can reveal a lot about the church and its culture. To defend the bride of Christ from man-made traditions we need to be bold in asking questions. Why is this particular thing done? Why is it done this way or at this time? Why is it done in this manner? How did this practice or ritual begin? Who started it and why?

Often I encounter one of two responses. People either do not know the origin or history of a specific tradition—"Why, we've had a potluck dinner on the last Sunday of every month for as long as anyone can remember"—or they know everything in exacting detail. This latter response usually indicates those who view themselves as "keepers of the tradition."

Asking questions about our traditions is important for understanding what we need to keep in our beautiful box. Questions can also reveal what may be standing in the way of a good church becoming a great church. Sometimes our local church traditions and practices need to be preserved but they need to be fully explained as well. There are others that have outlived their expiration date or which have a negative impact on the church's mission.

In one community all the churches of one denomination gathered together quarterly for an evening worship or activity. A beloved former pastor of one of the churches started the tradition. And it was started in a time when people from the different churches did not get to see each other very often. Even though the churches were separated by only eight to ten miles, at one time in history that was a significant amount of travel. Thus, the congregations did not interact with one another except at those quarterly gatherings.

The tradition of those meetings continues today even though a journey of ten miles is nothing to us now. Not only that, but telephone and e-mail communication revolutionized our ability to stay in touch with each other. The purpose of those gatherings has faded with the changes in society yet the churches continue to hold them every quarter. Only a small handful of members from the churches still attend and that number declines every year.

If you were the pastor or a key lay person in one of those churches you might be tempted to suggest ending those quarterly gatherings. After all, do we really need another evening worship service that basically duplicates what we did earlier that morning? It would seem a likely candidate for retirement, right?

Not so fast.

You had better make sure you pick the right battles to fight over man-made traditions.

Pick your battles!

BRINGING CHANGE TO any church is no easy task. Finding ways to gracefully retire troublesome traditions can be even more of a bugbear. That is why leaders are reminded to pick your battles. You have to decide what is worth fighting for and what is not. While you may prefer that quarterly Sunday evening free from obligations, terminating the gatherings may be a battle you do not want to engage in for two reasons.

First, if the gatherings are not negatively affecting the mission and purpose of the church, it will be difficult to substantiate a reason for their retirement. Those traditions which hinder the church's work and witness in the world—requiring a certain style of dress, only using one specific version of the Scriptures, refusing to help the poor and needy—have to be confronted and challenged if the church is to move forward. The quarterly gatherings are not an obstacle to ministry, they do not drain resources and some members still receive some benefit from them.

Second, those who do continue to attend will become defensive and hostile if it is suggested the gatherings end. There is no need to engender antagonism over something that has such a minimal impact. There will be future battles that *must* be fought over critical issues of ministry and mission, and some of these same people will be staunchly opposed to change. It is not wise to stir people up over smaller things that are negotiable when bigger battles loom.

If your church is experiencing decline, stagnation or even death as a result of man-made traditions, those are the things that need to be targeted. If the congregation insists that the Christmas Eve service has to be at 10:00 PM and there is proof this is a detriment to families with young children, this is a man-made tradition that should be addressed. However, if the Ladies' League, which has dwindled down to five women, still meets in the church parlor every second Tuesday it is not a good idea to tamper with it. As the Beatles sang, "Let it be." There is no reason to rile up the Ladies' League—and their friends and relatives in the church—when there is so little at stake.

Bear in mind that for every man-made tradition you seek to remove, keep at least one or two others in place—at least for the time being. This makes it easier to point to those traditions still in place as proof that the pastor is not, in fact, "trying to ruin our church!"

Also, explain the tradition and why it is troublesome at this point in time. Show how it no longer fulfills its original intent or causes added stress and decline on the church. Explain what its alternative might look like or how that alternative can continue to "carry the torch" for the retiring tradition. It is a basic rule of human behavior that we do not willingly give up something that benefits us for something else that has no proven benefit.

If we can say, for example, that we have talked with a dozen young families who would like to attend the Christmas Eve service, but cannot due to the time, we have a solid argument to make. We can show the potential benefit of changing the service to an earlier time: new families with children. This makes it harder for critics to argue against. After all, there are not too many people who can generate a sustained argument against new members.

We may not be Pope Francis or have the kind of influence he has but we can still do much to defend the bride of Christ from man-made traditions. It will take perseverance, compromise and a willingness to take an unpopular stand. But no change comes without hard work. No incident of bullying is ever a simple matter. If we truly desire to see our churches become healthy and free from embedded traditional bullies we will take seriously the need to differentiate between what is negotiable and what is non-negotiable.

CHAPTER 10
IDOLATRY WITH A VIEW

The bride of Christ is bullied
by buildings and land

"Thou shalt not worship thy buildings more than thy God."

Bill Easum

DURING MY COLLEGE career I took several art history courses as part of my major. One course was the art and architecture of the medieval world. The photographs of the great cathedrals of Europe fascinated me. The longer I studied them the more I desired to see them in person.

Over two decades later I found that desire fulfilled. In the summer of 2010 I took my first mission trip to the Czech Republic. Following the week of mission work, my oldest son, Brett, and I stayed a few extra days in Prague. We wanted to do some sightseeing together. Naturally enough, cathedrals were the one place I was continually drawn to.

The most impressive one we visited was St. Vitus Cathedral, located on the grounds of Prague Castle. This massive structure, dating back to the eleventh century AD, was used not only for religious services but also for the coronation of kings and queens. It is also the final resting place for provincial patron saints, noblemen and archbishops. Stepping into the imposing grandeur of St. Vitus is truly taking a step back in time. One is immediately engulfed by the immensity and reverential atmosphere produced by soaring stained glass and the vaulted ceiling.

The architecture of medieval cathedrals was designed to draw the worshiper's attention toward heaven. Every element was focused on pulling one's gaze upward. I would venture to say that it is impossible to walk into a cathedral such as St. Vitus and *not* look up at the ceiling.

The cathedrals of Europe also feature massive amounts of stained glass, statuary and gilded altarpieces. Again, these were intentional design decisions. The purpose was to create a semblance of heaven on earth. My son and I commented on how ostentatious it all looked. But again, the idea was to surround medieval worshipers with a sense of what heaven might be like. The intent was to create a place of awe and reverence where one could almost be transported into the presence of the Holy by sheer force of the architectural design.

I finally had the opportunity to see the kind of cathedrals I had read about in college. But I was not prepared for the mixed reactions I experienced as I stood beneath those buttressed walls and soaring spires. There was the overwhelming sense of scope—of majesty, power and glory. One cannot stand in such places without feeling it.

However, my other reaction was to question just how much all of that grandeur had cost. Who had financed all the gold on the altarpiece? Where had the funds come from to contract those gigantic stained glass windows? Who had paid the laborers to build the facade and the artisans to craft the statues?

And could all that money have been used to help the poor instead?

The early Church gathered in homes for worship, prayer, meals and to celebrate the Lord's Supper. They saw no need for specialized buildings for their own use. They felt that Jesus' return was imminent so there was little need for worldly items. It was not until the late third and early fourth centuries AD that great basilicas began to spring up. Emperor Constantine financed many of these as a way to curry favor for his empire-wide religion, as well as to enhance and perpetuate his legacy.

Christians throughout history have understood themselves to be a pilgrim people, travelers through this world but not permanent residents of it. As the 1771 hymn states, "Guide me, O thou great Jehovah, pilgrim in this barren land." We are strangers in a strange land, awaiting the promised return of Christ, who will carry us to that "land that is fairer than fair." So how did we come to be bullied by buildings and land?

It will come to you, this love of land

IN MARGARET MITCHELL'S 1936 novel *Gone With the Wind*, spoiled, narcissistic Scarlett O'Hara complains to her father, Gerald, about their home, the plantation Tara. She says the plantation holds no attraction for her because she desires to marry local beau Ashley Wilkes. Gerald responds, "Do you stand there, Scarlett O'Hara, and tell me that Tara—that land—doesn't amount to anything?" When Scarlett nods her affirmation, Gerald continues. "Land is the only thing in the world that amounts to anything...for ''tis the only thing in this world that lasts, and don't you be forgetting it! ''Tis the only thing worth working for, worth fighting for—worth dying for."

He goes on to tell her, ""'Twill come to you, this love of land. There's no getting away from it, if you're Irish."[12] Only later in the story, during the ravages of the Civil War, does Scarlett come to understand and appreciate the wisdom of her father's words.

Faithful Jews to this day hold the same attitude about the land of Israel. A love of the land is in their bones. A ragtag collection of tribes, brought together by Yahweh as his favorite possession in all the earth, was promised a beautiful, precious land of their own (Genesis 15:18-21; Exodus 3:8). God faithfully delivered them into that land (Joshua 1-5). Land is one of the key themes running throughout the Hebrew Scriptures. However, ownership of the land has always been a contentious issue, even up to the present day.

An in-depth exploration of Middle Eastern land quarrels is beyond the scope of this work. However, we should bear in mind

---

12 Margaret Mitchell, *Gone With The Wind* (New York: Scribner, 2011), p. 55.

the importance that land had in the Old Testament. One of the purposes of the Year of Jubilee (Leviticus 25) was to ensure that land, which had been disposed of to pay off debts, would be returned to its original owners. This would prevent perpetual cycles of poverty as every fiftieth year the generations would resume ownership of their ancestral property. In Leviticus 25:23, God instructed the people, *"The land must not be sold permanently, because the land is mine and you reside in my land as foreigners and strangers"* (there's the "pilgrim" concept).

The land was a gift from God, graciously bestowed upon the people. But God warned them that if they rebelled against him and did not obey his commands, they and the land would suffer. The sinfulness of the people would result in their being displaced from their land and carried off in captivity:

> *The Lord will drive you and the king you set over you to a nation unknown to you or your ancestors. There you will worship other gods, gods of wood and stone. You will become a thing of horror, a byword and an object of ridicule among all the peoples where the Lord will drive you. You will sow much seed in the field but you will harvest little, because locusts will devour it. You will plant vineyards and cultivate them but you will not drink the wine or gather the grapes, because worms will eat them. You will have olive trees throughout your country but you will not use the oil, because the olives will drop off. You will have sons and daughters but you will not keep them, because they will go into captivity. Swarms of locusts will take over all your trees and the crops of your land.*

(Deuteronomy 28:36-42; cf. Leviticus 26).

True to his word, God sent the people of the northern kingdom of Israel into captivity in Assyria in 740 BC (1 Chronicles 5:26; 2 Kings 15:29). The southern kingdom of Judah lasted a little longer, finally falling to the Babylonians in 587 BC (2 Chronicles 36:20-23; 2

Kings 24:1; Jeremiah 25:9-12). While the people were eventually allowed to return to their land, they remained pawns and vassals of neighboring nations. By the first century AD and the birth of Jesus, the Roman Empire ruled the land.

Scripture attests to the fact that early Christians owned land and property (Acts 2:45; 4:34). The first properties owned by the early Church were catacombs, used not only for the interment of the dead but as places of meeting and refuge during times of persecution. Today's church-owned cemeteries are descendants of the first real estate ever owned by the Church.

The place of God's presence

"CHURCHES FIND END Is Nigh: The Number of Religious Facilities Unable to Pay Their Mortgage Is Surging," declared a January 25, 2011 article in *The Wall Street Journal*. According to author Shelly Banjo, "Since 2008, nearly 200 religious facilities have been foreclosed on by banks, up from eight during the previous two years and virtually none in the decade before that, according to real-estate services firm CoStar Group, Inc. Analysts and bankers say hundreds of additional churches face financial struggles so severe they could face foreclosure or bankruptcy in the near future."[13] When the housing market collapsed in 2008 many churches were also affected. Having borrowed to build newer or larger facilities, the combination of a crippled economy, job loss and declining membership all combined to push churches into foreclosure.

Age, attrition and changing generational demographics have also contributed to many congregations having to bid their buildings goodbye. But this is not necessarily a bad thing. In fact, it may help many churches remember it is not the buildings but *the people* who are the true Church where God's presence dwells.

---

[13] Banjo, Shelly. *Churches Find End Is Nigh*, http://online.wsj.com/article/ SB10001424052748704115404576096151214141820.html?mod=WSJ_hp_MIDDLE NexttoWhatsNewsSecond

The first building in the Old Testament designed specifically for God's presence was the Tabernacle in the wilderness. Yahweh's glory filled the Tabernacle (Exodus 40:34) as a sign that he was not aloof, like the deities of Egypt. Instead, Yahweh chose to put himself right in the center of his people.

Once the Israelites took possession of the Promised Land the Tabernacle was set up permanently at Shiloh (Joshua 18:1). This was the gathering place for all the people and the *de facto* religious capital until David conquered Jerusalem. No longer did the Tabernacle move around as it had done in the wilderness. Worship and community gatherings were centralized in one location.

Generations later King David planned to build a temple to house the Ark of the Covenant, another physical symbol of God's presence. Having unified the entire Promised Land under his rule, David established Jerusalem as his capital city. The temple would be the social, political and religious centerpiece of Israel. However, due to the blood on David's hands it was his son Solomon who oversaw the construction of the temple (1 Chronicles 22). Solomon's Temple, as it was known, was completed sometime in the mid-tenth century BC. It stood as the focal point of God's presence until 587 BC when King Nebuchadnezzar of Babylon razed it to the ground and carried the people into captivity.

Following the Babylonian exile the Israelites returned to their own land and set to work rebuilding the temple. The second temple was completed and dedicated around 517 BC.

During the reign of King Herod the Great, the temple was rebuilt from the ground up as a way for Herod to perpetuate his legacy. While technically still the second temple it came to be known as Herod's Temple. This was how Jesus knew it during his lifetime. Herod's Temple stood until 70 AD when Jerusalem was besieged by Roman troops who completely demolished the temple. In some Jewish and Christian circles it is thought that the completion of a third temple will be a sign inaugurating the end times.

In the New Testament we find no directives to construct a temple or building. Existing locations such as Solomon's Colonnade (Acts 5:12) served as meeting space for the early Church in Jerusalem, while houses provided the main gathering places. The earliest extant house church, dating back to approximately 235 AD, was discovered at Dura Europos on the Euphrates River in eastern Syria.

By the end of the second century Christians were using other existing buildings (such as meeting halls) to gather in. As the Church grew, and as more wealthy and elite members of Roman society joined, buildings appeared that were specifically designed for Christian worship. Constantine's decree establishing Christianity as the empire-wide religion necessitated the raising of even more houses of worship, a trend that continues to this day.

Yet it is a trend that is finally beginning to show signs of weakening. In the very near future I predict we will see fewer church buildings being constructed. Not only are new sanctuaries and family life centers increasingly cost-prohibitive to build; they also require an immense amount of revenue to maintain. Utilities, insurance, heating and cooling, general maintenance, inspections and so on combine to take a huge chunk out of a church's budget. I also predict we will see more instances of different congregations sharing a single building.

A few years ago I was in San Diego for a conference. In my downtime I went searching for used bookstores and as I was walking through one neighborhood I came across a United Methodist Church. Wondering what sort of activities would be listed on their outdoor sign, I walked over to take a look.

I expected to see the times of the worship service and Sunday school, Wednesday evening activities, maybe even a pithy little saying like "God answers knee mail" or "To prevent sinburn use Sonscreen." What I found was a number of different congregations using the same facilities.

On Sundays at 7:00 AM an Eritrean Orthodox Coptic congregation gathered for worship. At 10:30 AM the United Methodist congregation met. They could not go on too long because at 12:30 PM a Slavic evangelical congregation was next in line. Finally, at 4:30 in the afternoon a Native American congregation gathered there. Four very different congregations using the same building. I believe this will eventually become the norm and not the exception.

Rising costs, dwindling support

THE REASON CHURCHES will need to share physical space is because the cost to maintain land and buildings continues to increase, and individual congregations are struggling to find the revenue to stay afloat. The once-reliable revenue stream has all but dried up due to changing generational demographics.

At an earlier time in American history the church building was the centerpiece of every community. Christendom gave the church a place of unparalleled importance. As recent as the 1950s—the last great period of growth for American mainline denominations—culture and society recognized and respected the voice and place of the church in the community.

Today's older generations planned, financed and helped build the churches we still use. If something was needed for the building—a new roof or piano, a coat of paint for the hallway, new tables and chairs for the children's rooms—previous generations gave liberally of their finances (as well as their time and talents) to see the need was met. There was little questioning. If something was needed, people gave. After all, it was for "God's house."

However, current and emerging generations no longer have the same level of commitment to church buildings as their predecessors did. They do not give financially due to their own mounting debt, because they have not been taught the biblical principle of giving, or to be blunt, because it is of little importance to them. As a result, existing churches are not only in numeric decline; financially they are unable to maintain their facilities. Buildings are falling into greater disrepair because the older generations—who historically could be counted on to keep the church solvent—are dying. Or they are physically and financially unable to do what they once did.

Younger generations often do not understand the emphasis that is placed on church buildings, especially when real people are struggling with real needs. If they give, they want to know that their contributions are being used to aid people and provide authentic ministry opportunities. Generally speaking, they are not terribly interested in keeping things fixed around the church building. They would rather see their gifts and talents used to help improve people's lives instead of putting in new carpet or repaving the parking lot.

I once had a conversation with a devoted man of God in my church. He shared his struggle with how much of his weekly offering went to institutional maintenance as opposed to actual ministry to those in need. I told him that I, too, have wrestled with that dilemma.

The majority of the weekly revenue in the local church goes to pay salaries and bills. Take a look at the budget of any small or medium-sized church. At least sixty percent—if not more—of the budget is for staff, upkeep and insurance. Many churches never get around to doing what Jesus did because all the resources that could be used for ministry go to keeping the doors open. And those resources now come from fewer and fewer supporters.

Today's church must not only contend with declining membership and the perception of irrelevance. She must also come to terms with the fact that soon her once-beautiful buildings will be sitting empty, or removed to make way for the next thing to arise in that location.

How church buildings get in the way of being Jesus

WHILE BUILDINGS PROVIDE many benefits for the local church they can also get in the way of being Jesus to the world. Let us look at a few of the ways in which buildings and land can bully the church.

First, as we have already noted, resources that could be used to help the poor and reach the lost are tied up in the physical facilities. I have seen far too many professed Christians intentionally ignore the poor around them but who are quick to shell out thousands of dollars for the building. Think of how much more the local church could do if it did not have to pay for utilities or insurance.

Prior to the mid-fourth century AD, the money and resources (clothing, food, etc.) that was collected by the church each week went directly to aid the suffering. This is one of the key reasons for the rapid spread of Christianity in the first few hundred years of its existence: Christians were known for their compassion and generosity toward all, especially widows, orphans, prisoners and the sick. What they took in, they gave away. In too many churches today the money from the offering plate rarely ever makes it past the front doors.

In the wake of a fire or other disaster that destroys a church building I have to confess that sometimes I get a little frustrated when I hear the pastor or church members say things like "We're already planning to rebuild." Secretly, I wonder to myself: *Why rebuild? Why invest all the time and expense reconstructing a building that, in a matter of years, will likely be unsustainable?* Instead, why not see the tragedy as an opportunity to return to the New Testament example? Rather than be encumbered with debt, utilities, insurance and the like, why not return to meeting in homes? After all, homeowners already pay the mortgages, utilities, insurance and upkeep! Financial resources could be channeled into providing practical aid to the needy and lost. And on Sundays, the congregation could worship in a school auditorium, café, storefront or another church sanctuary (like the church I described in San Diego).

Second, church buildings perpetuate an erroneous ecclesiology. The Greek word for "church" is *ekklesia*, which means "an assembly." It also means "to call out or be called out." Thus, the Church in the New Testament was a gathering (assembly) of those who were called out from the world. We are set apart as an alternative community of love, grace and reconciliation that points to and reveals the kingdom of God. The Church is the people, not a building.

Addressing Jewish and Gentile Christians, the apostle Paul wrote...*you are no longer foreigners and strangers, but fellow citizens with God's people and also members of his household, built on the foundation of the apostles and prophets, with Christ Jesus himself as the chief cornerstone. In him the whole building is joined together and rises to become a holy temple in the Lord. And in him you too are being built together to become a dwelling in which God lives by his Spirit* (Ephesians 2:19-22).

God's spirit indwells the members of the Church just as his presence resided in the Tabernacle and the temple. Only now there is no need for a physical building. God abides in each believer.

Paul made this clear in 1st Corinthians 3:16-17: *Don't you know that you yourselves are God's temple and that God's Spirit dwells in your midst? If anyone destroys God's temple, God will destroy that person; for God's temple is sacred, and you together are that temple.* Note that "you together" are God's temple. Or as we say in the South, "Y'all are God's temple." All believers coming together make up the Church.

Peter reiterated this principle: *As you come to him, the living Stone—rejected by humans but chosen by God and precious to him—you also, like living stones, are being built into a spiritual house to be a holy priesthood, offering spiritual sacrifices acceptable to God through Jesus Christ* (1 Peter 2:4-5). The more emphasis we place upon buildings the farther we move from a biblical understanding of the church. We perpetuate bad theology.

Third, church buildings keep Christians on the inside and everyone else on the outside. A major downfall of church buildings is that they keep members focused inside the walls rather than on the world which Christ calls us to engage. Many Christians prefer the tame, predictable confines of their buildings to being in ministry among people.

A building becomes an idol when we are unwilling to use the facilities to minister to those in need for fear of messing up the carpet or getting dirty handprints on the walls. It is okay for members Mr. & Mrs. Stippledopper to use the fellowship hall for their daughter's birthday party, but heaven forbid if an immigrant family wanted to use it for the same thing.

It is interesting that when Jesus stormed the temple and threw out the moneychangers and sellers, Matthew remarked, *the blind and the lame came to him at the temple, and he healed them. But when the chief priests and the teachers of the law saw the wonderful things he did and the children shouting in the temple courts, "Hosanna to the Son of David," they were indignant.*

"Do you hear what these children are saying?" they asked him (Matthew 21:14-16a).

The religious leaders were appalled. The handicapped and—*gasp*—boisterous children had invaded their temple! Why, something might get broken. Pages might be torn out of the hymnals. There would be food and dirt all over the carpet. Oh, the horror!

Jesus intentionally removed all impediments to the temple courts so that everyone could have access to God's presence. Those who most desperately needed the temple and its ministry—the weak and ill, the children—could come unhindered before Yahweh. After all, was that not what the temple had been built for?

I know a church that built a beautiful family life center. Plans were drawn up; fund-raisers and pledge campaigns were conducted. Everything came together smoothly. As the building was going up it was agreed upon that the purpose of the new building would be to serve the community. It would be a tool for ministry and outreach, open to the public, a witness of God's gracious hospitality to all.

However, within that church was a small group of members who had held positions of leadership and influence for many years. And they were decidedly against the new building being used for "outsiders." It was fine for Sunday school classes or any other church activity to be held there. But outside groups were limited to those who (a) would enhance the church's image in the community, or (b) who would make a sizable donation to the church for the opportunity to use the facilities. There were many heated discussions during administrative meetings about who could and could not use the building.

Church buildings keep too many Christians inside and too many non-Christians or pre-Christians outside.

Fourth, buildings continue to propagate an "attractional" form of doing church. "Attractional" church inverts the *missio Dei*. It does just what its name implies: it attracts people to the building. Remember, God incarnated himself in the person of Jesus Christ. He lived among the people, as one of the people, in order to show the way to the kingdom. We are to do likewise. And that means stepping outside our buildings and engaging the culture around us.

Attractional churches expect the lost to come to them rather than the other way around. They want to stay securely on their own "turf." We are the ones who are supposed to sacrifice, to inconvenience ourselves for the sake of helping others know Christ. But truthfully, how many Christians do you know who actually *go* to where the needs are? How many truly live out the incarnational presence of Jesus by taking their light into the darkness?

Church buildings hinder us from stepping out in faith, trusting God and following the guidance of the Holy Spirit. We would prefer to stay in our pews or fellowship halls and let the curious come to us. Regretfully, the decline in church membership and our irrelevance in today's society is a direct result of this sort of attitude. We are not called to "stay and sit" like some sort of religious lapdog. We are called apart so that we may be sent out to be salt and light (Matthew 5:13-16).

Fifth, church buildings foster too many issues of control. Like the group of members I described above, congregational bullies use buildings to control and dominate the church. With a few of their friends on key committees, especially the trustees, they have an overwhelming say in what does and does not happen in the building. Land and buildings can be significant leverage for immature members who want to push their own agendas.

Buildings also provide a convenient outlet for members to redirect their giving when something does not go their way. If the pastor does something to get on the wrong side of these people, what normally happens? Giving to the general budget declines. Disgruntled, bitter or vengeful members redirect their regular offering away from the pastor's salary and into the building fund or the new van fund. In this way they can still say they are giving to the church but are not allowing any of their money to be used for anything they disagree with.

This type of attitude cripples churches. While the building fund or new van fun shows nice growth, the Body of Christ suffers tremendously. Inappropriate control is exercised by a few in order to dictate terms to the many.

Paul's problem with idolatry

IT IS A safe bet that Paul did not have to contend with issues of buildings and land at Corinth. After all, it is bad taste to criticize the home in which your church meets! And since there were no church buildings like we are familiar with, there probably were not very many big shots in the congregation redirecting their money into the building fund. What Paul *did* have a problem with, however, was idolatry. It is something the contemporary church seriously needs to come to grips with, especially as it relates to our buildings.

Chapter ten of 1st Corinthians is a continuation of Paul's argument from chapter eight. As we saw, that chapter ended with

Paul stating he would not eat meat if it might cause another believer to stumble. In 9:19-23, Paul explained that he used his Christian freedom to reach people, and he followed that up in 9:24-27 with an illustration of the Isthmian games as an example of discipline and self-control. It was a lack of self-control that led to the Corinthian issues surrounding meat sacrificed to idols. It was also evident in how some in the church were attending the temple feasts in the city.

Following a sacrifice, temples opened their doors for people to come in and eat together. For Paul this was a serious concern. Diners gathered in the name of, and in the temple of, a Roman deity. They thanked the deity for the sacrifice and the meal. From Paul's perspective, by attending such feasts the Corinthian Christians were participating in an idolatrous practice.

First Corinthians 10:1-13 contains several examples, taken from Israel's history, of how God responded to idolatry among his chosen people. Paul used this to lead into his main point: *Therefore, my dear friends, flee from idolatry. I speak to sensible people; judge for yourselves what I say. Is not the cup of thanksgiving for which we give thanks a participation in the blood of Christ? And is not the bread that we break a participation in the body of Christ? Because there is one loaf, we, who are many, are one body, for we all share the one loaf* (10:14-17).

Once again Paul acknowledged that food itself was nothing and that the idol itself was nothing. However, *the spiritual realities behind the idol* were incredibly significant. Since Rome's gods were pagan, the spiritual realities behind them were demonic...the *sacrifices of pagans are offered to demons, not to God, and I do not want you to be participants with demons* (10:20).

Satan was the puppet master pulling the strings of the Roman gods. Therefore, when Christians sat down to eat in a pagan temple, they were, at some level, recognizing and celebrating evil. They were unknowingly opening themselves up to demonic influence. Paul told them they could not eat at the table of demons and at the table of Christ. The two are incompatible.

Since the Corinthian believers had repented—changed allegiances—from the worship of pagan deities to the worship of Christ, their conduct had to reflect that. By participating in temple feasts they were not only causing weaker believers to stumble; they were also flirting with idolatry. Paul made the consequences of this clear: *Are we trying to arouse the Lord's jealousy? Are we stronger than he?* (10:22).

The new converts to the Christian faith needed to exercise self-control. They were using their newfound freedom in Christ to do whatever they wanted. They were not thinking about the impact of their witness on others in the church or the community. They only wanted to continue their own selfish habits. This sounds suspiciously like controllers and dream-killers in many churches today.

The issue of idolatry is gravely important, especially where we make idols out of our buildings or land. Just because the building has a steeple does not mean it cannot become an idol. We trifle with God's anger by replacing our first love with something else. Churches today would do well to study, reflect on and practice the admonitions of Paul for selflessness and self-discipline.

CHAPTER 11
DEFENDING THE BRIDE OF CHRIST
FROM BUILDINGS AND LAND

"The church's greatest period of vitality and growth until recent times was during the first two centuries A.D. In other words, the church grew fastest when it did not have the help or hindrance of church buildings."

Howard Snyder

OF ALL THE bullies we have faced so far, that of buildings and land is the biggest—in terms of scale—and the most deeply embedded in our religious culture. Despite the fact that we know our physical facilities can be a significant hindrance to the accomplishment of Christ's mission, it is not as if we can just do away with them tomorrow. And even supposing we could, it would take a few years to dispose of everything properly. In addition, a great many Christians simply cannot imagine being the church without a building. Even if we do see fewer church buildings being constructed in years to come, or if multiple congregations start sharing space, church buildings are going to stay around. So for better or for worse we are stuck with our buildings.

We have seen how our fixation on physical facilities and real estate can prevent us from living out the gospel in authentic, incarnational ways. However, our need to have stained glass, steeples and sanctuaries is a symptom of a much deeper issue. The root issue is not the physical structures we possess and use. The underlying concern is the attitude and orientation of our hearts. We must deal with the sin of idolatry if we are to defend the bride of Christ from this bully.

Idolatry: how to make God angry

IDOLATRY IS THE worship of someone or something as a god. It is excessive or blind devotion and adoration. We often think of idolatry as bowing down before a statue or carved image, as the story of the golden calf in Exodus 32 illustrates.

A biblical understanding of idolatry is when we place anyone or anything higher than God. If we place the accumulation of wealth higher than God then wealth is our idol. If we seek recognition at the expense of others then attention or fame is our idol. Idolatry is not merely paying homage to a figure in a shrine. It is when we elevate anything that is not God to the position of God in our lives.

God condemned idolatry in the Old Testament through the first and second commandments of the law: *"You shall have no other gods before me.*

"You shall not make for yourself an image in the form of anything in heaven above or on the earth beneath or in the waters below. You shall not bow down to them or worship them; for I, the Lord your God, am a jealous God, punishing the children for the sin of the parents to the third and fourth generation of those who hate me, but showing love to a thousand generations of those who love me and keep my commandments" (Exodus 20:3-6).

The purpose of those commands was so the people of Israel would be different from all the other nations that surrounded them. They were not to make idols of Yahweh. All the cultures around them worshiped and served idols—physical representations of a deity—but not Israel. Yahweh wanted his chosen people to stand out, not through the worship of idols, but by their faithfulness to the covenant and obedience to his statutes. Israel would be unique. And because of that uniqueness, Yahweh would use Israel to draw other peoples and cultures to himself.

Unfortunately, the history of Israel is littered with the sin of idolatry. The people continually strayed from Yahweh and followed other gods. Worshiping false gods and setting up idols incurred God's wrath. In response God sent prophets to warn the people about their idolatry:

> *"You have done more evil than all who lived before you. You have made for yourself other gods, idols made of metal; you have aroused my anger and turned your back on me"*
>
> (1 Kings 14:9).

> *"This is what the Lord Almighty, the God of Israel, says: You saw the great disaster I brought on Jerusalem and on all the towns of Judah. Today they lie deserted and in ruins because of the evil they have done. They aroused my anger by burning incense to and worshiping other gods that neither they nor you nor your ancestors ever knew. Again and again I sent my servants the prophets, who said, 'Do not do this detestable thing that I hate!' But they did not listen or pay attention; they did not turn from their wickedness or stop burning incense to other gods."*
>
> (Jeremiah 44:2-5)

> *"Therefore say to the people of Israel, 'This is what the Sovereign Lord says: Repent! Turn from your idols and renounce all your detestable practices!*

> *"'When any of the Israelites or any foreigner residing in Israel separate themselves from me and set up idols in their hearts and put a wicked stumbling block before their faces and then go to a prophet to inquire of me, I the Lord will answer them myself. I will set my face against them and make them an example and a byword. I will remove them from my people. Then you will know that I am the Lord.'"*
>
> (Ezekiel 14:6-8)

> *"On the very day they sacrificed their children to their idols, they entered my sanctuary and desecrated it. That is what they did in my house."*

(Ezekiel 23:39)

"Put the trumpet to your lips! An eagle is over the house of the Lord because the people have broken my covenant and rebelled against my law. Israel cries out to me, 'Our God, we acknowledge you!' But Israel has rejected what is good... They set up kings without my consent; they choose princes without my approval. With their silver and gold they make idols for themselves to their own destruction."

(Hosea 8:1-4)

"Those who cling to worthless idols turn away from God's love for them."

(Jonah 2:8)

Idolatry is a sure-fire way of enraging a God who is jealous for his people and his covenant. Some people accuse God of being petty and insecure--of needing the affirmation of human beings--and claim that is why he condemns idolatry. They see God as incapable of dealing with any competitors for his affections. However, this is not the case.

God does not need the worship of human beings any more than he needs anything from us. He is fully and eternally complete in himself. God is not some clingy, jilted lover that must have our interactions. Rather, he knows that if we choose an idol in place of him we are setting ourselves on a path of ruin and alienation. It means we are settling for something far less than God's best for us. This is why God so strongly condemns idolatry. We exchange the opportunity to be in a relationship with the Creator for an allegiance to something that is created. By allowing our sinful nature to be in charge we forge our own path rather than trusting in God. We prefer the false promises of idolatry to the true promises of the Father.

We are spiritual beings; therefore, we were made to worship. It is part of our spiritual DNA. So it is not a matter of *if* we will worship because we most certainly will. The question becomes "*Who or what* will we worship?"

God desires that we worship him and live in a restored relationship with him—not because he is needy or greedy—but because he knows that we become like what we worship. Whatever captures our devotion eventually shapes us into its own image. God wants only the best for us. That best is found in a proper relationship with him, not throwing our hearts away after things that cannot satisfy us, no matter how much we are assured otherwise.

Israel repeatedly settled for less than God's best. When we in the Church emphasize our buildings more than our mission, or when we spend one thousand times more on land acquisition than we spend on those in need, we grieve the heart of God. And when we give our property greater reverence than we do the Lord it makes God angry.

When God is grieved and angry he has a way of making his displeasure known. He calls upon one of his servants to get people's attention in order to turn them back to his heart. God sends a prophet. The prophet is a much-needed (but much neglected) leader when it comes to confronting idolatry.

The Bible's weirdos?

WHEN WE HEAR the word "prophet," two images normally spring to mind. First, we envision someone who foresees the future—a clairvoyant or fortune teller. We may think of Nostradamus or a character like Merlin, or the man standing on the street corner holding a sign that reads REPENT! THE END OF THE WORLD IS NEAR! Or second, we think of a scraggly, brash outcast with a never-ending message of doom-and-gloom. We picture them in tattered clothes, with wiry, unkempt beards and wild eyes, the engineer of their own personal crazy train.

These images are reinforced by some of the peculiar actions God instructed his prophets to perform in the Old Testament.

Those prophetic demonstrations—what we might call "action sermons"—were designed to make a powerful visual impression upon the people and capture attention. They symbolized what God was saying.

For example, the prophet Isaiah was instructed to walk around naked and barefoot for three years (Isaiah 20:2). That *surely* made a strong visual impression! Jeremiah was told to make a yoke and wear it every day (Jeremiah 27). God called the prophet Hosea to marry a prostitute—to symbolize Israel's unfaithfulness to Yahweh—and to name two of his children "Not Loved" and "Not My People." I bet they were just a bundle of laughs at family reunions.

No Old Testament prophet had as many symbolic—and weird—actions to perform as Ezekiel. He was instructed to lay siege to a drawing of the city of Jerusalem (Ezekiel 4:1-3), to lie on his left side for three hundred ninety days (4:4-5), and to lie on his right side for forty days (4:6). While he was lying down Ezekiel baked his daily bread over a fire kindled with cow manure (4:15). In addition to this God instructed Ezekiel to shave his head and beard, and to divide the hair into thirds. One-third was burnt, one-third was struck with a sword, and one-third was thrown into the wind (Ezekiel 5:1-4).

In the New Testament the prominent prophets were John the Baptist and Jesus. When John arrived on the scene he was the first prophet that had been seen in Israel for several hundred years. John came out of the desert dressed in animal hair, subsisting on a high-protein diet of bugs and honey. He baptized people in the Jordan River for the repentance of their sins and declared the arrival of the Messiah. For a people who had not experienced a true prophet of Yahweh for many generations, John surely must have seemed like Amos or Isaiah or Elijah back from the dead.

Jesus fulfilled a prophetic role by declaring the arrival of the kingdom of God (Mark 1:15; Luke 4:18-19), manifested in him. He spoke and did what the Father instructed (John 5:19). Jesus urged the covenant people to change their allegiance and live in a new way, and he pointed out the hypocrisy and idolatry of the religious leaders.

A true prophet is not a fortune teller or psychic reader. Nor are they madmen-on-the-loose, ranting and raving about alternate realities. A prophet is someone who speaks on behalf of God. They have the spiritual gift of prophecy and are keenly attuned to the voice of God through Scripture, prayer and the Holy Spirit. The prophet delivers a message from the Lord in order to turn people back to God, to warn them away from sin and God's judgment, and to declare the will of God.

Authentic prophets have a difficult time because (a) their role has been complicated by frauds who do not truly speak on behalf of God, and (b) because the contemporary Church knows little about the prophetic gift, and even less about how the role of the prophet functions in the Body of Christ.

The fivefold offices

EPHESIANS 4:11-15 tells us,

So Christ himself gave the apostles, the prophets, the evangelists, the pastors and teachers, to equip his people for works of service, so that the body of Christ may be built up until we all reach unity in the faith and in the knowledge of the Son of God and become mature, attaining to the whole measure of the fullness of Christ.

Then we will no longer be infants, tossed back and forth by the waves, and blown here and there by every wind of teaching and by the cunning and craftiness of people in their deceitful scheming. Instead, speaking the truth in love, we will grow to become in every respect the mature body of him who is the head, that is, Christ. From him the whole body, joined and held together by every supporting ligament, grows and builds itself up in love, as each part does its work.

In order for the Church to be built up and to mature, Jesus gave *the apostles, the prophets, the evangelists, the pastors and teachers* for the explicit purpose of equipping the Church for service. Sometimes referred to as the "fivefold offices" or "fivefold ministries," these are functions of leaders in the Church.

The word *apostle* means "sent one" in the original Greek. An apostle is one who is sent on behalf of someone else. In ancient times a king would send an apostle to a neighboring kingdom as an emissary, authorized to speak and act at the behest of the king. In the political sphere a diplomatic envoy or an ambassador does something similar. They are sent as the living presence of a nation with full authority to carry out the tasks for which they were sent.

Apostles are like church planters. They move around frequently, led by the Holy Spirit to places where the gospel is needed. They establish new churches in areas where the gospel is just beginning to be heard, or where it has been neglected for many years.

Paul is the example we most think of, an innovator always seeking out the next place where God is at work. Author and missional church expert Alan Hirsch says, "At core, the apostolic task is about the expansion of Christianity both *physically* in the form of pioneering missionary effort and church planting, as well as *theologically* through integration of apostolic doctrine into the life of the individual Christians and the communities they are part of."[14]

Prophets follow apostles in bringing God's word and will to churches. They have the responsibility of helping people understand where they are and where God would have them be. Sometimes, in the event of a dysfunctional congregation, the prophet has to bring a hard word of challenge and correction.

---

[14] Alan Hirsch, *The Forgotten Ways: Reactivating the Missional Church* (Grand Rapids: Brazos Press, 2006), p. 154. Used by permission. All rights reserved.

"Prophets attack injustice, unethical behavior, oppressive regimes, and stereotypical barriers to what the Lord wants to do."[15]

The letter of Revelation was written to seven churches in Asia Minor at a time when persecution by the Roman Empire was brutal. The letter encouraged the Christians to persevere since the final outcome would be Christ's triumph and Rome's judgment.

However, in chapters two and three each church received a message with a prophetic component. For example, Jesus commended the church in Ephesus for their hard work and good deeds. But he followed this by saying,

> *"Yet I hold this against you: You have forsaken the love you had at first. Consider how far you have fallen! Repent and do the things you did at first. If you do not repent, I will come to you and remove your lampstand from its place."*
>
> (Revelation 2:4-5).

And to the church in Sardis, Jesus said,

> *"These are the words of him who holds the seven spirits of God and the seven stars. I know your deeds; you have a reputation of being alive, but you are dead. Wake up! Strengthen what remains and is about to die, for I have found your deeds unfinished in the sight of my God. Remember, therefore, what you have received and heard; hold it fast, and repent. But if you do not wake up, I will come like a thief, and you will not know at what time I will come to you."*
>
> (Revelation 3:1-3)

In both instances a warning was given if the churches did not repent and get back in line with God. There would be consequences

---

[15] Graham Cooke, *A Divine Confrontation: Birth Pangs of the New Church* (Shippensburg: Destiny Image Publishers, 1999), p. 31. Used by permission. All rights reserved.

if they failed to be obedient. It is the role of the prophet, by the direction of God, to make such statements. Prophets alert people and churches where they have gone wrong and help them make amends.

When we think of an **evangelist** most of us imagine someone like Billy Graham. The evangelist is gifted in making the gospel clear and understandable to the unchurched and lost. God uses evangelists—from the Greek *euangélion* (e-van-gel-e-on), meaning "messenger"—to carry the good news of Jesus Christ to those who need to hear and respond.

Pastors (sometimes referred to as "shepherds") are tasked with the spiritual nurture of the Church. These leaders are gifted in helping believers align their lives with the call of Christ through discipleship, prayer, study and worship. They oversee the care of the church community. **Teachers**, obviously, are those gifted to instruct the Church in the Scriptures, doctrines and ways of the Christian faith.

There can be overlap with these offices. For example, an apostle or prophet may also have the ability to teach. An evangelist may also make an excellent apostle. Pastor-teacher combinations are quite common.

A problem the contemporary Church faces—one it has inherited across the centuries—is a lack of differentiation between the offices. Think about the terminology used in the Protestant tradition for the ordained leader of the church: it is most always "pastor." While this is accurate much of the time, it perpetuates a false understanding of how God has gifted the Church to function.

We expect the pastor of our local church to fulfill all five offices. They should be going out into the unreached parts of our communities (apostle). They should be able to speak to the church (prophet), while at the same time delivering messages that result in new professions of faith (evangelist). We expect them to provide constant care and nurture to every person in the congregation (pastor), and be able to instruct with skill and knowledge (teacher).

Honestly, how many church leaders do you know who are capable of doing all those things?

None—exactly! Why is that?

It is simple: because God did not design the Church to be led by one person doing everything. The work of leading the Church is a cooperative of different gifts and abilities. Pay special attention to the fact that Paul said the role or purpose of these offices is *to equip his people for works of service* (emphasis mine).

In other words, *the people of the church* do the work of the church. General pastoral care, giving, serving, outreach, missions and communal life are the responsibility of the church members. It is not your pastor's job to do *your job* in the church. Church leaders are present to teach, lead, model and empower congregations to carry out the *missio Dei*. If you are expecting your pastor to do it all you are wrong. God will not hold your pastor accountable for how she or he did *your job*. He will hold you accountable for that. So quit trying to foist it off on the ordained leadership of your church. Get off your butt, allow yourself to be spiritually equipped, and get busy with what God has called you to do.

Churches tend to focus exclusively on the offices of pastor and teacher because (a) we want someone to take care of us when we get a boo-boo, and (b) we want someone to give us more knowledge. We do not truly seek *transformation* as much as *information*. Many self-professed Christians want to know *about* God but do not want to *know* God personally. Churches also like to have strong evangelistic messages, so that particular office is often included in the focus.

But when was the last time your church emphasized the office of apostle or prophet? I am guessing it has been a very long time, if ever.

To entertain the apostle means we are open about—and willing to step into—new, unreached areas. We are willing to plant new churches or ministries. We are willing to make whatever sacrifices are necessary in order to reach those deemed "unreachable."

We also do not entertain the prophet because, quite frankly, few church members want to hear what the prophet has to say. Most churches do not want to be challenged; even fewer are willing to change in response to God's Word. The prophet is viewed as a troublemaker, a rabble-rouser, someone who stirs things up that the church prefers to keep swept under the rug. *Best to keep away from prophets*, the thinking goes. *They are too fanatical*, we rationalize. *And besides, we're not THAT bad. We're doing just fine.* I imagine these are some of the things Israel and Judah also thought when Yahweh sent prophets to them.

Confronting idolatry in the church

TOO MANY CHURCHES have strayed from their biblical purpose. Instead of reaching the lost and making disciples they have become social clubs that cater to those ensconced within their walls. Despite having godly pastors, staff and leaders, many of these churches rarely look behind the Sunday morning façade. The risk of repercussion—to the budget, attendance or career—is too great. Thus, churches limp along making little forward progress because no one is willing to say what needs to be said. In order to confront idolatry in the church, we simply must have prophets.

It is the prophet's job to discern what God is saying to a particular church and then proclaim that message. Very often the message resembles what we saw in Revelation two and three: praise and encouragement for what is being done correctly, and the identification of what needs to be changed to come more in line with God's will.

We must not be afraid to speak the hard truths of God's Word no matter how painful it may be for us or for our congregations. Prophetic leaders have to say things that no one else wants to address. This is a demanding responsibility, one that causes many sleepless nights. There are times when prophets want to run away from that responsibility (remember Jonah 1:3?) because it would make their ministries, health and family life so much easier.

Unfortunately, prophets know they cannot do that. The Old Testament prophet Jeremiah understood this:

> *"Whenever I speak, I cry out proclaiming violence and destruction. So the word of the Lord has brought me insult and reproach all day long. But if I say, 'I will not mention his word or speak anymore in his name,' his word is in my heart like a fire, a fire shut up in my bones. I am weary of holding it in; indeed, I cannot."*

> (Jeremiah 20:8-9)

If prophets do not speak what God wants his Church to hear there are few others who will.

The following is part of a prophetic declaration a colleague with the gift of prophecy made to a key administrative committee in his church. I thank him for allowing me to use it here.

> "I believe that in being sent here God has assigned me the role of prophet. He has placed me here to present some very challenging, very uncomfortable things—just as he has used prophets throughout history.

> "After careful reflection, prayer and godly counsel—speaking prophetically—I do not believe God is pleased with this church. It has religion but no Spirit. It has function but no divine power. There is great sin present, most notably in the form of idolatry. Individuals are more interested in pleasing other people than in pleasing God. More attention is placed upon certain members, or the choir, or the building, or the budget, than upon letting the Holy Spirit move and do his work. There is no sense of hope or expectation that God will be encountered here. Faith seems to be a convenient word, not something exhibited by our actions and trust. I believe part of my responsibilities while I am here is to expose this so that God can begin a

loving, redemptive work in this place.

"You see, God's desire is for every one of us to return to our first love, to Jesus. He wants to draw us back to his own heart. To do this he must expose the sin, darkness and error among us. Each of us must carefully, honestly and painfully evaluate where our priorities truly are. God yearns to transform us; he is passionate about moving us to new life! I believe with all my heart that God wants to do amazing things in and through this church. But he cannot and will not while we are dominated by pride and rebellious disobedience.

"God is sending a very difficult message to this congregation. I have said this repeatedly in sermons in a variety of different ways. Much of what has been happening in past months is because God is sifting the hearts of his people. He is testing us to see who is truly committed to him and who is just here for show, or appearance or social obligation. God is desperately trying to draw this people back to himself. But if we refuse him and continue to live in rebellion then his Spirit will not dwell here. We will have a nice building with nice people and a few activities. But we will not be a church."

Some of you may be sitting there with eyes wide in amazement, aghast that a pastor would say such things. And you would be right in that most *pastors* would not. But keep in mind the role of the pastor is to guide and nurture the body of Christ. The role of the prophet is vastly different. It is to do what my friend did.

If we have been called by God to proclaim his word to the Church then we must do so, even if that word is one of rebuke, challenge or judgment. We cannot avoid those parts of God's message just because they may make us unpopular. We are not called to be popular. We are called to deliver the full counsel of

God's word and will. This does not only apply to ordained leaders. Sunday school teachers need to be sensitive to the Holy Spirit. There are prophetic words that must be brought out and addressed by teachers, committee chairs and other leaders as well.

If we are serious about defending our churches from idolatry we need to bear the following points in mind:

1. Once again, remember this is a spiritual battle. Idolatry is a tool of Satan, a way he deceives and alienates us from our relationship with Jesus. If the Holy Spirit leads you to share a prophetic word in your church, cover yourself with prayer before, during and after. Have faithful prayer warriors constantly lift you up. Satan does not want idolatry to be exposed in the church and he will *most definitely* lash out at you for doing so.

In the above example, my colleague told me that as soon as he finished his statement two members of the committee shot to their feet. One man accused my friend of calling him an "idolater," which he never did. The other man said he had never had a pastor say anything like that to him before (because as we said, a "pastor" would not). The man said he did not know if he would ever return to that church. He was faithful to his word, only showing up once or twice in the remaining years my friend served there.

Other members of the committee confessed that the words had been difficult to hear, but nothing had been spoken that was not the truth. Many people in that church knew the truth but had never had the courage, permission or support to speak it. Satan was not pleased by those prophetic words, as evidenced by some in the congregation who refused to hear. Thankfully, the majority did listen and started on the road to renewing their church. Expect a tremendous number of spiritual battles when confronting idolatry.

2. You must deal with your own idols first. Just as we noted about spiritual warfare, we must be sure we are not guilty of idolatry before bringing a prophetic declaration. If we have allowed anything else to take God's rightful place in our lives we have no authority from which to speak. A godly mentor or trusted Christian friend can help in this process. My colleague who spoke prophetically to the administrative committee had shared his words and his heart with three close, Godly brothers and sisters prior to making his statement. He sought their counsel, wisdom and prayers. Such friends and mentors can tell if we are not giving God the first, best and only place of importance in our hearts. As Jesus instructed us, we must deal with the speck in our own eye before trying to address the plank in the eye of the church (Matthew 7:5).

3. You must be secure in your identity in Christ. By this I mean you must be confident in who you are as a child of God, who you are as a follower of Christ, and who you are in your calling to serve God. The prophet has an incredibly difficult job.

As we know, few people are excited about the message the prophet bears. It is extremely easy for church members to turn their anger and venom onto the prophet. We only need to study the prophets of the Old Testament to see the hardships, suffering and frustrations they experienced. It is no different for prophets today. The old adage "Don't shoot the messenger" does not apply to prophets. These agents of God are routinely abused, battered and left for dead.

Anyone who brings a prophetic word before a committee or board, Sunday school class, or full congregation must be secure in who they are in Christ. They must know who has called them and why. They must be willing to say the things no one else will.

This is not an issue of ego or willpower. It is having a solid, biblical understanding of our regenerated identity as a co-heir with Christ (Romans 8:17). Many people will distance themselves from the prophet; some will drop all relationships because they cannot stand the message or the heat. Therefore, prophets need to be strong in their identity and willing to walk a path few others can or will.

In confronting the hypocritical behavior of the Pharisees, Jesus told them, *"Woe to you, because you build tombs for the prophets, and it was your ancestors who killed them. So you testify that you approve of what your ancestors did; they killed the prophets, and you build their tombs. Because of this, God in his wisdom said, 'I will send them prophets and apostles, some of whom they will kill and others they will persecute.' Therefore this generation will be held responsible for the blood of all the prophets that has been shed since the beginning of the world, from the blood of Abel to the blood of Zechariah, who was killed between the altar and the sanctuary. Yes, I tell you, this generation will be held responsible for it all"* (Luke 11:47-51).

Jesus was secure in who he was and in his relationship to the Father. He knew his identity and his mission. Thus, he was able to prophetically call out the self-righteous posturing of the religious elite.

4. Speaking prophetically is done for restoration. *This is critical!* Prophets may speak out of righteous anger, but they do not speak angrily. They do not rant and rave. They are not vindictive or manipulative. Their words are not punitive. The prophet declares the word of the Lord in order to restore people to a right relationship with God. It is done in love, with the goal of identifying sins and helping people confess and repent of them.

Prophets have compassionate hearts and spirits, with great affection for the Church. This compassion often looks a bit different from that of the pastor/shepherd. Prophets are not usually as nurturing compared to leaders with stronger pastoral gifts. Nevertheless, prophets are deeply committed to their relationship with Christ, to their call to preach and proclaim his word, and to the congregations they minister among. But if a prophetic word is not for the purposes of restoration it is valid to question the motives of the prophet.

5. Consider bringing in an outside prophet. Occasionally a church may choose to bring in a representative from a reliable prophetic ministry to assess the church and issue a prophetic word. We all know that our congregations get accustomed to hearing the pastor or other church leaders speak. By bringing in a guest speaker people are more apt to pay attention, and thus more likely to hear the prophetic word.

Our churches often bring in evangelists to lead a revival, teach or do a series of special services. Why do we rarely, if ever, bring in a prophet to speak? Is it because we are afraid of the repercussions within the church? Or are we just too afraid of the truth God has for us?

Since the prophetic gift has been neglected and ignored in the bulk of churches across our nation, it is not surprising that sinful attitudes and behaviors run rampant. The longer we avoid the corrective truths that come from prophets, the more ingrown we become. We become more alienated from the mission of the gospel.

Paul declared that prophets—just like all the leadership offices—come directly from Christ himself. When we avoid them we are avoiding the One who sent them. If we truly want to turn from an idolatrous emphasis on buildings and land we cannot continue to shun the prophet. We must make room for him or her alongside the pastor and teacher, the evangelist and apostle.

The only way our churches can escape their entrapment to idolatry is to humble ourselves and listen to what God says to us through his prophets, his word and the Holy Spirit. If we are unwilling to do that we have no business calling ourselves followers of Jesus.

CHAPTER 12
THE GOD THAT SPEAKS THE LOUDEST

The bride of Christ is bullied by money

"In Revelation we read of a book which no man could open. Some believe that was the pocketbook."

Anonymous

WE LIVE IN one of the most prosperous nations in the history of the world. According to the U.S. Department of Commerce Bureau of Economic Analysis, the market value of the nation's output of goods and services in the second quarter of 2013 was $16,633 billion.[16] This represented nearly twenty-five percent of the entire world economy. Only the European Union accounted for a larger percentage.

Did you know you can see exactly how rich you are in relation to the rest of the world? The web site globalrichlist.com allows you to enter your annual net income and it returns a list of data that shows where you are situated compared to other global citizens. For example, by entering an annual salary of $40,000 you can discover you are considered to be in the top 0.51% richest people in the world. That would make you the 33,982,065[th] richest person on the planet. The average Indonesian laborer would need fifty-three years to acquire that salary. You could work for two minutes and earn enough to buy a can of soda. A worker in Zimbabwe would need an hour's labor to purchase the same soda.[17]

While some may raise issues of accuracy with the site, it is designed as a fund-raising mechanism for the charity Care

---

16 National Income and Product Accounts: Gross Domestic Product, second quarter 2013, http://www.bea.gov/newsreleases/national/gdp /gdpnewsrelease.htm.

17 http://www.globalrichlist.com.

International UK. The point is not infallible precision with regard to financial income. It is a tool that allows users to recognize how much money we have at our disposal in the West. It is an interesting and eye-opening exercise. We may not be a Bill Gates or Warren Buffett, but compared to the majority of the world's population you and I are extremely wealthy.

Yet the majority of statistics indicate that the average American Christian gives approximately 2.5% of his or her annual income to the church. Only about five percent of all adults polled by organizations such as the Barna Group report tithing ten percent or more of their income.[18]

Even though economists say that over half of Americans carry credit card debt—and of that number one in ten carry debt of more than $15,000—we are still an extremely affluent society. We have access to just about anything and everything we want.

So why do our churches continually have money problems? A cursory glance around our parking lots on Sunday morning reveals a number of large and luxurious vehicles. We take nice vacations. We entertain ourselves by going to the theater, engaging in hobbies and shopping. It seems we can always find the money for another meal out, a cell phone upgrade, new wardrobe accessories or goodies for our pets. Is the church's problem *really* a lack of finances?

No, it is not. The issue many churches live with is *spiritual*, not economic. Our checkbooks and wallets have not been converted along with the rest of us. It is said that when some of the barbarian tribes of Europe were Christianized, the men would go into the river to be baptized with one arm held up straight. They would be immersed but would keep their sword arm up out of the water. They were not willing to let it be baptized for Christ. The warriors

---

[18] "American Donor Trends," Barna Group, https://www.barna.org/barna-update/culture/606-american-donor-trends#.UhF1mRbF_dk.

wanted their sword arms to remain under their control so they could continue to fight and kill.

We may do something similar when we are baptized. While we do not hold a sword arm out of the baptismal waters, we figuratively hold our checkbooks or personal possessions over our heads. We are willing to be baptized, up to a point. We are reluctant to surrender everything, especially when it comes to our wealth and possessions.

Money and things have a devastating power over us. We have already seen how overemphasis on buildings and land can derail the church's biblical mission. The same is true for money. How many times have you heard someone in the church make a statement such as "Nobody is going to tell me what to do with *my* money"? Or the old chestnut, "I'm not giving my money until (insert pastor or staff person's name) is gone."

People use their giving to bully the church. They not only withhold—they manipulate, coerce and browbeat others with their money. I have seen churches that could only do what the wealthy members of the congregation approved. Anything that did not sit well with them, that provided them no direct benefit or that might upset the status quo was quickly shot down. Normally all it takes is a few well-placed statements along the church's grapevine—"If the church votes to move forward with this idea, then they've gotten the last dollar out of me they're going to get"—to start the wheels spinning to pacify the givers.

The Greek playwright Aristophanes wrote a comedy entitled *Plutus* that was produced in 388 BC. Plutus was the Greek god of wealth. In the play, a poor man named Chremylus questions the random distribution of wealth in the world, only to find he has the blinded Plutus as a houseguest. Chremylus aids Plutus in regaining his vision and the god begins to dispense wealth helter-skelter to the noble and virtuous. This, of course, upsets the social and economic balance of things so badly that the gods of Olympus have to consider hiring themselves out as servants!

In line 230 of the play Chremylus invites Plutus into his home:

"Now, Wealth, you deity who wields the greatest power of all, you will please come inside with me because this is the house that by fair means or foul you're going to fill with riches this very morning."[19]

Aristophanes pinpointed an important truth: for many people, Wealth exerts "the greatest power of all." Money and the pursuit of wealth is the deity that possesses a staggering influence over us. In a comedy written nearly four hundred years before the birth of Jesus, Plutus personified the adage "money talks."

Several English words derive from Plutus and they all have to do with money. *Plutocracy* is governance by the wealthy. A *plutocrat* is one who rules by virtue of his immense wealth. *Plutolatry* is the worship of wealth. It is not difficult to recognize that some churches actually resemble a plutocracy more than the biblical Body of Christ. A group of prosperous people uses their riches to run the church. Nor do we need to look far to see evidence of plutolatry among some congregations. An overemphasis on budgets, affluence, greed and consumption are the preferred gods—not by confession or liturgy, but by actions.

Wealth has a seductive, formidable voice. It has not been stilled across the eons of human experience. And within the Church it may be the one god that speaks the loudest. If idolatry over buildings and land is the biggest bully in the church, then money is perhaps the most common.

Tithing x 3

IN TODAY'S SOCIETY we isolate and compartmentalize every aspect of our lives. We pigeonhole everything and do not often let those parts cross one another. For example, we have the "Sunday part" wherein we go to church and carry out all the expectations of

---

[19] Paul Roche, trans., *Aristophanes: The Complete Plays* (New York: New American Library/Penguin, 2005), p. 673.

cultural Christianity. Yet once Sunday comes to an end we put that part back on the shelf until the following week. We have different facets of our lives tucked away for friends and family, for work and play, for faith and science and intellect. Our worldview is shaped by American individualism and independence more than it is shaped by the life and teaching of Jesus.

A worldview of individualism was alien to the ancient Hebrew people. To them all of life was interconnected. Everything had an impact on everything else. Their faith was directly linked to their daily work, and their work was linked to their family of origin. Whereas we take one element of our worldview off the shelf, use it and put it back until it is needed again, a biblical worldview knows that nothing is compartmentalized because it all belongs to God.

In 2001, Bill & Pam Farrel authored a book titled *Men Are Like Waffles, Woman Are Like Spaghetti,* which explored some of the key differences between men and women. The Farrels described men as waffles because men tend to compartmentalize things in their lives. They keep everything in specific boxes and they work within one box at a time until the task is completed. Then they move on to another box/task. Woman, by contrast, have everything in their lives interconnected. There is little separation or pigeonholing because, like a plate of pasta, one thing connects to and touches many others. Our Western worldview today is like the waffle: individual little boxes in which we focus on one thing and one thing only.

The ancient Hebrew worldview was like spaghetti. Everything connected and related to Yahweh in some form or fashion. This worldview was expressed in Psalm 24:1—*The earth is the Lord's, and everything in it, the world, and all who live in it*—as well as Psalm 50:12—*If I were hungry I would not tell you, for the world is mine, and all that is in it.* There was nothing that did not originate from and return to Yahweh. Whether it was crops or crowns, water or weapons, animals or aunts, everything had a connection to the Lord.

This was not pantheism (the belief that everything is connected to God because everything IS God). The ancient Hebrews understood that God was sovereign and supreme, and all created things belonged to him. They did not subscribe to the idea that every single thing was divine. Only Yahweh was divine. All other things existed according to his will and were not his equal. Money and possessions—and the tithe—were not excluded from this worldview.

The word *tithe* means "one tenth." God instructed his people to give ten percent of their goods in recognition of the Lord's faithfulness and provision. In the Old Testament the overwhelming majority of people tithed the agricultural products they raised throughout the year. They also tithed every tenth animal from their flocks and herds (Leviticus 27:32).

There were actually three tithes required in the Old Testament. First was the agricultural tithe that went to support the priests and Levites:

> *"I give to the Levites all the tithes in Israel as their inheritance in return for the work they do while serving at the tent of meeting."*

(Numbers 18:21)

> *"Instead, I give to the Levites as their inheritance the tithes that the Israelites present as an offering to the Lord. That is why I said concerning them: 'They will have no inheritance among the Israelites.'"*

(Numbers 18:24)

Whereas the other tribes of Israel received a portion of the land, the Levites had no ancestral property to cultivate. Their role was to minister before the Lord; therefore, they were supported by the people's tithes.

But the Levites were also expected to tithe. Their tithe came from what had been given by the people. It was a tithe from the tithe:

The Lord said to Moses, "Speak to the Levites and say to them: 'When you receive from the Israelites the tithe I give you as your inheritance, you must present a tenth of that tithe as the Lord's offering. Your offering will be reckoned to you as grain from the threshing floor or juice from the winepress. In this way you also will present an offering to the Lord from all the tithes you receive from the Israelites. From these tithes you must give the Lord's portion to Aaron the priest. You must present as the Lord's portion the best and holiest part of everything given to you'"

(Numbers 18:25-29)

In this way everyone in Israel gave the same percentage to the Lord.

The second tithe was what I call the "vacation tithe." Every family was to allocate ten percent of their harvest for an annual family trip to the Tabernacle or the temple. This tithe is described in Deuteronomy 14:22-27:

"Be sure to set aside a tenth of all that your fields produce each year. Eat the tithe of your grain, new wine and olive oil, and the firstborn of your herds and flocks in the presence of the Lord your God at the place he will choose as a dwelling for his Name, so that you may learn to revere the Lord your God always. But if that place is too distant and you have been blessed by the Lord your God and cannot carry your tithe (because the place where the Lord will choose to put his Name is so far away), then exchange your tithe for silver, and take the silver with you and go to the place the Lord your God will choose. Use the silver to buy whatever you like: cattle, sheep, wine or other fermented drink, or anything you wish. Then you and your household shall eat there in the presence of the Lord your God and rejoice. And do not neglect the Levites living in your towns, for they have no allotment or inheritance of their own."

Since people were required to make the annual pilgrimage they were to set aside a portion of their agricultural income to take with them on that trip. We might think of it as saving up to take a family vacation. Everyone was to celebrate in recognition and praise of the Lord's bounty and faithfulness.

The third tithe is found in Deuteronomy 14:28-29. It was a tithe designed to provide aid to the poor:

> *"At the end of every three years, bring all the tithes of that year's produce and store it in your towns, so that the Levites (who have no allotment or inheritance of their own) and the foreigners, the fatherless and the widows who live in your towns may come and eat and be satisfied, and so that the Lord your God may bless you in all the work of your hands."*

Collected every three years and maintained in every local village, it was what we would call a benevolence fund for the most vulnerable people in society. Strangers passing through a community could be fed from this tithe. Widows and orphans who had no one to look after them could be cared for through this beneficence. By giving their tithes regularly the Israelites remembered God's goodness to them, that everything belonged to the Lord and that they were to care for those less fortunate.

As we might expect, the people often disregarded these instructions. One of the most (in)famous examples of this comes from the prophet Malachi. God held an imaginary conversation with the people:

> *"Will a mere mortal rob God? Yet you rob me.*
>
> *"But you ask, 'How are we robbing you?'*
>
> *"In tithes and offerings. You are under a curse—your whole nation—because you are robbing me. Bring the whole tithe into the storehouse, that there may be food in my house. Test me in this," says the Lord Almighty, "and see if I will not throw open the floodgates of heaven and pour out so much*

blessing that there will not be room enough to store it. I will prevent pests from devouring your crops, and the vines in your fields will not drop their fruit before it is ripe," says the Lord Almighty. "Then all the nations will call you blessed, for yours will be a delightful land," says the Lord Almighty.

(Malachi 3:8-12)

God was angry with his people because they were not giving to the Levities in honor of their services. There were not enough tithes being given (*"that there may be food in my house"*) for the Levites or the community benevolence fund. The people were guilty of withholding their tithes. Sadly, this is something that has not changed. Withholding money is a favorite tactic of church bullies.

Tithing and giving

WHEN WE TURN our attention to the New Testament we discover Jesus spoke more about money than about heaven, hell or salvation. He declared that wherever our treasure lies, that is where our heart will also be found, and that we cannot serve God and money at the same time (Matthew 6:21, 24; Luke 16:13). He instructed people to *"Give back to Caesar what is Caesar's and to God what is God's"* (Mark 12:17).

Jesus said that riches could be a barrier to entering and maturing in the kingdom of God (Matthew 13:22; Mark 10:23-27; Luke 8:14). The accumulation of possessions can cause ruptures in our most important relationships (Luke 12:13-15). In two extreme instances Jesus told those around him that they would need to divest themselves of all possessions in order to truly follow him (Luke 14:33; 18:22).

But throughout the gospels we never hear Jesus say anything about tithing. The only references to tithing in the New Testament refer back to the Old Testament examples. There is no scriptural evidence that Jesus or the apostles—or even the early Church in Act—taught tithing. This might be because tithing was an understood and accepted practice that the writers felt needed no elaboration.

Instead of an emphasis on tithing what we do find is an emphasis on *giving*. Giving is encouraged throughout the New Testament as the normal attitude and lifestyle of the Christian. We are encouraged to give cheerfully (2nd Corinthians 9:7), not out of fear or guilt. We are encouraged to give because we follow the example of Jesus.

The act of giving is an act of surrender and supreme trust. It is letting go of something important and valuable. This surrender and trust is exemplified in Luke 21:1-4 where Jesus and his disciples witnessed a poor widow giving all she had to the temple treasury. We also see this surrender and trust in the early church. Acts 4:33-35 tells us,

> *With great power the apostles continued to testify to the resurrection of the Lord Jesus. And God's grace was so powerfully at work in them all that there were no needy persons among them. For from time to time those who owned land or houses sold them, brought the money from the sales and put it at the apostles' feet, and it was distributed to anyone who had need.*

Paul was so confident of God's provision that he told the Philippian church that God would meet all of their needs through the richness of Christ's grace (Philippians 4:19).

A lifestyle of generosity and thankfulness was a defining characteristic of Jesus-followers. As the Church grew during its first few centuries it was Christian generosity that made an indelible and compelling testimony for the truth of the gospel.

The New Testament is also silent on a specific *amount* one should give. Only Paul offered any hint of an amount when he wrote, *On the first day of every week, each one of you should set aside* **a sum of money in keeping with your income**, *saving it up, so that when*

I come no collections will have to be made (1ˢᵗ Corinthians 16:2, emphasis mine).

The collection was to be taken to the Jerusalem church that was struggling through a severe famine at the time. The Corinthian believers were instructed to give in proportion to what they had received. Paul wanted them to allow the Holy Spirit to guide them in their generosity.

Today there are Christians who feel we should continue to tithe, just as described by the Old Testament. Others see the tithe as part of the law that Jesus fulfilled, and therefore is no longer binding under the new covenant. For our purposes, the point is not whether we use the term "tithing" and practice tithing. The point is that all we have in terms of wealth and possessions are gifts from God (James 1:17).

We do not truly own anything. The Christian worldview is derived from the ancient Hebrew worldview—that everything ultimately belongs to God. In his graciousness he has allowed us to be stewards over the wealth and goods we have. While we may have worked hard to earn the money to buy that boat, a bigger house, a vacation or a new wardrobe, all of it—the work, the money, the possessions—belongs to the Lord. That is why Jesus expects his followers to give without expectation of compensation (Matthew 5:42). It is why Christians are to take care of the poor (Matthew 25:31-46), to use their gifts in service to others (Matthew 25:14-30) and to not be greedy (Luke 12:13-21). It is not ours but his.

From this we can extrapolate the key financial issue within the Church: many Christians do not truly believe that all they have is a gift from God. They may acknowledge God's provision with their words but their behaviors say otherwise. They live in such a way as to deny the reality of God's sovereign ownership.

Three categories of givers

BECAUSE MONEY HOLDS a dominant influence over some in the Church it becomes the essential point of control. Financial bullies use various ways to govern the purse strings. Nowhere is this more evident than in the church budget.

Every church has to have a budget. As we discussed in chapter ten, there are insurance premiums and utilities to pay, buildings to maintain, and pastors and staff to compensate. Financial bullies use the budget to keep things under their thumb. They scrutinize every line item and every expenditure, cross-examining leaders and committees about what was spent and why.

While we need keen financial minds to serve in the church, a line is crossed when resources are hoarded and kept from important ministries. Some of us have been part of a committee meeting where influential people shot down ministry initiatives or budget requests. They did so because they did not want "their money" being used for things that did not directly benefit them. When such attitudes are present in leadership—which should not be allowed to happen in the first place—churches are well on the road to decline and death.

Those with selfish or immature financial agendas work hard to ensure their allies are consistently elected to positions of leadership. This is one reason why pastors seeking to revive and turn around a deteriorating church must see that the majority of entrenched committee members are replaced. A church cannot go forward by keeping the old leadership in place. It is often their manipulation of the budget, staff or buildings that has exacerbated the church's problems.

From a financial perspective there are basically three groups of people in the Church: big givers, faithful givers and non-givers. Big givers are those who can almost single-handedly float the whole church through a financial crisis. Big givers come in two categories.

The first is the wealthy person or family who gives selflessly and often anonymously. They have a heart that is right with Christ. They understand the wealth they have is a gift from God. They regularly use those resources to aid others inside and outside the church. These saints address emergency needs that arise in the church or community quickly and generously.

In one church I pastored there were two men whom God had blessed with very successful businesses. Both of them were committed to the cause of Christ and supported every endeavor to reach the lost and make disciples. They provided funds and supplies for mission trips, and participated on those mission teams as well. When an HVAC unit at the church went out, one of the men paid out-of-pocket to have a new one installed. He asked that I not say anything to anyone about what he had done. He did not want the publicity or attention. He simply wanted to serve the Lord and the church with the financial blessings he had received.

Having this type of big giver is a double-edged sword. While they can be counted on for their generosity and devotion, the problem is *they can be counted on for their generosity and devotion!* By this I mean that others can take advantage of their open-handedness. Normally, this is not done intentionally. It simply becomes a habit over the years.

In one church there had been a very wealthy, Godly man who died not long before I arrived. He had been responsible for launching a ministry to local children, giving to the construction of a new facility, and many other charitable acts. However, over the years the people of the church grew accustomed to his generosity. Everyone knew this man could be counted on if the collections were a bit low one month or if an emergency arose. As a result, people in the church became lax about their own giving. When that saint passed away the church quickly felt the financial pinch. They had gotten used to being bailed out. They became comfortable with someone else doing all the giving.

The second category of big giver is the person or family who bullies the church with their wealth. These givers may also help carry the church through a financial crisis—and they never let others forget it. They use their sizable contributions to make sure everyone dances to their tune. If someone—usually a pastor or staff person—does not want to dance that revenue stream is quickly shut off. In all likelihood you know of a church in your area that has a history of being intimidated and threatened by a few of these people. Churches have lost good pastoral leadership, gifted staff persons and sometimes members because a handful of people with money have always gotten their way.

This type of giver infests every church and they thrive on the power and fear they can instill if they threaten to stop giving. Author Robin Meyers makes this sobering observation, "In churches, the wealthiest members who contribute the most money are often coddled and feared. Their opinions are considered more important. Ministers recruit the wealthy with more vigor than they pursue those of more modest means because every church has to make its budget."[20]

* * * * * *

The second group of financial supporters in the church is the faithful givers. These people provide the backbone for the budget. They give regularly to the general fund and can also be counted on for special projects, youth fund-raisers and Sunday school donations. Their giving is normally known only to them and key financial representatives of the church. They do not flaunt their giving nor do they use it to manipulate the church. Most in this category understand the biblical perspectives on giving and seek to be as faithful with their resources as they can.

Finally, the third group is the non-givers. Their name identifies them completely. They give little to nothing toward God's work in

---

[20] Robin Meyers, *The Underground Church: Reclaiming The Subversive Way of Jesus*, p. 206. Used by permission. All rights reserved.

the world. Such persons may have been Christians for decades but they do not practice biblical giving and generosity.

Sometimes we are led to believe others are big givers when in reality they are anything but. I have found that whenever a turnaround or renewal is attempted in the local church, those who yell the loudest are usually those who give the least, if they give at all. This is because over the years other parishioners have come to assume that since Mr. Chiffalchimper has been a member of the congregation for over sixty years, he simply *must* be a big giver. Wrong. Non-givers often use *other* means to achieve their personal agendas in the church, such as gossip, longevity and deception.

In addition to withholding money, another tactic frequently used by financial bullies is controlled or directed giving. Instead of their offering going to the general budget it is designated to a different account. They exert control over how their money is used by keeping it out of the main bank account. When trying to get rid of a pastor or staff person this is the maneuver of choice. These givers can still feel pious because they continue to give to the church; however, they are refusing to let their money go to pay the salaries of church leaders they are seeking to remove. Sadly, a great many churches acquiesce to such foolishness, further cementing the power of the spiritually shallow. As a friend of mine once said about this approach, "That's not how God operates. That's how Satan operates."

Proverbs 11:24 tells us *One person gives freely, yet gains even more; another withholds unduly, but comes to poverty.* While the "poverty" spoken of here may mean a lack of physical resources—lacking the necessities of life—it also refers to spiritual impoverishment. When we withhold or designate our giving into the Roof Fund or Flower Fund (in order to have our way), we begin to suffer hardness of heart. Left unchecked, our hearts eventually become impervious to the voice of the Holy Spirit. Such people continue down a path of bitterness, hostility and self-deception, pulling impressionable members along with them and ruining churches.

Slaves to the credit

WE MUST ALSO contend with the specter of debt in our churches. This takes the form of individual as well as corporate debt. It is one of the greatest detriments to our wise and generous use of money.

Debt exists because we are imprinted by our culture to believe we must have everything we want, when we want, whether we can afford it or not. Young couples just starting out sink themselves in a morass of debt by purchasing large homes in order to keep up with their peers, or because of the cultural pressure to have it all and have it now.

We go shopping and whip out the credit card, promising ourselves we will pay it off next month. Yet when the next month arrives we can only make the minimum payment. More charges accrue, more fees are assessed and before long we are carrying a balance of four figures (and sometimes more). According to authors Daniel Ray and Yasmin Ghahremani at Creditcards.com, in 2012 the average credit card debt among low- and middle-income households totaled $7,145, down from $9,887 in 2008. Nearly two in five Americans (39%) carry credit card debt from month to month. And there is little difference between who spends: 55% of males and 60% of females are saddled with credit card debt.[21]

Some debt exists because most of us need our own transportation and vehicles are expensive. Student loans and medical bills account for large amounts of debt as well. Unemployment forces families to rely on credit cards in order to get by. While debt may be seen by some as a "necessary evil," or even as an acceptable part of our society, it is not God's will for anyone.

Proverbs 22:7 is a stark and truthful observation regarding debt: *The rich rule over the poor, and the borrower is slave to the lender.* Peter said it in a slightly different way: *People are slaves to whatever has*

---

[21] Ray, Daniel P. and Ghahremani, Yasmin. *Credit card statistics, industry facts, debt statistics,* http://www.creditcards.com.

mastered them (2 Peter 2:19). When we carry debt we are enslaved to the lender. They own us until we have repaid our debt. We are not free but under a contractual obligation to do what the lender says.

When in debt we cannot be generous as we are called to be. There is rarely any extra money left over at the end of the month. So instead of being able to use our money to bless and benefit others we are obligated to our creditors. One of the reasons our nation continues to send children to bed hungry, and to have families living in cars, is because we have not been good stewards of the financial resources God has given us. What could have gone to feed hungry children or aid homeless families is wasted by our conspicuous consumption or claimed by our creditors. If we use our resources properly God has designed it so that our extra becomes the help others need. After we take care of the necessities for ourselves and our families, some of what is left could be used to help express God's love and care for those around us.

Debt also chokes churches. In the same way it paralyzes and makes slaves of individuals, it likewise binds up the church. The freedom we should experience as followers of Christ cannot be fully realized while we have to panhandle for money to pay off the building debt or meet the budget. Some pastors and church leaders feel that anything that requires the church to go into debt should not be undertaken. It is a wise—and unfortunately scarce attitude in our day.

Church debt prevents the Body of Christ from addressing needs in the local community. We cannot give away food cards or utility vouchers because all our money is tied up in capital debt. We cannot support missionaries or send our own mission teams due to the fact that every dime is already earmarked to pay off our creditors. Church members grow tired of hearing about the need to generate more income.

Cash in Corinth

WAS MONEY A problem in the Corinthian church?

Probably not in the way we have discussed here. We know that wealthier members were using their position to undercut others at the Lord's Supper (1st Corinthians 11:17-34) but that indicates an issue of social stratification more so than using money to control the church.

Paul's only comments related to finances came at the end of his letter. In 1st Corinthians 16:1-2, he wrote,

> *Now about the collection for the Lord's people: Do what I told the Galatian churches to do. On the first day of every week, each one of you should set aside a sum of money in keeping with your income, saving it up, so that when I come no collections will have to be made.*

Paul showed no favoritism between churches. What he expected from the Galatians he expected from the Corinthians. He directed them to take a portion of their paycheck and tuck it away. That amount would be collected when Paul arrived and couriered to the church in Jerusalem (1st Corinthians 16:3).

Everyone was to participate, regardless of how big or small the paycheck. Each member was to set aside something for the love offering. Obviously those who earned more could give more. But no one was exempt. Everyone could do something to help.

We have to look into 2nd Corinthians if we want to see Paul's thoughts on money fleshed out a bit more. In what we would term a "fund-raising effort" Paul encouraged the Corinthian believers to give by lifting up the example of other churches:

> *And now, brothers and sisters, we want you to know about the grace that God has given the Macedonian churches. In the midst of a very severe trial, their overflowing joy and their extreme poverty welled up in rich generosity. For I testify that they gave as much as they were able, and even beyond*

their ability. Entirely on their own, they urgently pleaded with us for the privilege of sharing in this service to the Lord's people. And they exceeded our expectations: They gave themselves first of all to the Lord, and then by the will of God also to us.

(2nd Corinthians 8:1-5)

Paul held up the Macedonian churches as an example of how giving requires deep, abiding trust in God—especially in times of trouble. Despite the fact those churches were undergoing severe trials, their love and generosity compelled them to render whatever financial aid they could to their brothers and sisters. Even in the midst of harsh poverty they continued to give to the work of God's kingdom.

It has been my observation that whenever churches begin to experience financial difficulties the first things on the chopping block are benevolence, outreach and mission funds. In a fit of financial panic we start to scuttle the very ministries that are most designed to reach the needy and lost. The Macedonian churches did not panic but rather let their actions reflect their beliefs. They gave, even when they had little to give, because they trusted in the God who owns all things. Their belief was manifested in their generous actions.

Paul challenged the Corinthian church to imitate the selflessness of Christ, and to continue with the generosity they had previously displayed. What they started with enthusiasm should be carried on to completion. *For if the willingness is there, the gift is acceptable according to what one has, not according to what one does not have* (2nd Corinthians 8:12).

Here we find an echo of 1st Corinthians 16:2. Paul reminded them again that each person was to give what they were capable of giving. Great or small, each gift given to aid another was acceptable and pleasing in God's sight. Paul did not want the Corinthians sitting around, saying, "Well, if we only had more members, like they do in Macedonia, our giving would be better. We could take up a better love offering and do more benevolence assistance." All are to give according to the means that God has provided. God honors what we give when we do the best we can with what he has given us.

What God does not honor is stinginess. An attitude of "I'm not giving anything" is a childish rejection of the imitation of Christ. The person who can afford to give one thousand dollars but only gives ten dollars forces others in the church to do more than their fair share. This is why Paul also wrote,

> *Our desire is not that others might be relieved while you are hard pressed, but that there might be equality. At the present time your plenty will supply what they need, so that in turn their plenty will supply what you need. The goal is equality, as it is written: "The one who gathered much did not have too much, and the one who gathered little did not have too little.*
>
> (2nd Corinthians 8:13-15).

When everyone participates to the best of their blessing, no one is stretched beyond their means. As everyone does their part the church has more than enough resources for everything God brings to our attention.

No, Paul probably did not have to deal with financial bullies. However, he did take advantage of the love offering to express several key elements of Christian generosity:

(1) Every follower of Jesus should give (1st Corinthians 16:2);

(2) Every follower of Jesus should give what is in keeping with his or her income (1st Corinthians 16:2);

(3) Giving is done as an act of faith, trust and obedience to God (2nd Corinthians 8:2-3);

(4) True generosity comes from an authentic relationship with Jesus (2nd Corinthians 8:5);

(5) True generosity is manifested in practical aid to those in need (2nd Corinthians 8:5; cf., James 2:14-17);

(6) Authentic giving is an imitation of the sacrifice of Christ (2nd Corinthians 8:9);

(7) We are to give what we have, not lament what we do not have (2nd Corinthians 8:12).

The old saying "Money talks" is all too appropriate in many churches. In fact, money is often the god that speaks the loudest. If we aligned our hearts to the financial principles Paul advocated, and surrendered ourselves completely to the Lordship of Jesus Christ, there would be no money issues in our churches.

Or perhaps there would be one: trying to figure out how to use all the generous bounty God pours out on us for the advancement and glory of his kingdom. Would that this were so!

CHAPTER 13
DEFENDING THE BRIDE OF CHRIST
FROM MONEY

"Nothing that is God's is obtainable by money."

Tertullian

ONE BEAUTIFUL SUNDAY morning the pastor announced, "My brothers and sisters, I have with me today three sermons. The first is a one-thousand-dollar sermon that lasts five minutes. The second is a five-hundred-dollar sermon that lasts twenty minutes. And the third is a one-hundred-dollar sermon that lasts an hour. If our ushers will come forward we'll take up the offering and see which one I'll deliver."

Pastors, we would like to try that sometime, right?

A preacher announced from the pulpit, "I have some good news and some bad news this morning. The good news is that we have enough money to pay off our debt!"

Applause broke out across the congregation.

"The bad news," the pastor continued, "is that the money is still in your pockets."

While we chuckle at the cuteness of the jokes there is truth in them. All the money our churches need in order to do ministry and fulfill the *missio Dei* is sitting in the pews and chairs every week. The question becomes how do we get it out of the pockets and into the budget so it can be used?

Maybe we could try what one worship leader suggested:

When the time for the offering arrived the worship leader walked to the microphone and said, "All right, everyone, please stand. Now stretch your arms out in front of you. Grab the wallet of the person directly in front of you—and give like you've always wanted to give!"

217

Okay, that may not work either.

But what will get God's money out of our hands and into his work is a *cause*. People will give when they know their money is making a difference in the world. Mike Slaughter, pastor of Ginghamsburg United Methodist Church in Tipp City, Ohio, says in his book *Unlearning Church*, "...people are more inclined to give toward an organization or ministry that is involved in genuine life change. Money follows mission, not budget."[22] If we want people to share their financial resources we must show them a cause they can become immersed in. We must provide them with a reason to give, beyond just paying the bills or balancing the budget. There needs to be a way for people to see and know how their giving is making a real difference in the world.

If we want to keep the bride of Christ from being bullied by money it is time that our money becomes a tool for transformation instead of a weapon of intimidation. We should shift our focus from an attitude of scarcity to one of radical generosity. If we want to declaw the controllers and incapacitate the line item investigators, it is time we adopted a perspective—and practice—that shows exactly how God is using the weekly offering to change lives.

Show us the need

HOW OFTEN DOES the pastor or finance committee chair stand before the congregation and say, "We're in a bit of a financial crunch. We're behind in our giving and the budget is running into the red. If this pattern persists we'll have to take a serious look at some things in our budget. Therefore, we're asking each of you to prayerfully review your giving. If there is any way you can increase your giving—even by just a couple of dollars—it would help us out of this bind."

---

[22] Mike Slaughter, *Unlearning Church: Just When You Thought You Had Leadership All Figured Out* (Loveland: Group Publishing, 2002), p. 46. Used by permission. All rights reserved.

Or maybe you have taken part in a finance committee discussion about how to trim line items from the budget, how to save money on utilities or how a fund-raiser might help generate monies to pay the annual insurance premium.

While addressing this concept with my congregation I asked them to raise their hand if anyone enjoyed paying bills. As you can guess there were no responses. People are not motivated to pay bills. We know it is something we *have* to do in life. We have our bills at home. We have bills to pay if we are in business. We know the church has bills. But asking people to give just to keep the lights on or the bulletins printed becomes onerous.

In addition, it continues to foster a skewed understanding of giving. If I am only putting my money in the offering plate to pay the pastor or balance the budget, I can quickly assume that I should have a definite say in what the pastor does or does not do, or how the budget should be handled. And if I put in a considerable sum on a regular basis I can also assume that I am entitled to a greater say in such things.

Here is a paradigm shift for our financial thinking: the church needs to stop asking for money to pay the bills. Focusing only on paying bills wears our congregants out. We promote an unbiblical perspective on generosity. We reinforce bad theology. And we are constantly asking for more, more, more. Instead of badgering worshipers to give in support of the budget we need to let them see what their giving really means to people in need.

A perfect example of this approach is the child sponsorship organization Compassion International. Launched in 1952 by Reverend Everett Swanson, their goal is to rescue children from poverty around the world. When someone chooses to sponsor a child in need, Compassion International ensures that the sponsor is fully informed about how his or her monthly support is used. Givers know where their financial commitment goes and in what ways it is used to benefit the child (by providing medical care, clothing, food and so on). Sponsors receive information about their adopted child such as what the child studies in school, what they do for fun and what their country is like. There is also the opportunity to communicate directly with the child by letters passed through an interpreter. Compassion International makes it easy for sponsors to see what their monthly support does to improve the lives of children and their families.

In the United States it is easy for us to ignore the needs around us. We can redirect our steps to avoid coming in contact with the homeless. We can justify our lack of compassion toward the poor by accusing them of being lazy. We have many ways of desensitizing ourselves to the needs that exist everywhere.

However, when we come face-to-face with those needs we are confronted with a decision: will I help or won't I? The more we know about the need—the circumstances, the human beings involved in the situation—the harder it becomes to walk away. Proximity to need stirs us to action.

If we want to transition our churches from giving-just-to-pay-the-bills, or from being bullied by shallow believers with fat checkbooks, we need encounters with real people and real needs. When we can show our people how their giving benefits a single mother, or a family with no electricity, we generate hope, excitement and increased generosity. We know that our financial gifts are truly making a difference in the lives of others.

Church members will begin to appreciate regular updates on how their giving is benefitting the community. Needs they previously paid no attention to will become new opportunities for giving and serving. Visitors will be able to see our commitment to positive change through our financial giving. When we stop existing just to pay the bills and begin to live for the transformation of the world, people will take notice. The church becomes an unstoppable force that, as Jesus said, not even the gates of Hell can stand against.

I like to tell my congregations that if we are generous in helping those outside our walls, God will take care of the needs inside our walls. If we believe this and live accordingly, it does not mean we will get new computers for the office every few years or that we will be able to put new carpet in the sanctuary. Jesus will ensure the basic needs of his bride are taken care of when we begin to live as he has shown us.

At the end of my time in one church I encouraged them to continue focusing outside the walls, regardless of what the monthly financial report said. Looking at the chair of the finance committee I asked, "Over the past two years, since we made our turnaround and started in a new direction, has our budget ever worked out on paper?"

He shook his head. "No."

"So for the last two years," I continued, "we've run behind in our giving. Do you remember how much?"

"Well, two years ago we were about $12,000 behind. Last year we were about $3,000 behind at the end of the year," he replied.

"Let me ask you this: in those two years that we failed to balance the budget, did we ever lack anything we needed in order to do any outreach or missions project?"

Once again the finance chair shook his head, but this time with a smile. "No," he replied. "One way or another the money always came in."

That church did not collapse in on itself when it started focusing outward. It did not lock the doors when the budget was not met. Churches that focus exclusively on money never have enough. Churches that focus on missions, outreach and authentic ministry can rely on God's provision for whatever they need to do for the kingdom. Of course there were things we could not do inside the walls, like upgrading the office computers or installing an elevator. But those were not needs. They were *wants*.

When my wife visited India in 2005 one of the things she came to realize was the difference between a want and a need. Her mission team did a lot of work in the slums of Hyderabad. She discovered that a need is food, shelter and clothing. Anything beyond that is a want. Too many churches assume their wants are actually needs.

"Well, the choir *needs* new robes." Do they need those robes at the expense of starving children in the neighborhood? Which of the two would Jesus emphasize? I believe that if we commit to ending something such as childhood hunger in our local communities, we will discover that new choir robes are not such a pressing issue. When we can provide testimonies and hands-on experiences of helping end childhood poverty or hunger, there will be no shortage of money in our churches. People will be happy to give when they know children are being fed, when they know that children are doing better in school, and when they know that children are happier and families are being helped.

What basic needs are going unmet outside your church's walls? Can you identify one or two things in your neighborhood, town or county that Christ is calling you to focus your resources upon? Go for it because money follows mission, not bills.

There can be only one DNA

MOST CHURCHES HAVE fallen into a mentality of scarcity. Over the years they have come to believe their financial resources are limited, especially as older members pass away or are no longer able to support the church as they once did. With the death of each saint the financial panic becomes greater. If a church has relied upon the generosity of a single individual or family for significant monetary support, the fear of losing that person or family can be overwhelming.

Therefore, the church enacts legislation designed to protect the budget from needless expenditures. Normally one or two key people in the congregation are tabbed as unofficial watchdogs of the budget, like Cerberus guarding the entrance to Hades. While we must maintain financial integrity and live as good stewards of what God has entrusted to us, we are never called to just pay the bills and get by. We are not recipients of God's blessings so we can hoard them inside our buildings, afraid to use them for fear we will not have any more. In what ways does God want to use the finances of your church to see lives transformed to his glory?

To find answers requires that we spend deliberate time in the Scriptures, seeking God's expectations for the church. Most of our churches need refresher (or in some cases, introductory) courses in the Lord's heart for the poor, our call to biblically informed action, a sound theological perspective on wealth and possessions, and radical discipleship that exemplifies sacrifice and surrender. The committees and decision-making bodies of our churches— especially the finance committee—will need to look more like prayer gatherings and Bible studies than corporate business meetings.

Every living being contains a unique double-helix strand of DNA. The purpose of DNA is to carry and replicate a detailed set of organic blueprints for the reproduction of different parts of each cell. To use a different image, DNA is the recipe and ingredients that make us who we are.

The church is a living entity with its own DNA. It is composed of individual people just as our bodies are composed of individual cells. The DNA of the church is the *missio Dei*. Through our adoption into God's family, our submission to the lordship of Jesus Christ and our ongoing sanctification, we are imprinted with the missional DNA of God himself. The more we mature in our faith the more of the missional DNA we embrace.

However, if you take a close look at declining and dying churches you will find something that does not even occur in the natural order. You will discover competing strands of DNA within the Body of Christ. No organism could live and fulfill its purpose if it had multiple strands of DNA. The 1986 film *Highlander* was promoted with the tag line "There can be only one," referring to a group of immortals who had to battle one another in order to claim the prize and be "the one." Within the Body of Christ there can be only one strand of DNA, one set of blueprints, one recipe.

Yet in most churches we find evidence of different DNA strands, each in conflict with the others. The Senior Saints Sunday school class thinks the church should be focused on one thing (normally something that directly benefits the members of the class). The choir or an administrative committee wants something different. The pastor has a vision for the church but this is often overridden or ignored by the wealthy and influential constituents among the congregation. The board of elders or the trustees believe that resources should be allocated in a specific place and specific way, yet this draws funding away from the children's ministry or outreach team. Every group within the church has a different agenda.

As a result, the church can go nowhere because its parts are all pulling in different directions. Imagine the danger you would be in if different parts of your physical body started going off in opposite directions! On one level it would be somewhat comical to see arms, legs, feet, eyes and all the other parts disengaging from the whole to pursue their own way. But it would be no laughing matter because we would cease to exist if that happened.

This is the predicament of churches in the twenty-first century: too many years of different groups pulling in different directions, too many competing DNAs vying for supremacy. As Paul noted in 1st Corinthians 1:12, *One of you says, "I follow Paul"; another, "I follow Apollos"; another, "I follow Cephas"; still another, "I follow Christ."* Different Corinthian factions wanted the DNA of Paul or Apollos or Peter. While one group seems to have been committed to the missional DNA of Christ, others had competing agendas. They wanted the DNA of their group to be the one that ruled the roost. Churches today continue to struggle with the same problem.

If we are serious about confronting the bully of money it is imperative that we reclaim and reassert the DNA of the *missio Dei.* It is not optional. It is vital for the very survival of the church. The people who faithfully attend and support our churches must be led to see that their giving propels the mission of Jesus in the world. Everything in the church exists to support the missional DNA.

What are you doing with your blessing?

ON THE FIRST Sunday in my new church, at the beginning of my sermon, I held up a five-dollar bill. "Who would like to have this as a gift?" I asked. "Whoever wants it has to come forward and you have to tell me what you're going to do with it."

A ten-year-old boy was the first one out of his seat and down the aisle. When I gave him the bill and asked what he intended to do with it, he said he would use it to buy some fishing equipment. As he returned to his family I told the congregation there were basically three things he could do with the gift. He could spend it on himself. He could save it. Or he could use it for others.

"So let me ask you this," I said. "As individuals and as a church, what are you doing with your blessing? Every single day we receive good and precious gifts from our heavenly Father. As we just said, there are three things you can do with the blessings given by God. You can use them for yourself. You can hoard them. Or you can use them for the benefit of others."

Psalm 67 was a song used by the people of Israel in worship. It was a hymn of praise that asked for Yahweh's blessings upon the assembled people. Verse one begins, *May God be gracious to us and bless us and make his face shine on us*—the plural "us" identifies it as a prayer for the community of worshipers gathered together. Unlike cultural Christianity that causes us to approach worship with a "Lord, bless *me!*" attitude, this psalm calls for God's favor upon everyone.

To ask for God's face to shine on us is an image of receiving his goodwill and blessing. A bright, shining face reveals a person of pleasant disposition. It is an indication of inward peace and joy. In biblical times to turn one's face toward another was a sign of respect and favor. It meant there was a welcoming connection. We see examples of this throughout the Old Testament:

*"'The Lord bless you and keep you; the Lord **make his face shine on you** and be gracious to you; the Lord **turn his face toward you** and give you peace."'*

(Numbers 6:24-26)

*If you return to the Lord, then your fellow Israelites and your children will be shown compassion by their captors and will return to this land, for the Lord your God is gracious and compassionate. **He will not turn his face from you** if you return to him.*

(2 Chronicles 30:9)

*Restore us, Lord God Almighty; **make your face shine on us**, that we may be saved.*

(Psalm 80:19, emphasis mine)

In contrast, to turn one's face away from another was to dismiss that person, to demean them and write them off.

*How long, Lord? Will you forget me forever? How long will you **hide your face** from me?*

(Psalm 13:1)

*And the nations will know that the people of Israel went into exile for their sin, because they were unfaithful to me. So **I hid my face from them** and handed them over to their enemies...*

(Ezekiel 39:23, emphasis mine)

What do we tell our children when we want them to pay attention to us? "Look at me when I'm talking to you." To face another person is to respect them, to recognize their presence and to engage with them.

But why would Psalm 67 ask for the blessing of Yahweh's face upon the worshipers? The psalmist made it abundantly clear: *so that your ways may be known on earth, your salvation among all nations. May the peoples praise you, God; may all the peoples praise you.*

The reason the people of Israel asked for Yahweh's face to shine on them—the reason we should likewise seek this divine blessing—is so that same blessing may be shared with others. We ask God to bless us in order that his ways—his glory, his love—may be seen and experienced by all people. The reason we are blessed by God is so that we can be a blessing to others. God does not bless the church merely for our benefit. It is so we can give the blessing away in order to glorify God.

Due to the selfishness that permeates our society, we slip into the fallacy of believing that God's blessings are just for me, or my family, or my group or my church. This betrays a superficial, egotistic spirituality because God's blessings are to be shared with all the earth. Psalm 67 pleads for Yahweh's blessing so that even more people could praise God. That was the purpose of Israel's call as Yahweh's chosen people. Verse seven captures this: *May God bless us still, so that all the ends of the earth will fear him.*

What if our churches focused more on sharing God's blessings instead of hoarding them? What if we actually wanted all peoples and all nations—and the poor, homeless, rejected and alien who live around our buildings—to praise God?

Make a fist with one hand. Imagine you are holding a blessing in your fist. Now imagine God wants to put another blessing in your hand. But he cannot. Why? Because you are still clinging to the previous one. If you notice, you cannot give anything away when your hand is made into a fist. You cannot share a blessing with a closed fist. A punch is not much of a blessing!

If we go around with figurative clenched fists, refusing to release God's blessings, everyone suffers. The person for whom that blessing was meant suffers because she or he never receives it. We also suffer. We cannot experience the joy of generosity as we pass the blessing along, nor can we receive the next great thing God has for us. He cannot put a new blessing into a tight fist. To open our hands—to let go of the favors we have received—is to surrender to God's will. It is to be obedient. It is to extend an open hand to another, rather than a closed fist.

In one church I served we ended just about every worship service with the first verse of Psalm 67. It served as the perfect benediction as we said it aloud together: May God be gracious to us and bless us and make his face shine on us—so that your ways may be known on earth, your salvation among all nations. Amen.

In order to effectively save the Church from financial bullies the focus must transition from hoarding to giving away what we have. Psalm 67 should become our attitude and practice with regard to our financial resources. God will take care of all the stuff inside the walls if we will take care of the lost and hurting outside the walls.

Tips for transition

THERE ARE SOME things that all church leaders need to understand and accept when shifting from paying the bills to financing the mission.

First, such a transition is not likely to sit well with some of your big givers. You should be prepared for intimidation tactics and threats from them. They will be unhappy that the emphasis has moved away from their personal entitlements and power. You are likely to hear such things as

- "If this is how the church is going to use *my* money, I certainly won't be giving any more."
- "You tell that pastor that my family hasn't supported this church all these years just so he can turn it into a homeless shelter!"
- "If this proposal gets voted through rest assured that I will not give anything else to this church."
- "I intend to withhold my giving until this church gets a new pastor, someone who cares about the members who've built and supported this church."

There will be snide remarks and destructive comments made about the missional thrust. Some will believe that by redirecting their giving or withholding it altogether the church will eventually have no choice but to capitulate to their demands.

Let me be straightforward and blunt at this point. *Do not be intimidated by the big givers of your congregation. Anyone who uses their wealth to bully the bride of Christ does not have a heart that is right with the Lord.* They are not listening to or being obedient to the Holy Spirit. They are living out of their sinful, unregenerate nature. If they threaten to walk out because their demands are not met, *let them go.* The church does not need manipulated money.

One of the things that confound my congregations is that I am unfazed by financial threats. I have come to know that if someone is using their money against the church for their own selfish ends the church can get by just as well without that money. This strips the person of their leverage. It serves notice that the church does not cater to one person over another nor does the church negotiate with financial bullies. If a big giver cannot support the biblical mission and DNA of the church they are better off in a dead or dying church that will play by their rules.

Second, remember that God is the provider for your church, not the moneyed families or big givers. It is true that God will use those families or individuals if their hearts are fully submitted to the lordship of Christ. God enjoys nothing more than working through us to make his kingdom a reality in the world. He has blessed many people with wealth so they can use their financial blessing to aid others. However, God is equally capable of providing for the bride of Christ in other ways.

As soon as you begin to return your church to its missional DNA and some stop giving, you will discover others in the congregation who will step up. I have seen the owner of a grocery store chain donate all the food for weeklong mission trips. I have seen elderly ladies bring in candy for Halloween and Easter outreach events. People who desire to see the church make a lasting difference in the lives of others will share, donate and serve in any way they can to make that happen. This usually leaves the big givers standing there with stunned expressions and bloated checkbooks because the church did not come to a grinding halt without their money.

I have repeatedly told finance committees and administrative councils that God wants to receive the glory for the church's finances. It is not up to one individual or family to bail the church out. We are to turn our faces to God and seek him for our financial needs. When we do this—when we exhibit trust in his divine provision—God moves through the countless resources he has entrusted to his people. And sometimes he may also come through with miraculous, supernatural provision that *only* he can get credit for.

Third, identify areas of need in your surrounding community and pray about how God would like to use your church to address those needs. Projects do not have to be huge, in-depth or eternal. Select a few smaller needs that can be met quickly and easily. It might be diapers and baby supplies for low-income families or single mothers. It could be school supplies for immigrant children. It might be a weekly or monthly free meal for the community, rent assistance or a clothing closet. Throw your financial resources into whatever God places before your church. Then watch what God does.

Always make sure you provide ample space and time to celebrate when a need is met. Use testimonies, videos or print resources to keep the congregation informed about how their giving is changing lives. The majority of Christians want to make a difference in the world. They want to know their giving produces fruit. The more we can show them, the less we have to fret about money.

Fourth, let the mission dictate the money, not the other way around. It is time to stop limiting our mission because we do not think we have enough. What if we started dreaming about what we would like to do for God's glory? What if we sought his will and guidance, and dreamed some wild, God-sized dreams? Suppose we believe a particular project or event will help our church fulfill its mission, and suppose we look to God to provide for it. Rather than being confined by what we cannot spend or cannot afford we should start asking, "What does God want us to do, in this place, at this time?"

Church consultant Bill Easum writes, "Spiritually deep people don't look at their budgets to see how little they can spend; they look at their budgets to see if how they are spending money is bringing people to Christ. When God moves in their hearts to do something, they don't ask if they can afford it; they trust God to supply the funds!"[23]

If what we seek to do is expensive, outrageous, challenging or complicated, we look to God—the Source of all—to help us accomplish the mission. If it is something that is not in God's will it will not come to fruition, and our churches can turn to other ideas and options. If, however, it is of God we can count on his help and provision in bringing it about. A Pharisee named Gamaliel first offered this advice in the early days of the Church.

As the Jewish Sanhedrin debated about what to do with Peter and the other apostles who kept teaching about Jesus, it was suggested the Christ-followers be put to death. However, Gamaliel stood up and said,

> *"In the present case I advise you: Leave these men alone! Let them go! For if their purpose or activity is of human origin, it will fail. But if it is from God, you will not be able to stop these men; you will only find yourselves fighting against God."*
>
> (Acts 5:38-39)

---

23 Bill Easum, *A Second Resurrection: Leading Your Congregation to New Life* (Nashville: Abingdon Press, 2007), p. 59. Used by permission. All rights reserved.

If we allow our financial resources to dictate what we do as a church we will never possess the transformational power we should have. We will always worry about giving. We will be prisoners to a bank balance. We will allow less mature believers to call the shots.

It is time we understood budgeting and finances to be about the will of God and the work of the Holy Spirit, not something that will make our local banker proud. We need to finance the church's mission in the world, not cater to a handful of wealthy individuals. Churches will always experience problems with money and giving from time to time. Economics, changing demographics and unforeseen needs will exert stress on our budgets.

But if the bride of Christ is to show the world a better, alternative way of living and loving, we cannot continue with our current patterns of financial thinking. We are past due for a significant shift in our hearts, attitudes and wallets. It is time to let God be God, to trust and act as if Jesus really does know what is best for his bride.

Discover the mission God has for your church. Fund that mission so that lives can be transformed. Step forward with radical boldness and faith, recognizing that all we have comes from God, and that he knows how best to use it for his purposes. *May God be gracious to us and bless us and make his face shine on us—so that your ways may be known on earth, your salvation among all nations.*

CONCLUSION

"I have spoken with pastors and church staff who have been attacked by church bullies. While the bully brings them great pain, they have even greater hurt because most of the church members stood silent and let it happen."

Thom S. Rainer

AS WE HAVE seen throughout this book, and as you may know from personal experience, much of the turmoil and ineffectiveness in the local congregation stems from bullying situations. Self-professed Christians who bear little resemblance to Jesus use intimidation and manipulation to ensure their positions of power remain intact. They are more concerned about maintaining the status quo and their personal entitlements than in serving Jesus Christ.

Many pastors have been battered and abused by such behaviors. Some have left the ministry altogether, carrying scars and emotional wounds that run deep. Churches have earned reputations for grinding up pastors and staff, or as nothing more than social cliques. Church members have been mistreated for daring to speak in opposition to the controllers. We should not be surprised that the world considers us woefully inept, hypocritical, selfish and exclusive—because this is the image we have allowed to be perpetuated. To some degree or another, we are all guilty of allowing our local churches to become affected by bullies.

In his book *Leadership On the Other Side*, Bill Easum comments on how every church has a small group of people who "need to be kicked in the butt." He goes on to explain what he means, and I include it here with his permission:

"I've seen a disturbing pattern throughout all of my consulting ministry: most established churches are held hostage by one or two bullies. I keep hearing pastors say, 'If I tried that, I'd lose my job!' Some individual or small group of individuals are usually extremely opposed to the church making any radical change, even if it means the change would give the church a chance to thrive once again.

"Courageous pastors often ask, 'What do I do when one person intimidates the church so much that the church is not willing to try something new?' My response is always, 'Either convert them, neutralize them, or kick them out.' To which someone usually cries, 'That's not very Christian!' What they mean is, 'That's not very nice.'

"My response describes much of the wisdom of both the Old Testament and Jesus. Maturing Christians love so deeply that they will do anything, even not be nice, 'for the sake of the gospel.' Jesus was so compassionate toward others that he could not remain quiet when he saw people holding other people in bondage. Jesus called his best friend 'Satan' when he got in the way of the mission. He drove the money changers out of the temple. He went out of his way to upset the religious bullies of his time. Being nice is often nothing more than a lack of compassion for people. Church leaders are robbing people of their spiritual birthright when they allow dysfunctional people to bully the church.

"One of the basic lessons I'm learning as a consultant is that before renewal can begin, some person or group usually has to leave the church. Almost every time a dying church attempts to thrive once again, someone tries to bully the leadership out of the attempt. Almost every time, if a turnaround is to take place, these people are lost along the way because they are no longer allowed to get their way. When they can't get their way, they leave. Not even Jesus got through the journey with all of the disciples. Why should we expect to?"[24]

In order to defend the church from bullies it is *vital* that the pastor and key leaders have a support team in place. There is nothing in this book that can or should be done solo. Not only would that set the leader up for accusations of arrogance or tyranny; it makes him or her susceptible to every attack imaginable. There must be a group of supportive, Spirit-filled believers who can and will work with you for a better future.

A brief but important incident occurred in Exodus 17:8-13:

> *The Amalekites came and attacked the Israelites at Rephidim. Moses said to Joshua, "Choose some of our men and go out to fight the Amalekites. Tomorrow I will stand on top of the hill with the staff of God in my hands."*

> *So Joshua fought the Amalekites as Moses had ordered, and Moses, Aaron and Hur went to the top of the hill. As long as Moses held up his hands, the Israelites were winning, but whenever he lowered his hands, the Amalekites were winning. When Moses' hands grew tired, they took a stone and put it under him and he sat on it. Aaron and Hur held his hands up—one on one side, one on the other- so that his hands remained steady till sunset. So Joshua overcame the Amalekite army with the sword.*

Had it not been for Aaron and Hur the battle against the Amalekites would have gone a completely different way. Moses had his job to do: holding the staff of Yahweh aloft during the battle. Aaron and Hur had their jobs as well. They helped support the arms of Moses until the battle was over.

Every pastor and church leader needs a team of Aarons and Hurs around them for support. This is invaluable for emotional,

---

[24] Easum, Bill. *Leadership On the Other Side*, pp. 161-162. Used by permission. All rights reserved.

mental, physical and spiritual well-being. This team must be willing to take a stand against the controllers and bullies. They will have to bear some of the heat that is routinely directed toward pastors or other key leaders. Aarons and Hurs stand in the gap, helping to deflect Satan's fiery arrows and serving as a screen to help filter out negativity and animosity.

Aarons and Hurs exist in every church. Sometimes it takes a little while to find them but they are there. For years they have secretly been yearning for something to change in their church. They are not content to merely be on display in a museum or mausoleum. They desire to be part of a genuine movement. These are the followers of Jesus whose eyes light up when you talk about God's dreams for the future. Such people are willing to do whatever it takes to fulfill the *missio Dei*.

These people make God's kingdom their priority. They love the Lord and do not demand entitlements, control or recognition. They are willing to see new things and are willing to hear the truth about their church, even when it is uncomfortable.

Often these people are influential members of the congregation. They may be lifelong members, have ties to a key family or are people everyone else respects. They have voices that others will listen to and positive influence throughout the congregation.

If you do not know who these people are in your church, ask God to reveal them to you. When he does, invite them out for coffee or lunch. Share your vision with them—even if it is something as simple as changing the time of the Christmas Eve service or providing diapers for infants in low-income homes. Explain that you would like for them to be an Aaron or Hur in the congregation.

If you already know the supportive people be sure to train and educate them. Work together as a group to read and study a leadership or church growth book. Schedule casual meetings where everyone can come together and brainstorm or pray.

I have discovered and developed a team of such people in every church I have served. Not only were they emotionally and physically supportive; they caught God's vision for the church and worked to bring it about. They provided valuable feedback, encouragement, correction and were shields against those who would batter and abuse leaders.

One approach I have used is to gather these people into what I call a "future planning taskforce." You might select a name that better suits your context. I personally invite people who will serve as Aarons and Hurs—old and young, male and female, single, married, with children, without children, "lifers" and newer members. I have done this with groups as small as six and as large as fifteen. The key is to include a wide variety of personalities and outlooks from across the congregation who will make a commitment to the process.

I meet with this group for sixty to ninety minutes once a month. In between the scheduled meetings the participants have selected readings they are to review, reflect on and respond to for the next meeting.

Each monthly session (and subsequent readings) focuses on a different aspect of change or revitalization, as well as dreams for the future. Most Christians have forgotten how to dream something great for God. They have not been given permission to dream or their dreams have been ridiculed and shot down. Part of any turnaround involves giving people permission to imagine what dreams and goals God is placing before us.

Topics for your team might include such things as postmodernism, worship, the biblical mission and purpose of the church, discipleship, missions and outreach, and change, to name a few. One session that has proven to be quite valuable centers around the statistical data of the local congregation.

Most churches and denominational structures keep records of annual attendance and giving, demographic makeup of the congregation, members lost and received, and so on. Using this information I put together a twenty-year retrospective to share with the group. Naturally this takes a bit of time and digging, but it pays off when the participants see the pertinent data about their church. Facts do not lie. And despite our best attempts at denial, such information paints a true picture of the church's overall health and well-being. This session often generates the most discussion as participants come to grips with the truth about their church.

The team meets anywhere from eight to fourteen months, depending on how much training and education is needed. After this much time exposed to new perspectives and ideas they become the vanguard in dealing with the bullies. This team has seen the data (and they are encouraged to share that data with Sunday school classes, small groups, etc.). They know the congregation. They want to see their church fulfilling its biblical mission. Their voices help others understand the need for transformation or revitalization. Such leaders not only become carriers of the DNA; they also provide a shield for the pastor and leaders when things get a bit overheated.

＊ ＊ ＊ ＊ ＊ ＊

A great many issues developed in the Corinthian congregation that precipitated Paul's letters. We noted in the Introduction that the church in Corinth was not all bad. However, unchecked problems were pulling them down the wrong path. Paul gave sound—sometimes sarcastic, occasionally blunt—correction to those believers. The survival of the Corinthian church was at stake if their issues were not addressed. Their witness was compromised, their effectiveness hindered, their claims laughed at and rejected.

We also noted that your church is not all bad. But like Corinth, unchecked problems may have destabilized and paralyzed the church you love and serve. The survival of your congregation is at stake. You are painfully aware of how your church's witness has been compromised, its effectiveness hindered, its claims laughed at and rejected.

It took two letters (that we know of) for Paul to confront and attempt to realign the Corinthians' worldview. Yet despite his best efforts history tells us the Corinthian church continued to reject Paul's admonitions. In 96 AD, Clement of Rome—one of the earliest of the Western church fathers—wrote an extremely lengthy letter to the Corinthian church. At fifty-nine chapters it was twice as long as both of Paul's letters combined.

Clement was bishop of Rome from 92-99 AD and he received word that many in the Corinthian church had banded together and ousted several key leaders from the congregation. Clement reprimanded them, urging the believers to be united in love and humility. Sounds very much like what Paul told them nearly forty years prior.

In chapter three of his letter Clement said,

> "Every kind of honour and happiness was bestowed upon you, and then was fulfilled that which is written, 'My beloved did eat and drink, and was enlarged and became fat, and kicked.' Hence flowed emulation and envy, strife and sedition, persecution and disorder, war and captivity. So the worthless rose up against the honoured, those of no reputation against such as were renowned, the foolish against the wise, the young against those advanced in years. For this reason righteousness and peace are now far departed from you, inasmuch as every one abandons the fear of God, and is become blind in His faith, neither walks in the ordinances of His appointment, nor acts a part becoming a Christian, but walks after his own wicked lusts, resuming the practice of an unrighteous and ungodly envy, by which death itself entered into the world."[25]

This sounds suspiciously like some churches today: fat, happy and completely satisfied. Righteousness and peace are nowhere to be found. There is little fear of God and many do not behave in ways befitting a Christian.

Four decades after Paul's letters the Corinthian church still refused to listen. They remained divided over leadership. In Paul's day it was over the apostles. In Clement's day it was over leaders

---

[25] http://www.ccel.org/ccel/schaff/anf01.ii.ii.iii.html.

from within the congregation. The church continued to be bullied by private agendas, power and pride.

As church members and leaders we have a choice. We can continue to allow the bride of Christ to be intimidated and browbeaten. Or we can take proactive steps to release her to fulfill the *missio Dei*. If we choose to do nothing—and if our churches remain social clubs with faint religious overtones—we should not be shocked or saddened when they resemble the Corinthian church.

It is my prayer that we will all choose the harder path where we walk by faith and not by sight (2nd Corinthians 5:7). Where we confront dysfunctional attitudes and personalities firmly and in love. Where we allow the word of God and the presence of the Holy Spirit to dictate who we are and what we do. Where our churches truly achieve the fullness of God's blessing and favor as we display lives of contagious joy and obedience.

I encourage you as pastors and laity to devote yourselves to an intense study of the New Testament. Open your hearts. Join together in prayer. Listen to the voice of the Spirit. Jesus loves his bride and her task on earth is not yet complete. You would do everything possible to protect your loved one from a destructive situation. We should assume no less of Jesus. He desires to see his bride alive and free, giving and blessing, celebrating and transforming—an unstoppable force of grace and love that remains the best hope for the world.

Join me in helping to defend our churches from bullies!

> *Finally, brothers and sisters, rejoice! Strive for full restoration, encourage one another, be of one mind, live in peace. And the God of love and peace will be with you. Greet one another with a holy kiss. All God's people here send their greetings. May the grace of the Lord Jesus Christ, and the love of God, and the fellowship of the Holy Spirit be with you all.*

(2nd Corinthians 13:11-14)

APPENDIX 1
SCRIPTURES ON SPIRITUAL WARFARE

OLD TESTAMENT

Numbers 10:35-36

³⁵Whenever the ark set out, Moses said, "Rise up, Lord! May your enemies be scattered; may your foes flee before you." ³⁶Whenever it came to rest, he said, "Return, Lord, to the countless thousands of Israel."

2 Samuel 22:2-4

²He said: "The Lord is my rock, my fortress and my deliverer; ³my God is my rock, in whom I take refuge, my shield and the horn of my salvation. He is my stronghold, my refuge and my savior— from violent people you save me." ⁴I called to the Lord, who is worthy of praise, and have been saved from my enemies.

2 Kings 6:15-17

¹⁵When the servant of the man of God got up and went out early the next morning, an army with horses and chariots had surrounded the city. "Oh no, my lord! What shall we do?" the servant asked.

¹⁶"Don't be afraid," the prophet answered. "Those who are with us are more than those who are with them."

¹⁷And Elisha prayed, "Open his eyes, Lord, so that he may see." Then the Lord opened the servant's eyes, and he looked and saw the hills full of horses and chariots of fire all around Elisha.

Job 5:12

¹²He thwarts the plans of the crafty, so that their hands achieve no success.

Psalm 3:7-8

[7]Arise, Lord! Deliver me, my God! Strike all my enemies on the jaw; break the teeth of the wicked. [8]From the Lord comes deliverance. May your blessing be on your people.

Psalm 44:4-8

[4]You are my King and my God, who decrees victories for Jacob. [5]Through you we push back our enemies; through your name we trample our foes. [6]I put no trust in my bow, my sword does not bring me victory; [7]but you give us victory over our enemies, you put our adversaries to shame. [8]In God we make our boast all day long, and we will praise your name forever.

Psalm 118:12-14

[14]They swarmed around me like bees, but they were consumed as quickly as burning thorns; in the name of the Lord I cut them down. [13]I was pushed back and about to fall, but the Lord helped me. [14]The Lord is my strength and my defense; he has become my salvation.

Isaiah 43:1-3a

[1]But now, this is what the Lord says—he who created you, Jacob, he who formed you, Israel: "Do not fear, for I have redeemed you; I have summoned you by name; you are mine. [2]When you pass through the waters, I will be with you; and when you pass through the rivers, they will not sweep over you. When you walk through the fire, you will not be burned; the flames will not set you ablaze. [3]For I am the Lord your God, the Holy One of Israel, your Savior."

Isaiah 54:17

[17]"...no weapon forged against you will prevail, and you will refute every tongue that accuses you. This is the heritage of the servants of the Lord, and this is their vindication from me," declares the Lord.

Daniel 10:12-13, 20-21

¹²Then he continued, "Do not be afraid, Daniel. Since the first day that you set your mind to gain understanding and to humble yourself before your God, your words were heard, and I have come in response to them. ¹³But the prince of the Persian kingdom resisted me twenty-one days. Then Michael, one of the chief princes, came to help me, because I was detained there with the king of Persia."

²⁰So he said, "Do you know why I have come to you? Soon I will return to fight against the prince of Persia, and when I go, the prince of Greece will come; ²¹but first I will tell you what is written in the Book of Truth."

NEW TESTAMENT

Matthew 4:1-11

¹Then Jesus was led by the Spirit into the wilderness to be tempted by the devil. ²After fasting forty days and forty nights, he was hungry. ³The tempter came to him and said, "If you are the Son of God, tell these stones to become bread."

⁴Jesus answered, "It is written: 'Man shall not live on bread alone, but on every word that comes from the mouth of God.'"

⁵Then the devil took him to the holy city and had him stand on the highest point of the temple. ⁶"If you are the Son of God," he said, "throw yourself down. For it is written: "'He will command his angels concerning you, and they will lift you up in their hands, so that you will not strike your foot against a stone.'"

⁷Jesus answered him, "It is also written: 'Do not put the Lord your God to the test.'"

⁸Again, the devil took him to a very high mountain and showed him all the kingdoms of the world and their splendor. ⁹"All this I will give you," he said, "if you will bow down and worship me."

[10]Jesus said to him, "Away from me, Satan! For it is written: 'Worship the Lord your God, and serve him only.'" [11]Then the devil left him, and angels came and attended him.

Matthew 6:13

[13]And lead us not into temptation, but deliver us from the evil one.

Matthew 16:18

[18]And I tell you that you are Peter, and on this rock I will build my church, and the gates of Hades will not overcome it.

Matthew 18:18-20

[18]"Truly I tell you, whatever you bind on earth will be bound in heaven, and whatever you loose on earth will be loosed in heaven.

[19]"Again, truly I tell you that if two of you on earth agree about anything they ask for, it will be done for them by my Father in heaven. [20]For where two or three gather in my name, there am I with them."

Mark 6:7, 13

[7]Calling the Twelve to him, he began to send them out two by two and gave them authority over impure spirits.

[13]They drove out many demons and anointed many sick people with oil and healed them.

Luke 10:18-20

[18]He replied, "I saw Satan fall like lightning from heaven. [19]I have given you authority to trample on snakes and scorpions and to overcome all the power of the enemy; nothing will harm you. [20]However, do not rejoice that the spirits submit to you, but rejoice that your names are written in heaven."

John 8:44

⁴⁴You belong to your father, the devil, and you want to carry out your father's desires. He was a murderer from the beginning, not holding to the truth, for there is no truth in him. When he lies, he speaks his native language, for he is a liar and the father of lies.

John 10:10

¹⁰The thief comes only to steal and kill and destroy; I have come that they may have life, and have it to the full.

John 12:30-33

³⁰Jesus said, "This voice was for your benefit, not mine. ³¹Now is the time for judgment on this world; now the prince of this world will be driven out. ³²And I, when I am lifted up from the earth, will draw all people to myself." ³³He said this to show the kind of death he was going to die.

Romans 12:21

²¹Do not be overcome by evil, but overcome evil with good.

1st Corinthians 15:22-27

²²For as in Adam all die, so in Christ all will be made alive. ²³But each in turn: Christ, the firstfruits; then, when he comes, those who belong to him. ²⁴Then the end will come, when he hands over the kingdom to God the Father after he has destroyed all dominion, authority and power. ²⁵For he must reign until he has put all his enemies under his feet. ²⁶The last enemy to be destroyed is death. ²⁷For he "has put everything under his feet."

2nd Corinthians 10:3-5

³For though we live in the world, we do not wage war as the world does. ⁴The weapons we fight with are not the weapons of the world. On the contrary, they have divine power to demolish strongholds. ⁵We demolish arguments and every pretension that

sets itself up against the knowledge of God, and we take captive every thought to make it obedient to Christ.

2nd Corinthians 11:14-15

[14]And no wonder, for Satan himself masquerades as an angel of light. [15]It is not surprising, then, if his servants also masquerade as servants of righteousness. Their end will be what their actions deserve.

Ephesians 6:10-17

[10]Finally, be strong in the Lord and in his mighty power. [11]Put on the full armor of God, so that you can take your stand against the devil's schemes. [12]For our struggle is not against flesh and blood, but against the rulers, against the authorities, against the powers of this dark world and against the spiritual forces of evil in the heavenly realms. [13]Therefore put on the full armor of God, so that when the day of evil comes, you may be able to stand your ground, and after you have done everything, to stand. [14]Stand firm then, with the belt of truth buckled around your waist, with the breastplate of righteousness in place, [15] and with your feet fitted with the readiness that comes from the gospel of peace. [16]In addition to all this, take up the shield of faith, with which you can extinguish all the flaming arrows of the evil one. [17]Take the helmet of salvation and the sword of the Spirit, which is the word of God.

Colossians 1:13-14

[13]For he has rescued us from the dominion of darkness and brought us into the kingdom of the Son he loves, [14]in whom we have redemption, the forgiveness of sins.

Colossians 2:15

[15]And having disarmed the powers and authorities, he made a public spectacle of them, triumphing over them by the cross.

2 Thessalonians 2:9-12

[9]The coming of the lawless one will be in accordance with how Satan works. He will use all sorts of displays of power through signs and wonders that serve the lie, [10]and all the ways that wickedness deceives those who are perishing. They perish because they refused to love the truth and so be saved. [11]For this reason God sends them a powerful delusion so that they will believe the lie [12]and so that all will be condemned who have not believed the truth but have delighted in wickedness.

Hebrews 2:14-15

[14]Since the children have flesh and blood, he too shared in their humanity so that by his death he might break the power of him who holds the power of death—that is, the devil— [15]and free those who all their lives were held in slavery by their fear of death.

James 2:19

[19]You believe that there is one God. Good! Even the demons believe that—and shudder.

James 4:7-8

[7]Submit yourselves, then, to God. Resist the devil, and he will flee from you. [8]Come near to God and he will come near to you.

1 Peter 5:8-9

[8]Be alert and of sober mind. Your enemy the devil prowls around like a roaring lion looking for someone to devour. [9]Resist him, standing firm in the faith, because you know that the family of believers throughout the world is undergoing the same kind of sufferings.

1 John 3:8

⁸The one who does what is sinful is of the devil, because the devil has been sinning from the beginning. The reason the Son of God appeared was to destroy the devil's work.

1 John 4:4

⁴You, dear children, are from God and have overcome them, because the one who is in you is greater than the one who is in the world.

Revelation 12:7-11

⁷Then war broke out in heaven. Michael and his angels fought against the dragon, and the dragon and his angels fought back. ⁸But he was not strong enough, and they lost their place in heaven. ⁹The great dragon was hurled down—that ancient serpent called the devil, or Satan, who leads the whole world astray. He was hurled to the earth, and his angels with him.

¹⁰Then I heard a loud voice in heaven say: "Now have come the salvation and the power and the kingdom of our God, and the authority of his Messiah.

For the accuser of our brothers and sisters, who accuses them before our God day and night, has been hurled down. ¹¹They triumphed over him by the blood of the Lamb and by the word of their testimony; they did not love their lives so much as to shrink from death.

APPENDIX 2
SCRIPTURES ABOUT REMEMBERING

OLD TESTAMENT

Deuteronomy 6:12

¹²...be careful that you do not forget the Lord, who brought you out of Egypt, out of the land of slavery.

Deuteronomy 8:10-18

¹⁰When you have eaten and are satisfied, praise the Lord your God for the good land he has given you. ¹¹Be careful that you do not forget the Lord your God, failing to observe his commands, his laws and his decrees that I am giving you this day. ¹²Otherwise, when you eat and are satisfied, when you build fine houses and settle down, ¹³and when your herds and flocks grow large and your silver and gold increase and all you have is multiplied, ¹⁴then your heart will become proud and you will forget the Lord your God, who brought you out of Egypt, out of the land of slavery. ¹⁵He led you through the vast and dreadful wilderness, that thirsty and waterless land, with its venomous snakes and scorpions. He brought you water out of hard rock. ¹⁶He gave you manna to eat in the wilderness, something your ancestors had never known, to humble and test you so that in the end it might go well with you. ¹⁷You may say to yourself, "My power and the strength of my hands have produced this wealth for me." ¹⁸But remember the Lord your God, for it is he who gives you the ability to produce wealth, and so confirms his covenant, which he swore to your ancestors, as it is today.

Numbers 15:37-40

³⁷The Lord said to Moses, ³⁸"Speak to the Israelites and say to them: 'Throughout the generations to come you are to make tassels on the corners of your garments, with a blue cord on each tassel.

[39]You will have these tassels to look at and so you will remember all the commands of the Lord, that you may obey them and not prostitute yourselves by chasing after the lusts of your own hearts and eyes. [40]Then you will remember to obey all my commands and will be consecrated to your God. [41]I am the Lord your God, who brought you out of Egypt to be your God. I am the Lord your God.'"

1 Chronicles 16:12

[12]Remember the wonders he has done, his miracles, and the judgments he pronounced…

Psalm 63:6

[6]On my bed I remember you; I think of you through the watches of the night.

Psalm 77:11-12

[11]I will remember the deeds of the Lord; yes, I will remember your miracles of long ago. [12]I will consider all your works and meditate on all your mighty deeds.

Psalm 78:7

[7]Then they would put their trust in God and would not forget his deeds but would keep his commands.

Psalm 103:1-2

[1]Praise the Lord, my soul; all my inmost being, praise his holy name. [2]Praise the Lord, my soul, and forget not all his benefits.

Psalm 119:55

[55]In the night, Lord, I remember your name, that I may keep your law.

Isaiah 49:15-16

[15]"Can a mother forget the baby at her breast and have no compassion on the child she has borne? Though she may forget, I will not forget you! [16]See, I have engraved you on the palms of my hands; your walls are ever before me.

Lamentations 3:21-24

[21]Yet this I call to mind and therefore I have hope: [22]Because of the Lord's great love we are not consumed, for his compassions never fail. [23]They are new every morning; great is your faithfulness. [24]I say to myself, "The Lord is my portion; therefore I will wait for him."

Jonah 2:7

[7]"When my life was ebbing away, I remembered you, Lord, and my prayer rose to you, to your holy temple.

NEW TESTAMENT

Luke 22:19-20

[19]And he took bread, gave thanks and broke it, and gave it to them, saying, "This is my body given for you; do this in remembrance of me." [20]In the same way, after the supper he took the cup, saying, "This cup is the new covenant in my blood, which is poured out for you."

John 14:26

[26]But the Advocate, the Holy Spirit, whom the Father will send in my name, will teach you all things and will remind you of everything I have said to you.

John 15:20

[20]"Remember what I told you: 'A servant is not greater than his master.' If they persecuted me, they will persecute you also. If they obeyed my teaching, they will obey yours also."

1st Corinthians 11:2

[2]I praise you for remembering me in everything and for holding to the traditions just as I passed them on to you.

1st Corinthians 15:2

[2]By this gospel you are saved, if you hold firmly to the word I preached to you. Otherwise, you have believed in vain.

Hebrews 13:7, 16

[7]Remember your leaders, who spoke the word of God to you. Consider the outcome of their way of life and imitate their faith.

[16]And do not forget to do good and to share with others, for with such sacrifices God is pleased.

James 1:25

[25]But whoever looks intently into the perfect law that gives freedom, and continues in it—not forgetting what they have heard, but doing it—they will be blessed in what they do.

James 5:19-20

[19]My brothers and sisters, if one of you should wander from the truth and someone should bring that person back, [20]remember this: Whoever turns a sinner from the error of their way will save them from death and cover over a multitude of sins.

2 Peter 1:5-9

[5]For this very reason, make every effort to add to your faith goodness; and to goodness, knowledge; [6]and to knowledge, self-control; and to self-control, perseverance; and to perseverance,

godliness; [7]and to godliness, mutual affection; and to mutual affection, love. [8]For if you possess these qualities in increasing measure, they will keep you from being ineffective and unproductive in your knowledge of our Lord Jesus Christ. [9]But whoever does not have them is nearsighted and blind, forgetting that they have been cleansed from their past sins.

2 Peter 3:3-5, 8-9

[3]Above all, you must understand that in the last days scoffers will come, scoffing and following their own evil desires. [4]They will say, "Where is this 'coming' he promised? Ever since our ancestors died, everything goes on as it has since the beginning of creation." [5]But they deliberately forget that long ago by God's word the heavens came into being and the earth was formed out of water and by water.

[8]But do not forget this one thing, dear friends: With the Lord a day is like a thousand years, and a thousand years are like a day. [9]The Lord is not slow in keeping his promise, as some understand slowness. Instead he is patient with you, not wanting anyone to perish, but everyone to come to repentance.

Revelation 3:3

[3]Remember, therefore, what you have received and heard; hold it fast, and repent. But if you do not wake up, I will come like a thief, and you will not know at what time I will come to you.

APPENDIX 3
SUGGESTED READING ON
VISION AND LEADERSHIP

Advanced Strategic Planning—Third Edition
> Aubrey Malphurs (Baker Books, 2013)

Church Leadership: Vision, Team, Culture, Integrity—Revised Edition
> Lovett Weems (Abingdon Press, 2010)

Church Unique: How Missional Leaders Cast Vision, Capture Culture, and Create Movement
> Will Mancini (Jossey-Bass, 2008)

Cracking Your Church's Culture Code: Seven Keys to Unleashing Vision & Inspiration
> Samuel R. Chand (Jossey-Bass, 2010)

Developing a Vision for Ministry in the 21st Century
> Aubrey Malphurs (Baker Books, 1999)

Finding a Vision for Your Church—Assembly Required
> Michael Milton (P & R Publishing, 2012)

Giving Life to Vision: Moving the Church from Plans to Progress
> Marty Guise & Timothy H. Filston (Resource Publications (OR), 2012)

God's Vision, Your Decision: The Master's Plan For The Church, The Pastor, and You
> Jerome Stokes (LifeBridge Books, 2003)

Key to Your Church's Vision, The

John Cameron King (Xulon Press, 2009)

Making Vision Stick (Leadership Library)

Andy Stanley (Zondervan, 2009)

Making Your Vision a Reality: Proven Steps to Develop and Implement Your Church Vision Plan

Paul Cannings (Kregal Publications, 2012)

Priorities for the Church: Rediscovering Leadership and Vision in the Church

Donald MacLeod (Christian Focus Publications, 2003)

Strategic Vision: Embracing God's Future for Your Church

Frank Damazio (Regal Books, 2013)

Transforming Leadership: Vision for a Church in Mission

Norma Cook Everist and Craig L. Nessan (Fortress Press, 2007)

Visioneering: God's Blueprint for Developing and Maintaining Vision

Andy Stanley (Multnomah Books, 2005)

BIBLIOGRAPHY

Aristophanes. *The Complete Plays* (The New Translation by Paul Roche). New York: New American Library/Penguin, 2005.

Balda, Janis Bragan and Balda, Wesley D. *Handbook for Battered Leaders*. Downers Grove: InterVarsity Press, 2013.

Beckham, William A. *The Second Reformation: Reshaping the Church for the 21st Century*. Houston: TOUCH Publications, 1997.

Cooke, Graham. *A Divine Confrontation: Birth Pangs of the New Church*. Shippensburg: Destiny Image Publishers, 1999.

Easum, Bill. *A Second Resurrection: Leading Your Congregation to New Life*. Nashville: Abingdon Press, 2007.

Easum, Bill. *Leadership On the Other Side*. Nashville: Abingdon Press, 2000.

Halter, Hugh. *Sacrilege: Finding Life in the Unorthodox Ways Of Jesus*. Grand Rapids: Baker Books, 2011.

Hirsch, Alan. *The Forgotten Ways: Reactivating the Missional Church*. Grand Rapids: Brazos Press, 2006.

Hull, Bill. *The Complete Book of Discipleship: On Being and Making Followers of Christ (The Navigators Reference Library)*. Colorado Springs: NavPress, 2006.

Hull, Bill. *The Disciple-Making Church: Leading a Body of Believers on the Journey of Faith*. Grand Rapids: Baker Books, 2010.

Hunter III, George G. *Radical Outreach: The Recovery of Apostolic Ministry & Evangelism*. Nashville: Abingdon Press, 2003.

Kempis, Thomas à. *The Imitation of Christ*. Revised translation, edited by Hal M. Helms. Brewster: Paraclete Press, 1997.

Mitchell, Margaret. *Gone With the Wind*. New York: Scribner, 2011.

Meyers, Robin. *The Underground Church: Reclaiming the Subversive Way of Jesus*. San Francisco: Jossey-Bass; 2012.

Putman, Jim. *Real-Life Discipleship: Building Churches That Make Disciples*. Colorado Springs: NavPress, 2010.

Rowling, J.K. *Harry Potter and the Philosopher's Stone*. London: Bloomsbury, 1997.

Slaughter, Michael. *Unlearning Church: Just When You Thought You Had Leadership All Figured Out*. Loveland: Group Publishing, 2002.

Snyder, Howard. *The Problem of Wineskins: Church Structure in a Technological Age*. Downers Grove: InterVarsity Press, 1975.

Webber, Robert. *Ancient-Future Evangelism: Making Your Church a Faith-Formed Community*. Grand Rapids: Baker Books, 2003.

ONLINE RESOURCES

Carter, Chelsea J., Messia, Hada and Greene, Richard Allen. "Pope Francis, the pontiff of firsts, breaks with tradition." CNN.com

http://www.cnn.com/2013/03/13/world/Europe/vatican-pope-selection. Web. 14 March 2013.

Christian Classics Ethereal Library. "Chapter III.—The sad state of the Corinthian church after sedition arose in it from envy and emulation." CCEL.org

http://www.ccel.org/ccel/schaff/anf01.ii.ii.iii.html
Web.

Banjo, Shelly. "Churches Find End Is Nigh: The Number of Religious Facilities Unable to Pay Their Mortgage Is Surging." WSJ.com

http://online.wsj.com/article/SB1000142405274870411540457609615 1214141820.html?mod=WSJ_hp_MIDDLENexttoWhatsNe wsSecond
Web. 25 January 2011.

Brenner, Charles B. and Zacks, Jeffrey M. "Why Walking Through a Doorway Makes You Forget." Scientific American. N.P. 13 December, 2011.

http://www.scientificamerican.com/article.cfm?id=why-walking-through-doorway-makes-you-forget.

Web. 18 September 2012.

Ray, Daniel P. and Ghahremani, Yasmin. "Credit card statistics, industry facts, debt statistics." Creditcards.com.

http://www.creditcards.com/credit-card-news/credit-card-industry-facts-personal-debt-statistics-1276.php

Web. 7 August 2013.

"American Donor Trends." Barna.org

https://www.barna.org/barna-update/culture/606-american-donor-trends#.UhF1mRbF_dk

Web. 12 April 2013.

"National Income and Product Accounts: Gross Domestic Product, second quarter 2013." U.S. Department of Commerce, Bureau of Economic Analysis. bea.gov

http://www.bea.gov/newsreleases/national/gdp/gdpnewsrelease.htm

Web. 31 July 2013.

http://www.globalrichlist.com

Web.

57790237R00162

Made in the USA
Charleston, SC
25 June 2016